In the Company of William Hazlitt
Thoughts for the Twenty-first Century

Maurice Whelan studied philosophy, theology and sociology in Ireland. He trained as a social worker in England and worked in London for many years as a field social worker and as a psychiatric social worker. He has an MA in Criminology and Social Policy. He was a visiting academic lecturer at the Tavistock Clinic in London. He is a member of the British and Australian Psycho-Analytical Societies. Since 1992 he has lived in Sydney. His publications include *Special Education and Social Control – Invisible Disasters* (1981), with J. Ford and D. Mongon, and *Mistress of Her own Thoughts: Ella Freeman Sharpe and the Practice of Psychoanalysis* (2000).

In the Company of William Hazlitt
Thoughts for the Twenty-first Century

Maurice Whelan

MERLIN PRESS
LONDON

First published in the UK in 2005 by
The Merlin Press Ltd.
PO Box 30705
London
WC2E 8QD
www.merlinpress.co.uk

First published in 2003 by
Australian Scholarly Publishing Pty Ltd
Suite 102, 282 Collins Street, Melbourne 3000
PO Box 299 Kew, Victoria 3101

British Library Cataloguing in Publication Data is available from the
British Library

ISBN 0850365538

Cover design by Green Poles Design

Printed in the UK by Antony Rowe Ltd., Chippenham

For Louise

Those who have the largest hearts have the soundest understandings; and he is the truest philosopher who can forget himself.

William Hazlitt

Contents

Acknowledgements

Numerous people have helped me during the writing of this book and to them I wish to express my gratitude. I would like to thank the Literature Fund of the Australia Council for the Arts for providing a grant to assist publication. I have always found librarians to be the most consistently helpful people, and the staff of the State Library of New South Wales and Willoughby Library, Sydney provided endless assistance to me. Irina Dunn director of the NSW Writers' Centre gave invaluable advice at a crucial moment. I am indebted to Alison Clark and Deborah Tyler for their copy-editing skills, and to Peter Fullerton, Judy Griffiths, Philip Hewitt, Peter Holbrook, Dushan Mrva-Montoya, Richard O'Neill-Dean, Neville Symington, Louise Whelan and Bob White whose reading and discussion of sections of the manuscript provided invaluable encouragement, criticism and suggestions. Everyone who attended my series of lectures *On Living to One's Self*, organised by the Sydney Institute for Psychoanalysis in August 2002, helped me to believe that Hazlitt still had an audience. I am grateful to Nick Walker at Australian Scholarly Publishing in Melbourne for having faith in my work and publishing an Australian edition in 2003, and to The Merlin Press in London for making the book available to a wider market. Finally a special thanks to Ella and Tom who at times must have felt we had an additional unseen, but very present, member conversing at our family table.

Chapter 1

In the Company of William Hazlitt

In *My First Acquaintance with Poets* William Hazlitt described the events of 1798 that had a profound effect on his life. Samuel Taylor Coleridge, then aged 25, went to Shrewsbury to preach. Hazlitt woke before dawn on a raw, cold, comfortless Sunday and walked the 10 miles through the January mud from his home in Wem to hear him speak. The marvellous cocktail of religion, poetry, philosophy and spirituality delivered with great energy and conviction dazzled the 19 year old Hazlitt. Coleridge's voice was like a Siren's song that stunned and startled and rose Hazlitt from a deep sleep. 'The light of his genius shone in my soul,' was how he described the experience. Before meeting Coleridge Hazlitt knew that within himself he had a mind capable of profound thought. He also intuitively believed in the value of his ideas. He lacked the faith to express them. Coleridge helped Hazlitt to believe that he would find the proper means of expression. While future years and events would complicate the relationship between these two great men, Hazlitt would remain forever grateful for this gift on encouragement.

Later in the same year Hazlitt visited Coleridge at his home at Nether Stowey, Somerset. Coleridge took Hazlitt to meet William Wordsworth who lived a few miles away at Alfoxden, and during the three weeks Hazlitt spent in Wordsworth's company was convinced that he had met the most creative and innovative poet of his generation. Wordsworth could take ordinary things in nature and from them create extraordinary poetry. Hazlitt would later write of him that 'he gathers manna in the wilderness, he strikes the barren rock for the gushing moisture. He elevates the mean by the strength of his own aspirations; he clothes the naked with beauty and grandeur from the stores of his own recollections.'[1]

My first acquaintance with William Hazlitt had little of the dramatic impact of the experience described above. I was on the other side of the globe nearly 200 years later travelling by car over the Sydney Harbour Bridge o making my way on a beautiful spring morning to a conference center overlooking Hyde Park. I was a speaker and my subject the place of imagination and creativity within psychoanalysis. It was my good fortune on that day to have as a discussant Jane Adamson from the Australian National University. She presented a journey through the last 500 years of English literature outlining how great writers had thought about the place on imagination in their creative activity. I remember her describing William Hazlitt as an independently minded literary critic. I remember her also referring to a comparison which Hazlitt had made between Chaucer and Shakespeare. Chaucer's mind was described as consecutive, that he thought of one thing at a time, his ideas being ticketed, labelled, in pews and compartments by themselves. Shakespeare's mind was described as discursive. He saw everything by intuition and his mind was a dancing mind 'full of swift transitions and glancing lights'. He made infinite excursions to the right and the left. He made 'the commonest matter-of-fact float in a freer element with the breath of imagination'.[2]

I had not heard a Siren's song but soon Hazlitt's words were gathering momentum in my mind. Then I found and read *Table Talk* a collection of his essays written between 1821–2. This small green pocket book six inches tall struggled to hold its place on the bookseller's shelf, dwarfed by its neighbours. It smelt of almonds. As I read I was struck by the many things that appeared before me, his exquisite and vivid prose, the depth and breath of his thought, his personal style of open and candid communication and above all the contemporary relevance of his writing. Soon I would discover that Robert Louis Stevenson had said – 'Though we are all mighty fine fellows nowadays, we cannot write like Hazlitt' and I would think that there are a lot of fine fellows and ladies writing nowadays but who is writing like Hazlitt. But for now I was captivated by what appeared before my eyes. Those wafer thin pages crackled with ideas, their very delicacy holding the most weighty of thoughts. Besides his particular qualities as a writer and thinker I was intrigued by the introductory note to the text which informed me that many of these essays had been written during one of the most difficult times of his life.

I became very curious not only about his works but also about the man. I was aware from the beginning when reading his essays of the invitation by Hazlitt to be in his company, to enter into his world. The opening lines from his essay On *Living to One's Self* articulate this offer. This is how it reads:

I was never in a better place or humour than I am at present for writing on this subject. I have a partridge getting ready for my supper, my fire is blazing on the hearth, the air is mild for the season of the year, I have but a slight fit of indigestion to-day (the only thing that makes me abhor myself), I have three hours good before me, and therefore I will attempt it. It is as well to do it at once as to have it to do for a week to come.

If the writing on this subject is no easy task, the thing itself is a harder one. It asks a troublesome effort to insure the admiration of others: it is a still greater one to be satisfied with one's own thoughts. As I look from the window at the wide bare heath before me, and through the misty moonlight air see the woods that wave over the top of Winterslow, 'While Heav'n's chancel-vault is blind with sleet,' my mind takes its flight through too long a series of years, supported only by the patience of thought and secret yearnings after truth and good, for me to be at a loss to understand the feeling I intend to write about; but I do not know that this will enable me to convey it more agreeable to the reader.[3]

I therefore 'sit' with Hazlitt. I often find that I am not only watching the fire or turning towards the heath or becoming fixed on the woods that wave in the moonlight. Something has happened since I became acquainted with his writing and with the man. He has a habit of regularly knocking on the door of my mind. Sometimes he makes an easy and welcomed entry; often he provides excellent company. His words arrive as if they expect to find a place. 'Our unconscious impressions necessarily give colour to, and react upon our conscious ones; We are not hypocrites in our sleep … in dreams our passions and imagination wander at will; Life in indeed a strange gift, and its privileges are most mysterious … We are little better than humoured children to the last, and play a mischievous game at cross purposes with our own happiness and that of others … The griefs we suffer are for the most part of our own seeking and making' … There must be a spice of mischief and wilfulness thrown in the cup of our existence to give it its sharp taste and sparking colour … Each individual is a world to himself, governed by a thousand contradictions and wayward impulses … Every man, in reasoning on the faculties of human nature, describes the process of his own mind.'

He can be a disquieting presence and I can wish he would go away. If I stare in awe at him he is likely to become uneasy fearing my adulation. If I grasp and share his depth of taste I can become dumb struck, not able to find words, not in need of any. I can remember Coleridge describing him as –'a thinking, observant, original man … [who] sends well-headed and well-feathered Thoughts straight forwards to the mark with a Twang of the Bow-string. [And although] he is strangely confused and dark in his conversation and delivers himself of almost all his conceptions with a forceps, yet he says more than any man I ever knew … that is his own in a way of his own.'[4]

I feel in the presence of a very generous man. He can offer more thoughts in one page than are often found in a complete book. His ideas may sometimes come at me with a mighty ferocity, he may meet my best shots with a robust volley that forces me to find within myself an even better response, his thoughts may challenge long held and precious assumptions but I have become accustomed to valuing his opinion and savouring his wisdom. It has been said that Hazlitt straddled the 18th and the 19th centuries that he joined up the ages of Enlightenment and Romanticism, that in him reason and imagination co-habit. I agree with this. I also see him as a man of the 21st century, at home in a Freudian world, conscious of the complexities of human living, convinced that much of what we wish for lies beyond conscious control.

I believe that if you want to understand someone properly you have to acquaint yourself with their environment, with the context within which they lived. This includes a stepping into their historical times. But it also includes the more challenging task of entering into a person's emotional and mental environment, the area inside themselves where they felt and thought.

Hazlitt stubbornly refused to be confined to any single place. His restless interest in the nature of things became infectious. He is up and off to other places and it is necessary to follow him, to go with him from his Winterslow cottage, to accompany him on his long walks over the English countryside; to know what its like to feel so depressed that walking across a room requires an enormous effort; to compete with him in a fiercely competitive rackets game; to stand with him as the jilted lover on the pavement outside the home of Sarah Walker, mad with love, mad with hate; to be at his side and stare for a week at a single hand painted by Rembrandt; to accompany him along the bustling streets of London which he loved and hated. Engagement with him needs to be based on the principles he espoused, a reaching out towards the other in sympathetic identification. To do less is simply unfair. Hazlitt has fallen foul of many critics who fail to accompany him in this way. Some of his biographers do the same. In some instances I find it hard to recognise the man they describe from the person I meet within his own words. Some may have stepped into his historical times but have refrained from entering his emotional and mental environment that area within which he felt thought and lived. If he 'invites' me to his table and places himself and his innermost thoughts in my hands, I believe it is good manners to join him.

Hazlitt who was a keen walker and could cover 30 miles a day as he strode across the English countryside, can stop abruptly and say the unexpected. In one of his most famous essays *The Fight* Hazlitt gives an account of a bout between Bill Neate and Tom Hickman, and when the combat is complete and its often horrific nature laid out for us to see, Hazlitt anticipating the observer's distaste in a flash turns to you as if you were standing beside him and says,

> Ye who despise the fancy, do something to show as much *pluck*, or as much self-possession as this, before you assume a superiority which you have never given a single proof of by any one action in the whole course of your lives![5]

Hazlitt often played his favourite game of rackets stripped to the waist, propelling himself into the action with great ferocity, cursing himself if he fell short, hailing himself if he succeeded. His combative corporeality, his raw earthiness can cause us to shift uneasily in our seats. But without this participation we will fall short of the mark in our attempt to grasp the sense and essence of him and his 'gusto'. 'Gusto' is one of the words which define Hazlitt. I will be exploring what it meant to him later in the book, but for the moment let us turn to a modern poet to give us a sense of it.

Between my finger and my thumb
The squat pen rests.
'll dig with it.[6]

As Seamus Heaney writes this poem he is sitting in his upstairs room watching his father dig out the cool, hard potatoes. His mind stretches back to his grandfather digging in Toner's bog for the best sods of turf. The body is behind the task, the hands are in the soil. As a counter weight to his fine sensitivity we often find Hazlitt digging with his pen, his work smelling of hard manual labour, his hands in the soil of his words, his mind strenuously unearthing the solid thoughts. 'My ideas,' he wrote 'from their sinewy texture, have been to me in the nature of realities.'

★★★

I would describe Hazlitt as a psychoanalytically minded man. Like Shakespeare before him, Hazlitt impresses with a keen perceptiveness of the workings of the human mind, possessing an intuitive and acute psychological sophistication, a capacity for penetrating insight well in advance of most of his contemporaries. Consider the times in which he lived, a period of great social change, a period which produced many great literary figures. Hazlitt observes changes and literary creations. What he experiences, what he feels, what he thinks what he comes to write is not one-dimensional; it is not simply geared to whether a work will sell well or not, whether it will bring popularity to the author. He has an enormous breadth and depth to his own mind. He brings these capabilities to bear upon a piece of work. His criticism is not theory-driven, but it does have a theory behind it. His response is not idiosyncratic, yet it is deeply personal, as if he has allowed the work to enter into the depth of his soul. It seems to live inside him and the emerge from him. In this respect he did not spare himself and neither did he spare the work or the person of the author. He considers it dishonest to do otherwise. His repertoire included an interest in the psychological effect of creative art and literature upon the recipient. He uses his own inner soul to facilitate pathways of communication between the art, the observer and the artist, between the text, the reader and the writer. The implication of this is that he is very interested in the *person,* indeed the *character* of the writer. It was here in this space he made many enemies.

Unlike William Wordsworth and Robert Southey, John Keats could appreciate the creativity, the originality and the genius of Hazlitt's criticism. In writing to the painter Benjamin Haydon in March 1818 Keats, sweeping through the negativism and the envy of a number of his contemporaries wrote:

It is a great pity that people should by associating themselves with the finest things, spoil them … Hunt has damned Hampstead and masks and sonnets and Italian tales – Wordsworth has damned the lakes– Millman has damned the old drama – West has damned wholesale – Peacock has damned satire, Oliver has damn'd music – Hazlitt has damned the bigotted and bluestockined – how durst the man? He is your only good damner, and if ever I am damn'd – damn me if I shouldn't like him to damn me.[7]

In more recent times John Kinnaird addressed the paucity of this type of criticism in today's literary world. Commenting on the fact that, with few exceptions, Hazlitt's estimations of his contemporaries and of works of literature before his time has proved unerringly accurate, he goes on to say:

Yet the fact that his criticism meets the surest test of time evidently holds little or no interest for us. And that this should be so suggests to me the rather terrible irony that today the word 'criticism' is ceasing to mean judgement at all. Today we 'interpret' a writer, we look for 'structure' and 'conventions' in the work, we 'place' him in a 'tradition,' and we may wish to decide whether he is or is not 'important for our time' – but all this judiciousness is not really judgement; for it is never a praise that is also willing, as Hazlitt's or Johnson's was, to damn. We no longer conceive of literature as inviting a judgement on its values, especially our fashionable values of 'irony' and 'paradox'; indeed, I suspect that all our celebration of the 'autonomy' of the work of art means no more than that, an exemption from criticism in the old sense – from a public estimate of the writer's character. If Hazlitt can still exasperate us today it is, I believe, because he reminds us that criticism, no matter how systematic its methods of analysis may become, can never escape the risk of a personal judgement of another's mind in its personality. Ignore or deride him how we will, our memory of Hazlitt will always be there reminding us that literature and criticism, whatever else they may be, end in the act of reading, in a dialogue that ensues; and he reminds us that these selves have brought themselves to write and read in order to know and judge, not 'art' or 'reality' or 'the modern self,' but themselves.[8]

Here Kinniard takes us to the heart of the matter. He is articulating a problem that besets literary criticism. But within his thoughts I hear echoes of a problem that concerns 'psychology'. My contention throughout this book is that a dynamic psychology, and particularly psychoanalysis, has much in common with literary criticism. Both are primarily concerned with creativity. The literary critic must always have an eye for the presence or absence of creativity. In psychoanalysis while we can only fully understand ourselves and our life by looking backwards at the past we can only change it by creatively living in the present. Psychoanalysis seeks to discover and unearth the obstacles to creativity. If you step back from being a literary critic or a psychoanalyst, you find yourself standing in the same area, occupying common ground.

★★★

This book is not a psycho-biography. It is not an attempt to put William Hazlitt's 'psychology' or his 'mind' under the microscope in order to find some new secrets. Consistent self examination and evaluation was an essential part of life for Hazlitt. We have already heard him speak in *'On Living to Ones' Self'* about the great effort he took to be satisfied with his own thoughts. I therefore see myself as my sub-title suggests, writing in the company of Hazlitt. I let my eyes rest on what he points out to me; I let my ears hear the music of his words; I allow the taste of his cooking partridge and the smell of the burning wood to intermingle with the patience and impatience of his thought. To allow my senses such companionship does not preclude turning to look at him when necessary. Perhaps the point can also be made by reference to a book called *William Hazlitt: Painted by Himself* by Catherine Macdonald Maclean.[9] She introduces this work by comparing his self portrait, which hangs in Maidstone Museum, Kent, with other portraits painted by others. She notes the difference and proceeds to write as if Hazlitt had written it himself. We read 142 pages of text written in the first person. I think this is a very inadequate form of biography. The frame that holds another person's life can be touched and visited, but if it is grasped too tightly it is in danger of being destroyed. You cannot continually intrude into someone else's mind in that manner. But the other major problem with this style is that the biographer becomes totally submerged in their subject. Just as I do not intend to take you on a journey through Hazlitt's life in a chronological fashion, (many of his biographers have adequately covered that ground) neither do I wish to act as a simple mirror scientifically reflecting his image. Again some of his biographers have taken this approach to such an extreme that they analyse the man and his works to death! Perhaps an alternative title to this book would be 'Thinking *with* Hazlitt'. I am therefore not merely applying his ideas to modern issues but using the wisdom which is available in his works to think about contemporary issues of human importance.

My *Table Talk* did not remain the only Hazlitt publication on my book shelf for long, and I was soon collecting and reading many of his works. I was made aware of the broad sweep of his interests and although known to many as an essayist and a literary critic, he was also a painter, journalist, a social and political commentator, a lecturer, a historian, a biographer, a philosopher, a critic not just of literature but of art and drama, his collected writings filling 21 volumes. At the same time I got caught up in the slipstream of interest in him and began to read about him. With no systematic guide to direct me I began with what was then the most recent biography by Stanley Jones (1989). To read more then one biography of any person's life was new for me but I was soon reading P.P.Howe (1922) and John Kinnard (1978) followed by Herschel Baker (1962), Catherine Macdonald Maclean (1943; 1948), David Bromwich (1983), Roy Park (1971), Ralph Wardle (1971), Augustine Birrell (1902) Hesketh Pearson (1934) and Alexander Ireland (1889). Anthony Grayling's Biography (2000) would appear later. I was thus provided with a very challenging experience. I read Hazlitt's own words and there around him stood this array of biographers and commentators, distinguished men and women in the field of English Literature. In the positions taken up in relation to Hazlitt the sweep is wide. Some state their aim as a reporting of the facts of Hazlitt's life, supplying information by drawing on his own writings and the details supplied by his contemporaries. P.P. Howe is a case in point. He stands at the centre of modern Hazlitt biographers, his book *The Life of William Hazlitt* (1922) together with his compilation and editorship of *The Complete Works of William Hazlitt* (1928–32) has provided a reference point for all subsequent explorations. To other biographers Hazlitt seems to be an object of academic research, his genius will be acknowledged but a respectable distance will be kept from the subject. Others allow the man to enter into their lives from whence they deliver their scholarly texts but do not recount Hazlitt's effect on their being. Some biographers are quite partisan in their approach to their subject, defending or attacking him. It is tempting to take sides on these issues and try to reach a definitive stance about who is right and who is wrong. Such judgements and subsequent choice may be required, but for my part reading conflicting accounts adds intrigue and increases my curiosity in the man and his writings. Let us look at some examples.

Brimley Johnson wrote the introduction to the 1907 edition of Hazlitt's *Lectures on the English Comic Writers*. Here he says:

> It is undeniable that neither his most intimate friends nor his most sympathetic critics have spoken or written of William Hazlitt with enthusiastic abandon or with spontaneous affection … We think much and often of what he has written; little and seldom of the man himself … he repels us … he was dissatisfied, morbid and tempestuous … he never trusted a friend, yielding continually to petty suspicions and imagining himself slighted at every word.[10]

Such a reprobate is this man that Johnson needs – on no evidence whatsoever – to have Hazlitt finding God on his death bed. To William Wordsworth Hazlitt would become an outcast. In response to Hazlitt's criticism he wrote:

> The miscreant Hazlitt continues, I have heard, to abuse Southey, Coleridge and myself, in the Examiner. I hope you do not associate with the Fellow, he is not a proper person to be admitted into respectable society.[11]

Bryan Procter one of Hazlitt's contemporaries said this of him:

> It has been supposed that Hazlitt was dogmatical and fond of controversy, and that
> he resented any opposition to his opinions. This is an error. He liked *discussion*
> – fair, free talk, upon subjects that interested him; but few men ever yielded
> more readily to argument, for few ever sought truth more sincerely. He had no
> overweening sense of his own superiority; indeed, as far as I could perceive, he
> was utterly without vanity. He was very candid, and would hear his own opinions
> canvassed with the utmost patience. In his conversation he was plain, amusing,
> convincing. There was nothing of the ambitious or florid style which is sometimes
> perceptible in his writings. He was rarely eloquent. Once or twice, when stung
> by some pertinacious controversialist, I have known him exhibit eloquent and
> impetuous declamation; but in general he used the most familiar phrases, and
> made truth, rather than triumph, the object of discussion. He enjoyed anecdotes
> illustrative of character, spoke pithily upon occasion, and, when in good spirits
> and good humour, was the most delightful gossip in the world![12]

Like Procter John Hamilton Reynolds found Hazlitt's company extremely
stimulating and in his letter to Mary Pierce Leigh written in 1817, provides us
with a virtual portrait of the man. He wrote:

> He is indeed *great* company, and leaves a weight upon the mind, which it can
> hardly bear. He is full of what Dr. Johnson terms 'Good talk.' His countenance
> is also extremely fine: – a sunken and melancholy face, – a forehead lined
> with thought and bearing a full and strange sorrow, but kindling and living at
> intellectual moments, – and a stream of coal-black hair dropping round all. Such
> a face, so silent and sensitive, is indeed the banner of the mind.[13]

These quotations could be thought of as positioned on the ends of a straight
line. By plotting all the points in between it might be thought possible to arrive
at a neat picture of Hazlitt, but those who have gone down that road provide
a portrait which is out of focus with his writings. While engaged in copying
a Titian at the Louvre in 1803 Hazlitt met a fellow student whose technique
involved the division of his canvas into numerous small squares and having no
order in the sequence of his copying. This machine-like attempt at painting
by numbers or photographic duplication appalled him, because it lacked any
imaginative identification with, and feeling for, the subject. He laid great stress
on the use of the imaginative and emotive capacities in the task of knowing
another person.

Hazlitt will not fit into any neat classification that may be made for him. As
well as listening to others let us listen to him in one of his many open-hearted
reflections on himself:

I have often been reproached for considering things only in their abstract principles, and with heat and ill-temper, for getting into a passion about what no ways concerned me. If any one wishes to see me quite calm, they may cheat me in a bargain or tread upon my toes; but a truth repelled, a sophism repeated, totally disconcerts me, and I lose all patience. I am not, in the ordinary acceptation of the term, *a good-natured man*; that is, many things annoy me besides what interferes with my own ease and interest. I hate a lie; a piece of injustice wounds me to the quick, though nothing but the report of it reach me. Therefore I have made many enemies and few friends; for the public know nothing of well-wishers, and keep a wary eye on those that would reform them. Coleridge used to complain of my irascibility in this respect, and not without reason.[14]

★★★

How should we begin knowing such a person? To do him justice we must consent to meet him on his own ground. This means accepting his invitation to read him, to look, not just at his actions and his theories. As he stated 'the author's mind is seen in his writings, as his face is in the glass.' We are required to listen to him, and allow him to effect us. Part of my attraction to him is that when he spoke about his interest in 'Metaphysics' what he is often referring to is what we would call 'Psychology'. Grayling refers to his attention to issues of moral motivation and character and names it a 'moral psychology'.[15] When Hazlitt refers to 'Philosophy' he is often referring to an introspective philosophy. In *The Shyness of Scholars* he wrote 'Philosophy also teaches self-knowledge; and self-knowledge strikes equally at the root of any inordinate opinion of ourselves, or wish to impress others with idle admiration.'[16] Catherine Macdonald Maclean who apart from her book *William Hazlitt: Painted by Himself* also wrote a valuable biography called *William Hazlitt: Born Under Saturn*[17] and, who had no expressed knowledge of psychoanalysis wrote about Hazlitt's interest in the 'under-conscious' with which she says 'his later essays are saturated and which constitutes one of their chief preservatives and one of the chief sources of their power to interest'. This is substantiated by Hazlitt who wrote about 'the way in which I work out some of my conclusions underground, before throwing them up to the surface' and his stated aim that in his essays he set out to write 'a sort of *Liber Veritatis,* a set of studies from human life.' Because man is an intellectual animal he is an everlasting contradiction to himself. 'His senses centre in himself, his ideas reach to the ends of the universe; so that he is torn to pieces between the two, without a possibility of it being otherwise'. If we need further clarification, as to what falls within the rubric of 'Metaphysics' and 'Philosophy' as Hazlitt conceived of them, we can turn to his own words:

Physical experience is indeed the foundation and the test of that part of philosophy which relates to physical objects … but to say that physical experiment is either the test or source or guide of that other part of philosophy which relates to our internal perceptions, that we are to look to external nature for the form, the substance, the colour, the very life and being of whatever exists in our minds, or that we can only infer the laws which regulate the phenomena of the mind from those which regulate the phenomena of matter, is to confound two things entirely distinct. Our knowledge of mental phenomena from consciousness, reflection, or observation of their corresponding signs in others is the true basis of metaphysical inquiry, as the knowledge of *facts*, commonly so called, is the only solid basis of natural philosophy.[18]

★★★

When I acquired Hazlitt's *Characters of Shakespeare's Plays* I found his first words that I had heard. They appeared in his reflections on *Troilus and Cressida*. Chaucer had also written a play based on the same historical event, hence the direct comparison with Shakespeare. Hazlitt wrote:

Chaucer had a great variety of powers but he could only do one thing at once. He set himself to work on a particular subject. His ideas were kept separate, labelled, ticketed and parcelled out in a set form, in pews and compartments by themselves. They did not play into one another's hands, they do not react upon one another as the blower's breath moulds the yielding glass. There is something hard and dry in them. What is the most wonderful thing in Shakespeare's faculties is their excessive sociability, and how they gossiped and compared notes together.[19]

Hazlitt returned to the same subject in his *Lectures on the English Poets*, where he wrote:

The striking peculiarity of Shakespeare's mind was its generic quality, its power of communication with all other minds – so that it contained a universe of thought and feeling within itself, and had no one peculiar bias, or exclusive excellence more than another. He was just like any other man, but that he was like all other men … The passion in Shakespeare is of the same nature as his delineation of character … The human soul is made the sport of fortune, the prey of adversity: it is stretched on the wheel of destiny, in restless ecstasy. The passions are in a state of projection.[20]

I listen to these words is two ways. I hear a marvellous description of Shakespeare's imaginative powers. If I stand further back and realise that these are Hazlitt's words I can see the justification of William Bewick's comment when he described Hazlitt as 'the Shakespeare prose writer of our glorious country; he outdoes all in truth, style and originality'.[21]

There is however another side to the connection with Shakespeare. It is related not to style nor to original powers of imaginative expression, but to his 'delineation of character,' his ability to perceive the truth about human nature. Shakespeare is in my reading the pre-eminent psychologist of all time. As poet and playwright he has expressed and dramatised every shade of human character; he has understood the complexities of human beings and the manner in which opposites coexist in the one person. There are many instances of this in his writings. One of my favourites in when he has Richard II speak:

> Thus play I in one person many people,
> And none contented.

It may seem a bold assertion but Hazlitt approaches Shakespeare in his understanding of human character. He never wrote a verse of poetry or a single work of fiction but his distinctive prose is inhabited by a Shakespearean spirit in its appreciation of the complexities of life. All great interpreters of Shakespeare have listened to his famous words spoken by Polinus in Hamlet:

> To thine own self be true,
> And it must follow, as the night the day,
> Thou canst not then be false to any man.

Hazlitt was always his own man, but he was not ashamed of the awe he felt for the man from Stratford. Such awe is not something to apologise for, if it is an expression of the greatness of the man and not an idolisation of him. Shakespeare's greatness rests on his ability to grasp truth and express it. That truth is something bigger than himself. Hazlitt is not just a passive conduit through which Shakespearean gems pass, nor is he another writer elaborating on Shakespeare. He stands on his own, an independent spirit. We might also imagine him standing beside Shakespeare. Through words written two hundred years ago by Hazlitt and four hundred years ago by Shakespeare we can travel back in time. The words of both men have lasted because they speak to us in our present life. As you progress through this book you will find the Shakespeare is never far away, with frequent reference will be made to his writings. To express the same sentiment as Shakespeare about being true to oneself Hazlitt found his own words. In his work as a dramatic critic he was once accused of being too personal. His reply:

My opinions have been sometimes called singular: they are merely sincere. I say what I think: I think what I feel. I cannot help receiving certain impressions from things; and I have sufficient courage to declare (somewhat abruptly) what they are. This is the only singularity I am conscious of.[22]

★★★

If 1798 had begun in dramatic fashion for Hazlitt the following year would open on no less profound a note. In the spring he visited an exhibition of old Italian Masters at Pall Mall in London. If the light of Coleridge's intellectual genius had begun to shine in his soul and if Wordsworth's poetry could cloth the naked with beauty and grandeur, Hazlitt would be dazzled and delighted with what his eyes were to behold as he walked among these great paintings. Here began a life long love of art, and his first steps towards becoming a renowned art critic. It also points us to one of the great secrets of Hazlitt's prose, his ability to paint pictures with words. In this he will become a master of the imaginative his speculative mind will become married to the picturesque. If Hazlitt was in awe of these timeless paintings that hung on gallery walls it was because he saw in them a representation of the everlasting, everyday truths of human living. This was another aspect of his writing which struck me from the beginning, the manner in which he brought people to life. I think of him as a gifted guide in an art gallery; as we look at this framed object, at those still figures that lived generations before us, set forever on canvas, and listen to his words, soon they become living objects, the people seem to move, the paint seems wet, the blood is flowing through their veins, and their skin feels moist. The faces, like those of the living who stand beside us might talk, might transport us to timeless moments in a shared past. Hazlitt continually painted picture portraits of his subjects. But let us go back to Pall Mall and to his account of the exhibition. This is how he described his exhibition:

> I was staggered when I saw the works there collected, and looked at them with wondering and with longing eyes. A mist passed away from my sight: the scales fell off. A new sense came upon me, a new heaven and a new earth stood before me. I saw the soul speaking in the face —'hands that the rod of empire had swayed' in the mighty ages past —'a forked mountain or blue promontory,'

> 'with trees upon't
> That nod unto the world and mock our eyes with air.'

> Old Time had unlocked his treasures, and Fame stood portress at the door … We had heard the names of Titian, Raphael, Guido, Domenichino, the Caracci – but to see them face to face, to be in the same room with their deathless productions, was like breaking some mighty spell – was almost an effect of necromancy! From that time I lived in a world of pictures. Battles, sieges, speeches in parliament

seemed mere idle noise and fury, 'signifying nothing,' compared with these mighty works and dreaded names that spoke to me in the eternal silence of thought.[23]

★★★

If you look up into a cloudless night sky in the southern hemisphere the stars of the constellation Cruz are clearly visible. These stars are popularly called The Southern Cross because they make a shape of a cross with the north/south axis pointing to the South Pole. For many years I naively presumed these stars stood side by side, as if their actual position somehow matched the way they appeared on the Australian flag. By visiting the Sydney Observatory where I could see a model of the stars relationship to each other I learned their true positions were not at all as I had presumed. Far from being aligned side by side they are set at great distances from each other. So distant are they that as I look up in the year 2003 from my Sydney home their true positioning is as follows. The light which I see from the nearest star Gamma, set out for earth in the year 1898 while Epsilon began its journey in 1843. Delta's light set out three hundred years earlier in 1543, Beta's in 1513 and the light from Alpha the last and furthest began its long journey in the year 1482, a decade before Christopher Columbus set sail for the Americas. The nearest is therefore more than 400 light years from the furthest.

At the Observatory I had to adjust pre-conceptions and allow my mind to enter into a different sense of time. The magic and the mystery of the written word allows us humans to traverse great expanses of time in a mere instant. People from distant eras live on through their words, and if we can make the necessary adjustments, we can hear them talk with the necessary freshness of living speech. Hazlitt lived in such a world. Already we have seen how alive Shakespeare was to him. When he walked through the woods or sat down to eat or write he felt the presence of those from ages past. We shall hear him describe their company and their presence. When I read Hazlitt's frequent references to works of literature, I listen to them in this vein. They are not merely the inclusion of a text to bolster his arguments or to display his knowledge of a subject; they arrive as if they know their place. As I look back in time I see not only Hazlitt and his luminaries, but those who have come after him who spoke with the same voice. Together they form a unified constellation; they illuminate life, and we need their texts and their company. They have addressed the same perennial human questions and their invaluable wisdom should not be lost, nor should the truths they spoke be extinguished by a narrow preoccupation with our earthly present. So while this book is not following the daily footsteps of Hazlitt's life, it nevertheless has an order and coherence, and reading it may require of you an adjustment similar to the one I was required to make in the Sydney Observatory. Welcome aboard!

Chapter 2

Hazlitt's Life and Times

William Hazlitt's father, who was also called William, was an Irishman who came from Shronell in County Tipperary. William senior was born in 1737 and his parents were Presbyterians who had moved from County Antrim in the North of Ireland. They were poor farmers but had a determination to provide their children with a good education. Excluded from Oxford and Cambridge, the only universities in England, because they did not belong to the established church, their two sons attended Glasgow University, where William senior graduated and became a minister in the Unitarian church.

William Hazlitt's mother was an Englishwoman. Her name was Grace Loftus. She was born in 1746. She was the daughter of an ironmonger in Wisbech, Norfolk. William and Grace married in 1766 when he was 29 and she was 20. Their first child, John, was born the following year. He was followed in 1768 by a second son, Loftus, who would die two years later. In 1770 Margaret was born and the family moved to Maidstone, Kent, where they would live for the next ten years. It was there that William, the subject of this book, was born in on 10 April 1778.

William senior was outspoken on political matters and, as his support for the American War of Independence made him unpopular with some of his congregation, he decided to leave England. He returned with his family to his native country in 1780 where he was appointed as minister to a small community in Bandon, County Cork. Bandon was a garrison town and the Rev. Hazlitt soon became aware of the cruel treatment of the American prisoners of war by the British army. He had the ear of powerful people in London and succeeded in having the matter investigated by the authorities. However, not only did he make himself unpopular with the military, but some of the townspeople who depended economically on the presence of the British regiments resented the threat to their livelihood. He decided to move on. With a missionary intent and in search of a more tolerant society the family emigrated to the USA in 1783. But their hopes for a better life were not realised. William senior's liberality conflicted with the Calvinistic orthodoxy of New England and he found it difficult to get a suitable post. The family encountered many other difficulties and four years later they returned to England to settle in the village of Wem in Shropshire, where William grew up.

William was now 9 years old and the family had been on the move since he was 2. He attended the local school and was also tutored by his father. Biographers have variously described him during his school days as intelligent, intense, priggish, precocious, delightful. In 1793, at the age of 15, he went to the

Unitarian New College at Hackney, London. He was able to keep in touch with his brother John who was living nearby in Long Acre and working successfully as a painter. Hackney College was by any standards a progressive educational establishment set up for the sons of Unitarians. Some, but by no means all, of the students were studying for the ministry. William seems to have had aspirations in that direction, but these did not last long. The college provided a liberal education and had some prominent thinkers and teachers on its staff, but its future was always a precarious one. While he was there William was exposed to ideas from many sources. He found it difficult always to follow the curriculum, but engaged in intense private study. One significant moment in his life came when he failed to produce a piece of work as required. Instead of reprimanding him, Mr Currie, his tutor, asked to see what he had been writing, and the young man produced an essay on civil justice (which he would later expand and publish as *A Project for a New Theory of Civil and Criminal Legislation*).[1] With some inkling that he was not dealing with an ordinary mind, Currie did not discourage the boy's explorations.

But Hackney College did not last, and when it was closed in 1796, William left London and returned to Wem and to private study for a few years. In 1798 he met Coleridge and Wordsworth. In the same year he moved back to London and tried to develop a career as a portrait painter, schooled in part by his brother John, and in the following year the exhibition of the Italian Masters presented him with the wonderment of the visual on canvas.

He was commissioned to make some copies of the great masters at the Louvre and in 1802, during a period of peace between France and England, he spent some months in Paris. On his return to England he managed to make a meagre living as an itinerant portrait painter. In 1803 he met Charles Lamb who would remain one of his most constant friends. In 1805 his first publication appeared in a book on Philosophy called 'An Essay on the Principles of Human Action'. He began his writing on social policy and in 1806 published *Free Thoughts on Public Affairs: or, Advice to a Patriot*. In 1807 he wrote a *Preface to an Abridgement of Abraham Tucker's Light of Nature Pursued*. Also in that year he published *The Eloquence of the British Senate* and *A Reply to Malthus's Essay on Population*.

In 1808 he married Sarah Stoddart. For the next four years they lived between London and Winterslow on Salisbury Plain. He wrote *A New and Improved Grammar of the English Tongue* in 1810. In 1811 his only child to survive, also called William, was born. In 1812 he gave his first public lectures on English Philosophy and got his first job as a parliamentary reporter with the *Morning Chronicle*. He had now given up hope of being a good enough painter. (One of Hazlitt's paintings, the portrait of Charles Lamb, is in the National Portrait Gallery in London. All his other works are in the Maidstone Museum in Kent.) *Memoirs of Thomas Holcroft* appeared in 1816. His writing and critical career began to expand with work for the *Champion*, the *Examiner* and the *Edinburgh Review*. By 1817 he was a major essayist, art and drama critic and political commentator. He met and became a strong influence on the young John Keats. His major books began to appear, *The Round Table* (1817), *Characters of Shakespeare's Plays* (1817), *Lectures on the English Poets* (1818), *A View of the English Stage* (1818), *Lectures on the English Comic Writer* (1819), *Political Essays* (1819), *A Letter to William Gifford, Esq.* (1819) *Lectures on the Dramatic Literature of the Age of Elizabeth* (1820). His marriage broke up and he became infatuated with Sarah Walker. He wrote *Table Talk* (1821–22). *A Reply to 'Z'* written in 1818 was published in 1823. This was followed by *Liber Amoris; or, The New Pygmalion* (1823), *Characteristics: in the Manner of Rochefoucauld's Maxims* (1823), *Sketches of the Principal Picture Galleries in England* (1824), *The Spirit of the Age* (1825). He married Isabella Bridgewater in 1824 but three years later they separated. He wrote *Notes of a Journey through France and Italy* (1826), *The Plain Speaker* (1826), *The Life of Napoleon Buonaparte* (1828–30) and *Conversations of James Northcote* (1830). He died in Soho, London on September 18 1830. He was fifty two.

★★★

What we identify as the age of Romanticism was named by Coleridge as the 'age of anxiety'. Vast numbers of people in England lived a precarious existence, seldom knowing where the next meal would come from. In his maiden speech in the House of Lords in 1812 Byron said 'I have been in some of the most oppressed provinces of Turkey, but never under the most despotic of infidel governments did I behold such squalid wretchedness as I have seen since my return in the very heart of a Christian country'. When John Keats went walking in Scotland and Ireland in 1818 and observed the appalling poverty around him he blamed the political system pronouncing it 'a barbarous age'.

Hazlitt was a thorn in the flesh of the establishment all his life. If the battles on the fields of Europe during the Napoleonic wars were fierce, the conflicts on the pages of the British press were equally ferocious. Hazlitt was in the thick of the fray; a corrosive sublimate eating out despotism, battering down the privileges seized at the expense of the poor. In Australia we are all too familiar with the draconian penal system that fuelled transportation which was central to the modern birth of this country.

To understand Hazlitt some appreciation of history and the society in which he lived is necessary. What I am about to provide are brief literary snapshots intended to give a sense of the tumultuous times in which he lived – a period in history characterised and shaped by three powerful events, the French Revolution, the Napoleonic Wars and the Industrial Revolution. In chapter 12, I will be dealing with Hazlitt's political thought in greater detail.

In 1793 William Pitt the younger, then Prime Minister, fearing or pretending to fear an insurrection, moved to crush reformist agitation. A meeting of reformers in Edinburgh was halted by the police and the leaders charged with sedition. Five were found guilty and sentenced to deportation. In the spring of 1794 Pitt suspended Habeas Corpus and Thomas Hardy, founder of the London Corresponding Society (a group of lower and middle class Dissenters), along with 11 others, including Thomas Holcroft, John Thelwell and Horne Tooke, was charged with treason. Pitt had made the public discussion of public affairs a capital offence and his attorney-general said it was high treason for anyone to campaign for 'representative government'. The intervention of the political reformer William Godwin turned public opinion against Pitt and the accused were acquitted. The British historian George Macaulay Trevelyan [2] wrote that 'This timely check saved England from a course of bloodshed, and perhaps ultimately from a retributive revolution'. Pitt would suspend Habeas Corpus again in 1798, pass the Treason and Sedition Acts in 1795, the Unlawful Oath Act in 1797 and ban the Corresponding Societies in 1799. While larger political freedoms were to be suppressed so also were any moves by an increasingly industrialised and urbanised work force to organise and unionise itself.

Prominent publications which supported reform were always in the government's sights. The *Examiner* owned by John and Leigh Hunt was a very successful paper selling 8000 copies a week in 1812. In 1810 the government made its first unsuccessful attempt to sue, and it failed again the following year. The offence on the second occasion was to reprint an article on military flogging which had already appeared in a provincial journal, the *Stamford News*. In 1813 however the proprietors were not so lucky. Leigh and John Hunt, as owners of the *Examiner*, were charged and found guilty of libelling the Prince Regent, sentenced to two years imprisonment and fined £1000. The offending piece they had published was:

> What person, unacquainted with the true state of the case, would imagine that … the delightful, blissful, wise, pleasurable, honourable, virtuous, true and immortal prince, was a violator of his word, a libertine over head and ears in disgrace, a despiser of domestic ties, the companion of gamblers and demireps, a man who has just closed half a century without one single claim on the gratitude of his country, or the respect of posterity.

Hazlitt met John and Leigh Hunt in 1812. He shared strong political affiliations with both men. Leigh might have been too much of a showman for Hazlitt's liking, and he personally felt more at ease with the quiet, steady John. Hazlitt dedicated his *Political Essays*, published in 1819 by William Hone, to John Hunt whom he described as a 'tried, steady, zealous, and conscientious advocate of the liberty of his country'. John Hunt was again imprisoned for a year in May 1821 under the Six Acts of 1819.

The population of England and Wales at the 1811 census was 10,488,000. London had 1,050,000 inhabitants. Tom Paine, whose sermon prompted Edmund Burke to write 'Reflections on the Revolution in France', summed up the situation when in 1794 he stated that 'the town of Old Sarum, which contains not three houses, sends two members to Parliament and the town of Manchester, which contains upwards of 60,000 is not admitted to send any. Is there any principle in these things?'

The 'Rotten Boroughs' was the name given to the urban electoral constituencies. The system was medieval, and despite great social, economic and demographic changes, had remained in place. Very few people were entitled to vote, in some cases only the Mayor and Alderman. Corruption was rife, a seat in parliament could be bought at the right price or bestowed by a powerful landowner as payment for services rendered. Inside Westminster there was a corruption of a similar kind with votes bought and sold. As to the administration of the executive business of government, sinecures and pensions as payments for favours were the order of the day.

Twenty-five years after Paine's remarks little had changed. In 1819 on August 16 at St Peter's-Field in Manchester a large crowd gathered to protest against the fact that they were still unrepresented in Parliament. This peaceful meeting of 80,000 men, women and children was set upon by a contingent of the Manchester Yeomanry Cavalry who hacked into the crowd and in ten minutes two women, a child and eight men were dead and 413 people wounded. This became known as the Peterloo Massacre. The action of the magistrate who ordered the troops to break up the meeting was praised in Parliament and further repressive laws called the Six Acts passed into law. Hazlitt did not live to see the great Reform Act of 1832 which abolished the rotten boroughs and broadened the franchise.

We can step forward a dozen years after Hazlitt's death to see how people who had been caught up in the industrial revolution lived. In the year 1842 the Royal Commission on Mines, when reporting on the conditions in the mining industry, revealed that children under five often worked alone in the darkness and provided the following report from a Lancashire woman: 'I have a belt around my waist and chain passing between my legs, and I go on my hands and feet. The water comes up to my clog tops, and I have seen it over my thighs. I have drawn till I have the skin off me. The belt and chain is worse when we are in the family way.'[3]

A snapshot of the life of one individual might illustrate the nature of the times. As you walk into the Botanical Gardens in Sydney you see a plaque to one Joseph Gerald. Gerald was born in 1760 in the West Indies of an Irish father and an English mother. He was a barrister and had practised law in America where he had observed the emergence of democratically elected government. Gerald moved to live and work in England. He was a brilliant man, an eloquent speaker and a reformer and was therefore considered dangerous by the Tory government. He was charged with 'sedition' on four counts. They were: using French words, using the word 'citizen' (perhaps heard in the same way as 'comrade' was in the USA in the 1950s), attending illegal meetings, and using arguments in support of reform of the electoral system. He was found guilty and sentenced to fourteen years' transportation. He arrived in Sydney in 1796 but died of consumption aged 36 a few months later.

The English penal system had developed into a sprawling mess. During the reign of George II and for much of the reign of George III capital offences multiplied at more than two a year. Two hundred different types of crime were punishable by death. This haphazard evolution often arose out of extreme moral indignation to one particular offence but the end product was an absurd and unjust system. To steal a boat from a river was a capital offence, but it was not if one stole it from a canal. To cut down trees in a garden was punishable by death. Justices of the Peace were often laws unto themselves and the most significant feature in many cases was not the offence or the evidence but the character of the particular Justice hearing the case. (When Sir Robert Peel as Home Secretary in 1823 introduced reform he removed the death penalty from over 100 different offences.) It was in 1829 that Peel established the first organised police force, the Metropolitan Police in London. The sheer inefficiency of the legal system is exemplified by the position of debtors. In any year 40,000 debtors were gaoled. (Hazlitt himself was briefly incarcerated for debt but speedily released by a friend.) Debtors were placed in the hands of gaolers who ran their gaol as a business. Inside they had to pay for their food and often ran up further debt to the gaoler, sometimes leading to the absurd position whereby the prisoner was acquitted or had served his time but languished for years without release because he was unable to pay his debts to the gaoler.

Anglicanism was the state religion and the universities excluded the non-conformists. Of Oxford and Cambridge, the only two universities in England, Trevelyan has written that 'instead of being the national centres of learning and instruction, they were little more than comfortable monastic establishments for clerical sinecurists with a tinge of letters.'[4] Joseph Priestley, a prominent Dissenter, wrote to Pitt saying 'The universities were pools of stagnant water secured by dams and mounds and offensive to the neighbourhood, whereas the non-conformists schools were rivers, which, taking their natural course, fertilise a whole country.' [5] Priestley also described Anglicanism as 'a fungus upon the noble plant of Christianity'. The Dissenters' colleges, like Hackney where Tom Paine was head, usually flourished around a charismatic individual and then folded with the death or departure of its leader. It is important to recognise that religion and religious affiliation was often the only way open to many people not only to get some education, but also to be part of a political constituency. The established church was primarily interested in maintaining its own privileges. Its attitude to change is perhaps best expressed by Bishop Horsley who in 1795 said, 'the mass of the people had nothing to do with the laws but to obey them'.[6] Not surprisingly, during the latter part of the 18th century membership of religious groups like the Methodists, Baptists, Congregationalists and Unitarians increased dramatically.

Besides the terrible poverty of large sections of society (then awaiting the pen of Charles Dickens to dramatise it) and the need for electoral and parliamentary reform and the removal of discrimination from those who did not follow the state religion, other social and political issues of significance were the persecution of the Irish Catholics, the slave trade and the draconian penal system. William Wilberforce was a good example of a person whose evangelicalism enabled him to be a leading light in the abolition of the slave trade. Prior to his conversion he mixed in the best society and was a friend of Pitt and many of the ruling class. With a foot in different camps he managed to unite opinion to effect one of the greatest social changes in the history of mankind. As the American colonies had been lost, Lord Sydney, Home Secretary in 1786, persuaded Pitt to use Australia as the new destination for the transportation of convicts, and the First Fleet sailed into Botany Bay in January 1788 when Hazlitt was almost ten years old.

Having expanded as a war machine up to 1815, the British economy fell into recession creating an estimated two million beggars. Hazlitt was not alone in the belief that the Lake Poets had taken 'the king's shilling'. He was deeply disappointed with Coleridge in whom he had seen the potential as a spokesman for reform. The repressive political regime which maintained the status quo was in 1818 supported by Wordsworth and Robert Southey. The liberal lawyer Henry Brougham, who had defended the Hunts, stood for a seat in parliament against the Tory candidate Lowther, the son of Wordsworth's patron William Lowther, Earl of Lonsdale. Wordsworth actively campaigned against Brougham, much to the disgust of Hazlitt, Keats and others of more liberal mind. Expressing his reasons for standing for parliament Brougham said that with the suspension of basic rights 'everyone who rose in a meeting, or sat down at his desk, to attack the measures of his majesty's ministers, now knew that he did so with a halter about his neck.'

Lord Lowther owned so much land in the north of England that it was said he could walk from coast to coast and never need to step off his own property. He had an income of £200,000 a year. This was at a time when less than fifteen percent of the country had an income of over £50. Until Brougham stood as a candidate the seat had not been contested. The Lowther camp did not expect to be opposed, as if the seat belonged to them by family right. William Wordsworth lived on property given to him by Lowther. Wordsworth was on a visit to

London when he heard the news of Brougham's candidacy. He immediately wrote to Lowther telling him the news and pledging his support. John Keats's walking tour of the Lake District coincided with the election and he wrote of his disgust at Wordsworth's behaviour.

The whole fabric of society was under stress from many sides. The poor and starving clamoured for food only to find the price of bread rising dramatically with an almost three-fold increase in the decade leading up to the year 1800. As the King drove in his carriage to open Parliament in 1793 his coach was attacked by an angry mob crying 'No War! No King! No Pitt! Peace! Peace! Peace! Bread! Bread!' Nor were those who sat in Parliament immune from drama and pressure. Edmund Burke made a dramatic resignation from the Whigs by flinging a dagger into the floor of the House of Commons in 1792, only to be followed by a weeping Charles James Fox. In the 30 years leading up to 1820, 19 Members of Parliament committed suicide and another 20 were pronounced insane. In 1811 the Prime Minister Perceval was assassinated in the House of Commons. Uncertainty and fear was spread throughout the reformist sections of society by the government system of maintaining spies and *agents provocateurs* who both incited and fabricated revolt among the poor and working class. In 1822 Peel as home secretary formally abolished the system.

In 1817 *The Round Table* was published containing 52 essays, 12 by Leigh Hunt and 40 by Hazlitt. They had previously been published in the *Examiner*. A review in the *New Monthly Magazine,* which was a mouthpiece for the Tory government, said the title was misleading and it should be called '"The Dunghill" or something still more characteristically vile; for such an offensive heap of pestilential jargon has seldom come our way'. It described the essays as 'raked together from the common sewer of a weekly paper called the *Examiner,* and they who after that information can have any relish for the feculent garbage of blasphemy and scurrility, may sit down at *The Round Table*, and enjoy the same meal with the same appetite as the negroes in the West Indies eat dirt and filth'.

Hazlitt wrote stridently against slavery and although the slave trade was abolished in1807, it was not until 1833 that slavery itself was made illegal. He believed that the treating of a minority in an uncivilised manner was a sign of a primitive or a collapsed civilisation. Writing about the Jewish madam who controlled the young prostitutes around the theatres in London, Hazlitt detested her abuse of them, but as always has an eye to the larger picture:

> We throw in the teeth of the Jews that they are prone to certain sordid
> vices. If they are vicious it is we who have made them so. Shut out any
> class of people from the path to fair fame, and you reduce them to grovel
> in the pursuit of riches and the means to live … You tear up people by the

roots and trample on them like noxious weeds, and then make an outcry that they do not take root in the soil like wholesome plants, you drive them like a pest from city to city, from kingdom to kingdom, and then you call them vagabonds and aliens.[7]

The fierceness of Hazlitt's criticism of Robert Southey is often referred to by those who highlight what they call Hazlitt's 'spleen'. Certainly his broadside on the poet laureate in 1818 illustrated that Hazlitt was a formidable enemy to make. But here again an understanding of the context is important. Southey was actively supporting the right-wing Tory government in their suspension of Habeas Corpus and the passing of the Sedition Act. He referred to Hazlitt and Hunt as men who 'live by calumny and sedition; they are libellers and liars by trade', and said that they should be arrested and transported. How would we react today if we read Southey's words (written in 1814) calling for the French to be castigated as 'the Jews of Europe, a people politically excommunicated and never to be forgiven, and above all never to be trusted'.

In 1803 when England again declared war on France Hazlitt condemned the general warmongering which was in fashion and in particular the activity of Wordsworth who in his sonnets was calling the nation to war and to its supposed glories. To Hazlitt this was an example of a long narrowing of the mind. A nation must defend itself and Hazlitt did not exempt himself from playing a role in such an emergency. What he most criticised was extolling of the glory of war and taking delight in the destruction of one's fellow man. When this point is reached everyone becomes a loser. Men have lost the awareness of their common humanity. This is an issue central to Hazlitt's politics which will be returned to in chapter 12 but he did not believe that wrongs would right themselves. 'Society' he wrote, 'when out of order, which it is whenever the interests of the many are regularly and outrageously sacrificed to those of the few, must be repaired, and either a reform or a revolution cleanses its corruptions and renew its elasticity.'[8]

Chapter 3

The Hand That Rocks the Cradle Rules the World

But for those first affections,
Those shadowy recollections,
Which, be they what they may,
Are yet the fountain-light of all our day,
Are yet a master-light of all our seeing.
William Wordsworth, 'Ode to Immortality'

In the previous chapter I mentioned the events of William Hazlitt's life that are usually found in introductions to collections of his essays, that he was born in Maidstone, Kent in 1778, he was the youngest of three children, having a brother John who was ten years older and a sister Margaret, often called Peggy, who was seven years older. His father and William's relationship with him have figured with reasonably regularity in many biographies. In some instances we find a whole chapter, even two, devoted to recounting the father's influence on his son. On the other hand Hazlitt's mother Grace, (née Loftus) who outlived William by seven years has rarely been mentioned in accounts of his life and the amount of information provided about her in half a dozen books would not stretch beyond a brief paragraph. Catherine Macdonald Maclean[1] proves to be an exception in this regard and gives some space to the relationship between mother and son. Macdonald Maclean recounts the difficulties which the family encountered during William's early years as they moved from England to Ireland, to the USA and back to England. However she does not depart from another commonly accepted view that despite the many upheavals and traumas endured by the family, the young William had a blissful childhood.

I begin this chapter with two questions. Why has his mother been given so little thought? Is it true that he had a wonderful childhood? There are a number of reasons why the early years of his life merit more attention. The plain facts about his childhood require enlargement. He was not one of three children but one of seven. There were four others who did not survive beyond their second birthdays. Loftus died in Maidstone aged two. Three others were born and died between William's second and fifth year of life, one in Ireland and two in the USA. In addition there is an unexplained gap in his mother's child bearing years. She gave birth to her first child John when she was twenty and had three children by the time she was twenty-three. There are then seven years when no children are recorded. From 1778 to 1783 she has four more children. William was the only survivor. Thomas was born in County Cork, Ireland, in 1780 and died there aged two. Harriet was born in the USA in 1782 and died the following year. Esther was born (also in the USA) on 1 August 1783 and died six weeks later.[2] This was his mother's last recorded pregnancy. She was then thirty-five. (Her own mother was 35 when Grace was born). In outline, William's family history is as follows:

Father, William Hazlitt, born 1737, Tipperary Ireland.
Mother, Grace Loftus, born 1746, Norfolk, England. Married 1766.
1770, moved to Maidstone, Kent, England.
John born 1767.
Loftus born 1768. Died age two of a putrid throat and fever (buried in
    Maidstone).
Margaret (Peggy) born 1770.
William born 1778.
1780, moved to Bandon, Cork, Ireland.
Thomas born 1780. Died 1782 (buried in Cork).
Harriet born 1782. Died 1783 of croup.
1783, moved to the USA.
Esther born 1783. Died 1783, dropped by nurse.
1787, returned to Wem, Shropshire, England.

William's early life can be viewed in stages:

1770–1780 Maidstone
William Hazlitt aged 0–2
1780–1783 Cork
William Hazlitt aged 2–5
1783–1787 The USA
William Hazlitt aged 5–9
1787–1793 Return to the UK
William Hazlitt aged 9–15

At 15 he left home to live as a boarder and study at Hackney College, London.

Apart from the loss of four children there is the question of why no births are recorded during the seven-year period from age 23 to 30 as all the evidence suggests she had little trouble getting pregnant. Did she have miscarriages or still births during that time? Alexander Ireland has stated that in Maidstone 'more children were born, but none of them survived except the youngest' [William].[3] This suggests that Loftus was not the only one who died.

Another important fact is the disruption and dislocation which the family endured from the time William was a toddler to their return to England when he was nine years old. I will enlarge on all these events with a view to exploring the stress that the family endured during William's childhood, with a particular emphasis on the effects of loss, both on his mother and on himself. The effect of loss and separation may not have been recorded or studied systematically in earlier generations, but this is no argument for saying they were not important and had no impact on peoples' lives. Human experience exists before any theory about it becomes formulated.

To the objection that this is an imposition of ideas from a later age unto an earlier time and an earlier life I would suggest that these ideas were not at all foreign to Hazlitt himself. He was interested in early life. He was acutely aware of the effect of loss on a person's emotional make-up and wrote very poignantly about it. Part of my fascination with him is how 'modern' his psychology is, and I will be systematically exploring this in chapters 4 and 5, and it will remain as a theme throughout the book. But I will now turn to the document which has stood as the centrepiece for exploration of his childhood. This was a journal which his sister Margaret began to write at the age of 65 in 1835, five years after William Hazlitt's death, while she lived in Crediton, Devon. It was written for her 24-year-old nephew, another William, the son of William Hazlitt. Margaret's journal however never found its way into the hands of the person for whom it was intended. But before approaching the content of the journal and the circumstances in which it was written, the history of the manuscript deserves some comment. It was dedicated before completion to Mr and Mrs Johns. In 1821, six months after the death of Margaret's father the Rev. Hazlitt, John Johns came as Presbyterian minister to Crediton. It seems he lodged with Margaret and her mother, both before and after his marriage in 1833. The dedication at the front of the journal reads 'To my good friends Mr. And Mrs. Johns from theirs affectionately Margaret Hazlitt, Crediton, Decbr. 10th 1836.'[4] The Johns left Devon to live in Liverpool in 1836. After the death of her mother in 1837 Margaret went to live with the Johns in Liverpool, where she spent the last four years of her life. When Margaret died in 1841 the manuscript remained with the Johns. The Rev. John Johns died in 1847. After his death the family returned to live in Devon before emigrating to Australia and the manuscript seems to have travelled with them. In 1884 one of the Johns' daughters brought it to the attention of William Carew Hazlitt the grandson of William Hazlitt. It became a valuable source for two books he wrote about the history of the Hazlitt family, *Four Generations of a Literary Family*, 1897, and *The Hazlitts: An Account of Their Origins and Descent*, 1911. Margaret's journal disappeared again until the late 1940s, when it was found in a New York bookshop, and in 1949 was purchased by the University of Delaware. In 1967 it was edited, annotated and published by Ernest J. Moyne. Margaret's journal is important because it is, as I have indicated, the source of most of the information that has been available to historians and biographers about William Hazlitt's childhood.

Turning to the contents, we read Margaret's opening words which tell us that she is starting to write on 18 April 1835. This, she informs us was the birth date of her father, who died 15 years earlier. As she begins she does not tell us that she is living with her mother, then aged 89. The journal as a whole tells us very little about her mother's life and a lot about her father. We are left having to make inferences about her mother's and Margaret's states of mind. Throughout the text she makes reference to the beauties of the places she lived in and visited in the USA and the rich human qualities of her life there. But invariably when she is at the point of exposing more of her inner world, and the loss she experienced, she draws a curtain over the event, usually by the adoption of a pious attitude of acceptance and resignation. In the midst of this there is also a repeated expression of a religious belief that those people whom she enjoyed and loved are not lost forever, but a joyful re-union will take place in a future life. But what of the reality of her life? About 90 per cent of her journal deals with events and people up to November 1787. This was the month the Hazlitt family moved back from the USA to live in the village of Wem in Shropshire. A few hundred words in the penultimate part of the journal cover her life in Wem, even though, having moved there as a young woman of 17, it would be the place where she spent a large part of her life, a total of 26 years from the ages 17 to 43. Margaret never married and lived with her parents all her life. William senior retired in 1813 and the three moved from Wem to Addlestone in Surrey. They moved again, to Devon, in 1818.

It is not unusual for the history of the period to lack a woman's point of view but here we have a woman who does sit down to write but then becomes silent. Why does she draw the curtain at that particular stage? Why does she not write about life after 1787? Perhaps as a pointer to explore this question we could look at the final part of her journal and the events that surround it. She started writing in April 1835, and drew on a collection of family letters and other documents. She wrote over a period of 18 months and then stopped in October 1836. In June of 1837 both her brother John and her mother died. In October 1838 having written nothing for 2 years she again takes up her pen.

> It is now two years since the last page of these notes was written; I wrote them with a pleasure I shall never feel again, for my dear mother was sitting by my side, and she was amused with what I wrote! But the spirit for the work is gone with her, and the brightness of my heaven is become dim.[5]

The final brief section of the journal is explicitly about her brother William. The prevailing sense in this section is of her trying to summon up energy to write.

The narrative jumps around and does not have the historical accuracy of the rest of the journal. In editing her journal for publication in 1967 Moyne observed that Margaret's account of the family's history 'is on the whole remarkably accurate and trustworthy'. Yet this final section is full of inaccuracies. She claims that in 1808 William Hazlitt was well known and had good prospects. This was not the case and it would be some more years before he established himself. She writes of William returning to London in 1810 and giving lectures at the Surrey Institution. He gave lectures in 1812 and did not speak at the Surrey Institution until 1818. Let us turn to what she says about William:

> The first six years after our settlement at Wem he devoted to study, and under his father's guidance he made a rapid progress. He was at this time the most active, lively, and happiest of boys; his time, divided between his studies and his childish sports, passed smoothly on. Beloved by all for his amiable temper and manners, pleasing above his years, the delight and pride of his own family, he felt, not like the rest, *the sad change from the society of the most agreeable and worthy friends to the dullness, petty jealousies, and cabals of a little country town.* Of the time passed here he always spoke with pleasure. The scenes of childhood are dear to all, and while safe under the parents' care, their years glide on, in innocence, without one anxious thought or fear of the storms that await them in after life. So it was with this dear boy.'[6] (my italics)

Many biographers have accepted at face value the picture of Hazlitt's early life which his sister presented here. We might compare it with various comments made by Hazlitt himself, which paint a different picture. In *On the Conduct of Life; or, Advice to a School Boy* written in 1822, a veiled communication to his son then aged 11, he counsels against working too hard and writes:

> Books are but one inlet of knowledge; and the pores of the mind, like those of the body, should be left open to all impressions. I applied too close to my studies, soon after I was of your age, and hurt myself irreparably by it.[7]

Perhaps his life was not as rosy as Margaret presents it? There is evidence to suggest he was not ideally happy and there are pointers to the fact that the Hazlitt household might not have been a place of total peace. We hear from William himself, at the age of 16 writing home to his parents from Hackney College:

> With respect to my past behaviour, I have often said and I now assure you, that it did not proceed from any real disaffection, but merely from the nervous disorders to which you well know, I was so much subject.[8]

The 'nervous disorders' to which he 'was so much subject' suggests to me a long-standing problem We also know from Margaret that he studied so hard that when he was 15 he brought on a fit, and it was a long time before he recovered.

I think some time needs to be spent in exploring Margaret's state of mind. How accurate were her perceptions of his childhood? To what extent did she go beyond outward appearances to know what was going on inside her brother's mind and heart? I am wary of accepting her narrative as the whole truth. As an instance of how out of touch she could be with his internal emotional life let us turn to her account of the death of William's infant son. This happened in 1810. She writes in her journal of his marriage and his move to Winterslow and continues:

> The next year his first child was born, and died soon after. The loss of this child was a severe stroke to him. I arrived there a day or two after, and never can I forget the look of anguish which at the first moment passed over his countenance, but his grief, though deep, was silent, and he applied [himself] to his literary pursuits with the greatest diligence. [9]

Here is Hazlitt's own account:

> I have never seen death but once, and that was in an infant. It is years ago. The look was calm and placid, and the face was fair and firm. It was as if a waxen image had been laid out in the coffin, and strewed with innocent flowers. It was not like death, but more like an image of life! No breath moved the lips, no pulse stirred, no sight or sound would enter those eyes or ears more. While I looked at it, I saw no pain was there; it seemed to smile at the short pang of life which was over: but I could not bear the coffin-lid to be closed – it seemed to stifle me; and still as the nettles wave in a corner over his little grave, the welcome breeze helps to refresh me, and ease the tightness at my breast! [10]

She sees anguish in his face and a deep sadness in his eyes but no words pass between them. She thinks he deals with it by applying himself 'to his literary pursuits with the greatest diligence'. She sees him repeating what she saw him doing as a young teenager, when 'he attended too closely to his studies that his overexertion brought on a fit', but he is left to get on with it by himself. William wrote about the death of his infant son 11 years after the event, as if he had not moved from the spot. Seeing the coffin-lid being closed stifled him; the same tightness remains in his breast.

In Margaret's journal major losses are dealt with in a summary fashion, as when she recounts the family's early months in the USA. The family had arrived on 26 May 1793:

On the 25th of June my beautiful little sister Harriet died of the croup. She was born at Bandon, and was an year and [a] half old. This was a sad stroke and was sudden and unexpected. On the first of August the same year another girl was added to the family, of whom we were soon deprived by the carelessness of a nurse who let the baby fall, which occasioned her death on the 12th of September. She was called Esther. This was another sad trial to my parents, but others awaited them, though not exactly of the same kind. I forgot to mention my brother Thomas, who was born and died at Bandon in 1780. [11]

In thinking of these events I am reminded of Margaret's comments on how she was affected by her own mother's death. 'The spirit of the work [i.e. writing] is gone with her, and the brightness of my heaven is become dim'. I have in mind also the context in which she compiled her journal. She wrote it, she tells us 'with a pleasure I shall never feel again, *for my dear mother was sitting at my side, and she was amused with what I wrote.*'(my italics). How could a mother be 'amused' by the re-telling and re-living of the death of four of her children?

Let us pause for a moment and turn to another mind which has engaged itself with Margaret Hazlitt. In his book *The Day-Star of Liberty* Tom Paulin described his visit to Maidstone Museum and his exploration of the various items of Hazlitt memorabilia on show and in the storerooms. He had looked at the various portraits of Hazlitt and his father. He takes up the story and writes:

> Then I found a miniature of Margaret Hazlitt, the sister who stayed at home to look after their parents. John's full-length portrait of Margaret hangs near Hazlitt's self-portrait in the main part of the museum, so I recognised her thoughtful, sensitive, strong-willed, rather Irish face. This miniature had more expression, more feeling, than the others in the box. Maybe that was why I looked at it for a bit longer, and then, on a sudden impulse, turned it over and found a bunch of plaited hair behind the glass back. Almost bay red, fresh, as though it had been newly cut, her hair looked just as it did in the portrait. For a moment, I felt in touch with the dead, with that family of painters and idealists, for Margaret painted too, and some of her work is in that store-room. [12]

What went on behind the strong-willed Irish face? Why did her account of her life at Wem not proceed beyond the month of arrival? Why has she told us so little about herself? But in an indirect way she reveals what was behind the face. William, she has told us, did not like the rest of the family feel 'the sad change from the society of the most agreeable and worthy friends to the dullness, petty jealousies, and cabals of a little country town'. She is lamenting the return from New England to Old England. Her father had turned down a number of offices or been rejected for positions. But one which was held by a friend the Rev. Gay would, in Margaret's opinion, have suited him perfectly. In relating the circumstances of their return she writes:

> At length [my father] made up his mind to return to England in the autumn and
> try to get settled before we arrived, as we were to follow him in the spring. A most
> unfortunate resolve! Had he staid over that winter, it is probable that we should
> never have left that dear country. For but a few months after he had sailed, old Mr
> Gay died … Instead of this happy end of our many wanderings in this changing
> world, it was our evil destiny to pass the best of our days in a little, disagreeable
> market town where we could not see the green fields and scarcely the blue vault
> of heaven. What a contrast to our transatlantic and sylvan abodes.[13]

She proceeds to blame her father's intransigence for their predicament. In
editing Margaret's journal Ernest Moyne notes this 'accusation' and his response
is to wonder why she has 'forgotten' that her father could not get employment
in the USA.

I think it is necessary to look further than a lapse of memory to get some
understanding of her state of mind. Why did she bury herself in such a dull
place? Why did she allow herself to be buried? Why did she not rebel? In her
writing she suggested that if her father had not left Cork in 1783 he could well
have become involved in the Irish rebellions which were fueled by centuries of
British misrule in Ireland. The French Revolution was to inspire insurrection in
Ireland and the uprising of 1798 saw many clerics executed and killed in action.
Margaret had good reasons to hold these views as her father's outspokenness
on the American War had offended some of his congregation in Maidstone and
contributed to his moving to Cork. There as we have read in chapter 2 he took
up the cause of the American prisoners and their cruel treatment at the hands of
the local English regiment. His complaints brought about the censure of some
officers, but he became unpopular in the local community and this hastened
his move to the USA. While this is true it was she who became friends with
Catherine Emmet whose uncle Robert Emmet, an Irish rebel, was executed for
treason in Dublin in 1798. Why, when the Irish servant girl, Honour, who had
travelled with the Hazlitt family to New York, only to run away on arrival, did
Margaret in effect take her place? When they were in Boston in 1786, before he
set out alone on his return trip to England, the Rev. Hazlitt placed his wife's
hand in Margaret's and told his daughter to look after her mother. Again in 1820
on his death bed he would put their hands together and instructed her again to
take care of her mother. Why did Margaret accept? Commenting on these events
Grayling wrote:

> That affecting action had bound poor Peggy to a spinster's lifelong service to her
> parents, and if she ever felt a pang about that fact, she must have remembered it

again then – although by this time, as a woman in her late forties (which in that period meant she was already an old lady) the time for repining had passed.[14]

Margaret's grandmother Grace Pentlow (1703–1801) lived to the age of 99, and although she married Thomas Loftus in 1725 at the age of 22 she did not give birth to Margaret's mother Grace until she was 43, in 1746. When Hazlitt senior died in 1820 Grace was then 74 and she lived to 91 so in what way would Margaret be considered an old lady? Why would her time for repining be past? Obviously the time for repining was not past. Fifteen years after her father's death when she is no longer in her late forties but in her mid-sixties she is still lamenting the lost opportunities in her life. Did she live for decades in silent resentment suppressing her tendencies to become morbid and tempestuous and develop a fiery and fitful temper? But through her life when her parents are still alive she keeps it all to herself. Was it left to William to be the one to develop the fiery and fitful temper? Did she paint a rosy picture of William's years in Wem for her own needs? I hear the words of a woman who was angry and bitter. Dutiful resignation does not dispose of resentment; it merely masks it. In telling us how much Hazlitt loved Wem she is also telling us how much she hated the place, the house, the village the countryside, the people. 'It was,' we have heard her say '*our evil destiny* to pass *the best of our days* in a little, disagreeable market town where we could not see the green fields and scarcely the blue vault of heaven.' Strong words from the girl who stayed at home to dutifully care for her parents. Whose hand shaped the evil destiny? Within the lifetime she spent with her parents did she ever allow into her mind thoughts about the family such as those expressed by her brother William in 1822 when he penned this snapshot of Hazlitt family life?

> One would think that near relations who live constantly together, and always have done so, must be pretty well acquainted with one another's characters. They are nearly in the dark about it. Familiarity confounds all traits of distinction: interest and prejudice take away the power of judging. We have no opinion on the subject any more than of one another's faces. The Penates, the household gods, are veiled. We do not see the features of those we love, nor do we clearly distinguish their virtues or their vices. We take them as they are found in the lump, – by weight, and not by measure. We know all about the individuals, their sentiments, history, manners, words, actions, everything; but we know all these too much as facts, as inveterate, habitual impressions, as clothed with too many associations, as sanctified with too many affections, as woven too much in the web of our hearts, to be able to pick out the different threads, to cast up the items of the debtor and creditor account, or to refer them to any general standard of right and wrong. Our impressions with respect to them are too strong, too real, too much sui generis, to be capable of a comparison with anything but

themselves. We hardly inquire whether those for whom we are thus interested, and to whom we are thus knit, are better or worse than others – the question is a kind of profanation – all we know is they are more to us than any one else can be. Our sentiments of this kind are rooted and grow in us, and we cannot eradicate them by voluntary means. Besides, our judgements are bespoke, our interests take part with our blood. If any doubt arises, if the veil of our implicit confidence is drawn aside by any accident for a moment, the shock is too great, like that of a dislocated limb, and we recoil on our habitual impressions again. Let not that veil ever be rent entirely asunder, so that those images may be left bare of reverential awe, and lose their religion; for nothing can ever support the desolation of the heart afterwards.[15]

And how are we to read this piece written to his son?

It was my misfortune perhaps to be bred up among Dissenters, who look with too jaundiced an eye at others, and set too high a value on their own peculiar pretensions. From being proscribed themselves, they learn to proscribe others; and come in the end to reduce all integrity of principle and soundness of opinion within the pale of their own little communion. Those who were out of it, and did not belong to the class of *Rational Dissenters*, I was led erroneously to look upon as hardly deserving the name of rational beings. Being thus satisfied as to the select few who are 'the salt of the earth,' it is easy to persuade ourselves that we are at the head of them, and to fancy ourselves of more importance in the scale of true desert than all the rest of the world put together, who do not interpret a certain text of Scripture in the manner that we have been taught to do. You will (from the difference of education) be free from this bigotry, and will, I hope, avoid every thing akin to the same exclusive and narrow-minded spirit. Think that the minds of men are various as their faces – that the modes and employment of life are numberless as they are necessary – that there is more than one class of merit – that though others may be wrong in some things, they are not so in all – and that countless races of men have been born, have lived and died without ever hearing of any one of those points in which you take a just pride and pleasure – and you will not err on the side of that spiritual pride or intellectual coxcombry which has been so often the bane of the studious and learned![16]

Perhaps these windows into family life will lead us to turn our eyes and thoughts to Grace Loftus. As I have said she has continually been assigned a minor place in William's life, in some cases not even deserving of an index entry. The details of her life are to be found here and there as asides to the main story. They lie about the place with little or no attempt to gather them in and find her an integral place in the formation of William's life. Consider these lines from Augustine Birrell: 'Grace Hazlitt, who, like her mother, lived to a great age, had many charms, and was reckoned very good-looking, though her marked resemblance in nose and lip to the younger Pitt is not by itself recommendatory of her person, and must have been a great trial to her son.'[17] Such a comment is nothing short of speculative rubbish. Birrell is to my knowledge alone in seeing a likeness between Grace and Pitt and there is also been no evidence to suggest that his mother's features were a great trial to her son on this or any other account.

But who was she? She has been referred to as 'William's mother', 'Mrs. Hazlitt'. 'The Rev. Hazlitt's' wife. We know that she was the ironmonger's daughter from Wisbech, Cambridgeshire. She was from a family of Dissenters and she met and married William Hazlitt when she was 20 and he 29 in 1766. Her beauty has been remarked upon including the attention given to her by the captain on the sea voyage from Cork to New York. Mention has been made of her popularity in the Boston area, after her husband returned ahead of the family to England. Visitors to the family home during the years in Wem spoken of her as delightful company. We also know that her family had connections with the Godwins and that the broadening of William Hazlitt's mind beyond his father's theological world into a wider culture and sense of aesthetics stems from her side of the family.

From the many accounts of William's life that I have read I am now and again offered a snapshot, a brief view of this woman. It is similar to the experience of being taken on a guided tour of the family album, catching occasional glimpses of a figure only to find that the page has been turned and another figure is quickly placed in your line of sight.

Let us run against the tide, let us insist that the page remain unturned and let us look at this face. It is the face at the centre of William's first affections. It is time to look at her life and her state of mind throughout William's childhood. As a starting point let us consider her position as she set sail from Cork to travel with the family to New York in April 1783. She left behind one dead son Loftus, buried in Maidstone. A second son, Thomas, who had also died before his third birthday, is buried in Bandon. She left behind her 80-year-old mother in Peterborough, England. They never expected to meet each other again. She began the six-week Atlantic voyage five-months pregnant, not knowing where the family are going to live or how they are going to be supported. Many friends advised against emigration but she has a husband who is adamant in pursuing his mission. On arrival in New York, worn out with seasickness, she finds the accommodation which had been promised not available and their Irish servant girl, who was of little help during the journey, runs away. The family are soon living an itinerant existence and four weeks later her daughter Harriet dies of croup. This is the third time in her life when she is pregnant and has to deal with the death of a toddler. Loftus died when she was 24 and pregnant with Margaret: Thomas died when she was pregnant with Harriet. Meanwhile her husband was offered a position in Carlisle 'with three hundred a year and a prospect of being president of a college that was being erected,' [18]but he turned it down. The congregation required a confession of faith but 'he told them he would sooner die in a ditch than submit to human authority in matters of faith.'[19] Five weeks later she gave birth to Esther, who died within six weeks. Soon after Esther's death her husband left to preach in Maryland 160 miles away. He became ill with yellow fever and his son John, then only 16, had to travel alone on horseback to find him and bring him home. On first hearing her husband was ill she believed he was dead and she was in a very fragile mental state. Would we nowadays say she had a mental breakdown? He was very ill and weak for months and the family had to endure a very severe winter awaiting his recovery.

After four years of struggle the decision was made to leave the USA and to return to England. Her husband decided to return on his own to get the family set up. This does seem rather an odd thing to do. He left her with all the children for ten months. Why did he need to go ahead? Surely, as they were returning to their own country, preparations could have been made by mail? She made the return journey by sea with the children and when she arrived in London she was again on the edge of a breakdown and her 84-year-old mother needed to come to help her and the family.

Perhaps I ask too many questions and more than I can answer. If answers are thought of in terms of new historical evidence then I have none. But mothers and daughters and sisters and wives have walked this earth for a long time. Social conventions have prevented many of them finding a public voice. For every Mary Wollstonecraft, Mary Shelley, Jane Austin or George Elliot there are a million who rest in unvisited tombs. All these women may be unknown and invisible to us. But only a fool would claim they were irrelevant. The hand that rocked the cradle has long left a strong imprint on the emotional world. The Margarets and the Graces of this world lived every day and played their part in life. How are we to know them? I try to know Grace Loftus by using something which her son prized so highly, a sympathetic imagination. If we hesitate and are unsure as to how we should proceed her son might be of help to us. An imaginative entering into the life and mind and heart of another is essential if we are to know them.

Roy Park has stated that 'the importance of childhood for Hazlitt lay in its symbolic fecundity and its subsequent symbolic richness'.[20] What is meant by symbolism in this context? Is it an internal capacity to represent something mentally? I would accept Park's observation if it is allowed to include emotional states and emotional relationships. Of crucial importance for the infant and child is the development of the capacity to symbolise their inner emotional experience. I would also point to the fact that it is not just the case that childhood provides the raw material which is to be put to the exclusive use of adult productions, but the rawness of these pristine states remains part of us all and has its place in the richness of life's texture. As Hazlitt said 'we are little better than humoured children to the last'.

I call upon some people who form part of the constellation which enlightens my life. They have taken one part of nature and through their genius have shown us some truths. To meet my first luminary I go to the middle of the twentieth century when the effects of loss and separation on peoples' lives began to be studied in a systematic fashion. I will then move backwards in time before Hazlitt's lifetime or that of his parents to a writer whose grasp of the effects of loss and separation on the shape of the personality has a distinctly contemporary ring to it.

John Bowlby studied the effects of loss and separation on the lives of human beings for fifty years. A seminal influence was Freud's 1917 paper *Mourning and Melancholia,*[21] where the idea of depression as the turning of anger upon oneself was explored. Bowlby's interest was signalled by the publication of his 1944 monograph called *Forty-four Juvenile Thieves.*[22] He noted that a high percentage of young delinquents did not have a consistent mother figure during early childhood. Bowlby was a child psychiatrist and psychoanalyst. He was commissioned by the World Health Organisation to carry on his research and in 1951 published *Maternal Care and Mental Health.*[23] His findings are summarised by his statement that 'it is believed to be essential for health that the infant and young child should experience a warm, intimate and continuous relationship with his mother (or mother substitute who steadily mothers him) in which both find satisfaction and enjoyment'. There followed his trilogy *Attachment,*[24] *Separation, Anxiety and Anger* [25]and *Loss, Sadness and Depression.*[26] Together with another worker in this field, Colin Murray Parkes,[27] Bowlby outlined the sequence through which adults who suffer a significant loss will pass. There are five phases. The initial reaction to the loss is shock and a sense of being numbed. This is followed by distress and anger. The third phase involves a searching for the lost one, a yearning for the person to live again and the status quo to be re-instated. When this does not take place there is a sense of despair and one's life, and indeed the whole self, feels disorganised. The final stage is one in which an acceptance of reality can take place. This is the pathway back to life where mourning has taken place.

Circumstances may contrive to cause a person to get stuck at any of these stages. (These 'circumstances' can come from within or from outside, or as is more often the case from both.) A state of shock can continue for years, indeed for a person's whole lifetime. To the casual eye and the casual acquaintance such an individual may present as normal and happy. But if anyone ventures into the area of their intimate emotional life they find a withdrawn numbness. Similarly a state of overt or covert anger can persist. When the lost person cannot be relinquished the mourner is left clinging to a dead 'object'. The outward manifestations of this internal state may be dourness, depression or a melancholic disposition. But it may also be more subtly present within a lack of creativity. The person stands still, and is unable to make anything new, unable to work, unable to love.

Bowlby worked in conjunction with James and Joyce Robertson who were social workers and psychoanalysts. In their work with children who were separated from their parents the Robertsons observed the same phenomena. However they not only studied children who suffered a major and permanent loss such as the sudden death of a parent. They were interested in children who in every respect were regarded as normal and well cared for. They observed children who were placed in temporary full-time care when their mother was admitted to hospital to have another child. Despite the period of separation being relatively short, sometimes only one week, they discovered that many of these children became deeply distressed. Believing their private observations would not be believed they decided to film the children, where the level of distress which they experienced was clear for all to see. Their actions contributed to a major change in hospital policy in the western world. When an infant or young child is admitted as an inpatient it is accepted practice that they be accompanied by a parent who will take up residence in the ward with their child. But they also contributed to a more radical change in people's minds. Here was proof that children experience loss in the same way as adults and they have the same need to mourn.

But let us now wind the clock back, not to Hazlitt's day but beyond, to the early part of the 18th century. Let us go to London and pick up a copy of the *Tatler*.[28] There we read an essay called 'On Recollections of Childhood'. The writer is Richard Steele (who would become a significant figure in shaping Hazlitt's literary style). Hazlitt wrote of Steele that he had never been surpassed in his ability to write about 'the heart-rending pathos of private distress'. [29] Let us listen to Steele's understanding of loss, his insight into the experience of being separated from someone precious and important, and his knowledge about the formation of the human mind.

The story is self explanatory and needs no further introduction.

The first sense of sorrow I ever knew was upon the death of my father, at which I was not quite five years of age; but was rather amazed at what all the house meant, than possessed with real understanding why nobody was willing to play with me. I remember I went into the room where his body lay, and my mother sat weeping alone by it. I had my battledore in my hand, and fell a-beating the coffin, and calling Papa; for I knew not how, I had some slight idea that he was locked up there. My mother catched me in her arms, and transported beyond all patience of the silent grief she was before in, she almost smothered me in her embraces; and told me in a flood of tears, 'Papa could not hear me, and would play with me no more, for they were going to put him under ground, whence he could never come to us again.' She was a very beautiful woman, of a noble spirit, and there was a dignity in her grief amidst all the wildness of her transport; which, methought, struck me with an instinct of sorrow, that, before I was sensible of what it was to grieve, seized my very soul, and has made pity the weakness of my heart every since. The mind in infancy is, methinks, like the body in embryo; and receives impressions so forcible, that they are as hard to be removed by reason, as any mark with which a child is born is to be taken away by any future application. Hence it is that good-nature in me is no merit; but having been so frequently overwhelmed with her tears before I knew the cause of any affliction, or could draw defences from my own judgement, I imbibed commiseration, remorse, and an unmanly gentleness of mind, which has since ensnared me into ten thousand calamities; and from whence I can reap no advantage, except it be, that in such a humour as I am now in, I can the better indulge myself in the softness of humanity, and enjoy that sweet anxiety that arises from the memory of past afflictions.[30]

Richard Steele had a deep appreciation of loss. He also had a theory of mind, a set of ideas and hypotheses which were useful to provide an explanation of a person's behaviour and of their emotional state. Here he has a theory of mind about what it is like to lose someone who is emotionally significant. He knew how the traumatic separation affected a person and shaped their life. 'I imbibed commiseration, remorse and an unmanly gentleness of mind.' He knew something about how things get *taken in* to a person's internal world.

However we could on first reading make the mistake of only seeing the boy and the traumatic effect of his father's death at such a tender age. But the piece quoted is not just about his father. His mother figures prominently and we are presented with the complicated interactions that involve all three. When he wrote that the mind in infancy is like the body in embryo and internalises forceful impressions, he is directly referring to his mother, to her grief, her dignity, her ability to allow her emotions to be openly expressed. The little boy has the direct unmediated experience of finding that his father is dead, and also the sense of that death as it is mediated by his mother. As Steele looked back through his life he could tell us that despite the unmanly gentleness of mind which became part of his character, he values the sensitivity which enables him to touch the softness of humanity, and while this leaves him open to suffering and vulnerable to calamities he can 'enjoy that sweet anxiety that comes from the memory of past afflictions'.

If we still hold in our hand the photograph of Grace Loftus what do we see if we turn back and allow the face to come alive? This is the face of Hazlitt's first affections. Is it the guiding light of all his day, the master light of all his being? Is this the face, the person with whom the infant William first learned about love? As you have been listening to Bowlby, Steele and the Robertsons have you imagined that she might be listening also? As she listened to the stages of mourning being outlined might there have been signs of recognition on her face? Having lost child after child and buried them in three different countries did she seem to understand what Steele was talking about? Did she even give a sign that she might have once read the very same essay? Can we see her as the mother of one of the greatest essayists in the language, speaking and using a version of his words, the words I have already quoted above? 'I have seen death many times in my children. The look was calm and placid, and the face was fair and firm. It was as if a waxen image had been laid out in the coffin, and strewed with innocent flowers. It was not like death, but more like an image of life! No breath moved the lips, no pulse stirred no sight or sound would enter those eyes or ears more. While I looked I saw no pain was there; it seemed to smile at the short pang of life which was over: but I could not bear the coffin-lid to be closed – it seemed to stifle me; and still as the nettles wave in a corner over their little graves, the welcome breeze helps to refresh me, and ease the tightness at my breast!'

To the murmurs of discontent that I am inventing a personality, that I read too much into something, I must turn, as Hazlitt turned in *The Fight*, and ask you. Have you ever known such suffering? Have you ever lost someone precious to you? You tell me that life was cheap two hundred years ago, that children died all the time! My answer is that people therefore suffered more. If infant life was cheap, can we find lines from a modern writer that rival Hazlitt's sentiments as he watched over the body of his precious dead child? Is there an account in a modern book which contains wisdom greater than Steele's? William Hazlitt's robust masculinity is much in evidence in his writings. But he also possessed a sensitive femininity of mind which enabled him, like Steele, to be aware of the softness of humanity. If we are to understand these qualities we need to accept that William Hazlitt was the son of two parents.

Chapter 4

A Freudian John the Baptist

We waste our regrets on what cannot be recalled, or fix our desires on what we know
cannot be attained. Every hour is the slave to the last; and we are seldom masters
either of our thoughts or of our actions ... Even in the common transactions and
daily intercourse of life, we are governed by whim, caprice, prejudice, or accident. The
falling of a tea-cup puts us out of temper for the day; and a quarrel that commenced
about the pattern of a gown may end only with our lives.
> *Friends now fast sworn,*
> *On a dissension of a doit, break out*
> *To bitterest enmity.*
We are little better than humoured children to the last, and play a mischievous game
at cross purposes with our own happiness and that of others.[1]

There are those who believe that modern dynamic psychology had its origins in
the mind of one man during the latter years of the 19th century, that Sigmund
Freud on his own discovered, even invented, the unconscious. Freud had an
undeniable genius. He was a discoverer and an inventor. But can we draw a
line on the sand where everything on one side is pre-Freud and old-fashioned
and dated and everything beyond is new and vital? He himself deplored such a
narrowness of mind. To claim that everything psychologically dynamic began
in 1897 does little more than display our ignorance of things past and our
unfamiliarity with the history of ideas. In 1925 Freud wrote that, 'The poets and
philosophers before me discovered the unconscious. What I discovered was the
scientific method by which the unconscious can be studied.'[2] Freud knew he
had gathered together many of the great insights of those who had gone before
him. As they were funnelled through his mind his genius transformed them.
What did emerge from his mind and is indisputably his is the creation of the
psychoanalytic setting and it has been inventively used and developed by many
people during the 20th century.

My aim is to show the modern relevance of Hazlitt's psychology. I indicated
in chapter one how I saw Hazlitt as a psychologically minded man and how
his insights found their way into my mind. When I found this happening, I
expected to find within the hundred years of psychoanalytic thought and writing
some references to him. In my search I turned to the library of psychoanalytic
books and journals, but found little knowledge or interest in the man and his
writings. Freud made no mention of Hazlitt. The single reference of substance
was in the first volume of the *International Journal of Psychoanalysis* in 1920. The
writer was L. C. Martin from the Sorbonne, Paris; the paper 'A Note on Hazlitt'.

Martin listed many aspects of Freud's thought that are to be found in Hazlitt's writings including repression, denial, projection, introjection, the importance of childhood and infantile life and dreaming. He then adds:

> A more than usually sustained habit of enquiry and gifts of insight and analysis much beyond the average gave to Hazlitt's Freudian suggestions something like the character of a consistent and dynamic though loosely woven theory of the unconscious.[3]

He concludes his valuable piece by writing that:

> These sporadic anticipations furnish a striking instance of the manner in which a whole new system may remain latent in the mind of an individual and without influence on the progress of human thought and society, for lack of the will or the opportunity to carry an original idea to its final and logical conclusions. Yet though Hazlitt did not attain, it is something that he experienced and bore witness to an unusually clear vision; and it would be both uncritical and anachronistic to blame him now for the want of the constructive intention and the scientific method which would have drawn these threads closely together into a coherent and ordered mental theory.[4]

Martin's understanding of the history of psychoanalytic ideas is that pre-Freudian literature and thought are cast in the role of John the Baptist, voices in the wilderness, preparing the way. If we follow Hazlitt's thinking through all of his writings we find a consistency and a growing maturity. The spontaneity of his expression and his imaginative leaps should not be confused with randomness. He was very conscious in the writings of his essays, especially so during the latter part of his life, of mapping out the workings of human minds. That his outline did not conform to some grid-like system does not render it any less accurate. The mind of man, he would say, is not like the palm of the hand, smooth and flat, but should be compared to the back of the hand, rough and uneven.

Turning to Martin's belief in psychoanalysis as the more advanced if not the ultimate truth perhaps it is understandable that a new body of knowledge in its early period of maturation might need to forcibly assert its distinctiveness. There is however a need to guard against the assertion of a pre-eminent position. Perhaps in the 1920s it was hard for some within the psychoanalytic world to consider the possibility that the writers and artists and philosophers might not only have anticipated much of what Freud was saying, but were in fact ahead of him. If this is the case we have a reversal of positions. Psychoanalysis today is trying to catch up with literature. Maybe their proper place is together in a maturing partnership!

One of Hazlitt's earliest biographers, Alexander Ireland, pointed to the centrality of introspection or self-analysis in his understanding of himself. Describing the coaching inn at Winterslow Hutt on the border of the Salisbury Plains where Hazlitt wrote many of his essays, Ireland wrote:

> It was his favourite haunt when he wished to secure that entire solitude and seclusion from the world which he found so favourable to thought and quiet literary work. It was here that he drew upon his recollections of books and pictures, recalling what he had observed of men and things, probing his own character unshrinkingly, and extracting an infinite amount of self-knowledge from his own infirmities.[5]

Hazlitt referred to himself time and again as a 'metaphysician' and a 'philosopher,' but in the terminology of the 21st century his 'metaphysics' and 'philosophy', can more properly be called a 'psychology'. In this psychology he had a dynamic view of the human mind, with a depth and breadth that anticipates a psychoanalytic perspective. The word 'unconscious' is part of his regular vocabulary, and he conceives of that part of the mind as a vibrant entity, not a mere passive warehouse of memory and experience.

> Our unconscious impressions necessarily give a colour to, and re-act upon our conscious ones; and it is only when these two sets of feeling are in accord, that our pleasures are true and sincere; where there is a discordance and misunderstanding in this respect, they are said (not absurdly as is pretended) to be false and hollow. There is then a serenity of virtue, a peace of conscience, a confidence in success, and a pride of intellect, which subsist and are a strong source of satisfaction independently of outward and immediate objects, as the general health of the body gives a glow and animation to the whole frame, notwithstanding a scratch we may have received in our little finger, and certainly very different from a state of sickness and infirmity. The difficulty is not so much in supposing one mental cause or phenomenon to be affected and imperceptibly moulded by another, as in setting limits to the everlasting ramifications of our impressions, and in defining the obscure and intricate ways in which they communicate together. [6]

This is a very Freudian unconscious. Closely linked to it was Freud's idea of free association, which lies at the centre of the practice of psychoanalysis. The German words (used by Freud) 'freir Einsall' are more properly translated as 'an idea occurring to the mind spontaneously'. Having abandoned hypnosis Freud encouraged his patients to say whatever came to mind. He believed a direct approach to elicit the person's deepest wishes would meet with an internal prohibition and resistance. One got around this by granting full freedom of expression. The analyst or Freud in this instance undertook to listen to and take seriously everything the patient said, however insignificant. This was the corner stone of Freud's therapeutic method and technique and remains so to this day.

In 1920 Freud wrote a short paper called 'A Note on the Prehistory of the Technique of Analysis'[7] where he mentioned the work of the poet and philosopher Friedrich von Schiller. In 1908 Otto Rank had drawn Freud's attention to Schiller's use of a method of free association and in that year Freud added a new paragraph to *The Interpretation of Dreams* quoting Schiller. The piece in question was a letter Schiller wrote on 1 December 1788 to the poet Karl Körner. Körner had writer's block and was struggling to work productively. Schiller offers the following advice.

> The ground for your complaint seems to me to lie in the constraint imposed by your reason upon your imagination. I will make my idea more concrete by a simile. It seems a bad thing and detrimental to the creative work of the mind if Reason makes too close an examination of the ideas as they come pouring in – at the very gateway, as it were. Looked at in isolation, a thought may seem very trivial or very fantastic; but it may be made important by another thought that comes after it, and, in conjunction with other thoughts that may seem equally absurd, it may turn out to form a most effective link. Reason cannot form any opinion upon all this unless it retains the thought long enough to look at it in connection with the others.[8]

However Freud had not read Schiller and instead traced a connection to the Swedish writer Ludwig Börne. In 1823 Börne had written an essay called 'The Art of Becoming an Original Writer in Three Days'. Börne's advice was:

> Take a few sheets of paper and for three days on end write down, without fabrication or hypocrisy, everything that comes into your head. Write down what you think of yourself, of your wife, of the Turkish War, of Goethe, of Fonk's trial, of the Last Judgement, of your superiors – and when three days have passed you will be quite out of your senses with astonishment at the new and un-heard-of thoughts you have had. This is the art of becoming an original writer in three days.[9]

In 1819, four years before Börne wrote the essay which Freud referred to, Hazlitt published his book 'Lectures on the English Comic Writers', where he wrote the following piece about the great French essayist Michel de Montaigne (1533–1592).

> Montaigne was the first person who in his Essays led the way to this kind of writing among the moderns. The great merit of Montaigne then was, that he may be said to have been the first who had the courage to say as an author what he felt as a man. And as courage is generally the effect of conscious strength, he was

probably led to do so by the richness, truth, and force of his own observations on books and men. He was, in the truest sense, a man of original mind, that is he had the power of looking at things for himself, or as they really were, instead of blindly trusting to, and fondly repeating what others told him that they were … he got rid of the go-cart of prejudice and affectation, with the learned lumber that follows at their heels, because he could do without them. In taking up his pen he did not set up for a philosopher, wit, orator, or moralist, but he became all these by merely daring to tell us whatever passed through his mind, in its naked simplicity and force, that he thought anyways worth communicating. He did not, in the abstract character of an author, undertake to say all that could be said upon a subject, but what in his capacity as an inquirer after truth he happened to know about it. He was neither a pedant nor a bigot. He neither supposed that he was bound to know all things, nor that all things were bound to conform to what he had fancied or would have them to be. In treating of men and manners, he spoke of them as he found them, not according to preconceived notions and abstract dogmas; and he began by teaching us what he himself was.[10]

The place of dreams and dreaming in mental life is closely allied to ideas of the unconscious and free association. In the preface to the third English edition (1931) of *The Interpretation of Dreams* Freud wrote, 'This book with the new contribution to psychology which surprised the world when it was published (1900), remains essentially unaltered. *It contains, even according to my present day judgement, the most valuable of all the discoveries it has been my good fortune to make. Insight such as this falls to one's lot but once in a lifetime.*' (my italics)[11]

If we turn to Hazlitt we find the following piece written in 1823.

The power of prophecysing or foreseeing things in our sleep, as from a higher and more abstracted sphere of thought need not be here argued upon. There is, however, a sort of profundity in sleep; and it may usefully be consulted as an oracle in this way. It may be said, that the voluntary power is suspended, and things come upon us as unexpected revelations, which we keep out of our thoughts at other times. We may be aware of a danger, that yet we do not choose, while we have the full command of our faculties, to acknowledge to ourselves: the impending event will then appear to us as a dream, and we shall most likely find it verified afterwards. Another thing of no small consequence is, that we may sometimes discover our tacit, and almost unconscious sentiments, with respect to persons or things in the same way. We are not hypocrites in our sleep. The curb is taken off from our passions, and our imagination wanders at will. When awake, we check these rising thoughts, and fancy we have them not. In dreams, when we are off our guard, they return securely and unbidden. We may make this use of the infirmity of our sleeping metamorphosis, that we may repress any feelings of this sort that we disapprove in their incipient state, and detect, ere it be too late, an unwarrantable antipathy of fatal passion. Infants cannot disguise their thoughts from others; and in sleep we reveal the secret to ourselves.[12]

Hazlitt and Freud are largely in agreement. Dreams are meaningful. They provide us with understanding. We repress that which we cannot allow into consciousness. Central to Freud's understanding was the belief that through dreaming we give expression to a wish. Our secret desires find representation and we imagine ourselves to be who or what we wish to be. But Hazlitt goes beyond Freud and to a modern understanding of dreaming. Dreaming can be an attempt at thinking. Our unconscious mind engages in a form of primitive thought. That which our reason cannot comprehend is engaged with by another part of our mind.

Apart from Martin, the only other person who seems to have made a significant link between Hazlitt and Freud was Albert Mordell. In 1919 he published a book entitled *The Erotic Motive in Literature*. In it he wrote the following:

> One English writer who gave almost complete expression to the views of Freud was William Hazlitt. In his essay 'On Dreams' in *The Plain Speaker*, he stated the theory. It may come as a surprise to Freud – probably as a greater surprise than when he learned that Schopenhauer had written about repression.[13]

Mordell cited the passage on dreams given above and proceeded to say that 'Freud's work may also be called a commentary on this extraordinary passage of one of England's greatest critics.'[14] But if we search through all of Freud's works we find no reference to Hazlitt. Does this mean he never heard of Hazlitt? Not so. He knew the above passage from *The Plain Speaker* because Freud read Mordell's book and wrote to him on 21 May 1920. Mordell's book was not well received in America but in England Havelock Ellis had reviewed it favorably. This is what Freud wrote:

> Dear Mr. Mordell:
>
> I have indeed read your book with great interest and I am glad you were able to do for the English–American literature something similar to what Rank did for the German in his book on Incest Motiv. I should also like to tell you not to take so hard the attacks and unfavourable criticisms. At present there is nothing else to be expected, and besides one good criticism by Havelock Ellis outweighs a couple of dozen bad ones. I hope you will continue with your literary studies and often give us pleasure with their results. With hearty greetings and respect.
>
> Freud [15]

For a few years around 1920 we have these brief glimpses of Hazlitt in the psychoanalytic literature and then it seems as if the curtain is drawn. Martin's paper has the distinction of being the first and the last to mention Hazlitt in the *International Journal of Psychoanalysis*. A few minor sideward glances appear in other psychoanalytic journals but we find nothing of substance. Even though in 1922 P. P. Howe published the first substantial biography of Hazlitt, and between 1928 and 1932 assembled and published *The Complete Works of William Hazlitt*, thus ushering in a new era of Hazlitt studies in literary circles, the psychoanalytic literature would remain virtually silent.

There is a final issue raised by Mordell's book and Freud's letter to him. As Freud read the book he knew about Hazlitt's knowledge of dreams, yet no mention is made in later editions of *The Interpretation of Dreams*. It seems also likely that Freud had read the first volume of *The International Journal of Psychoanalysis* in which the Martin article had appeared. In that volume of 1920 Freud himself had three papers published, 'One of the Difficulties of Psycho-Analysis', 'The Psychogenesis of a Case of Female Homosexuality', and 'A Child is Being Beaten'. An oversight perhaps?

In May 1922 Freud wrote to the writer Arthur Schnitzler (1862–1931). Schnitzler had trained as a doctor and a neurologist but turned from medicine to literature. I reproduce part of that letter below. It is self-explanatory as an expression of Freud's sentiments.

> I think I have avoided you from a kind of awe of meeting my 'double'. Not that I am in general easily inclined to identify myself with anyone else or that I had any wish to overlook the difference in our gifts that divides me from you, but whenever I get deeply interested in your beautiful creations I always seem to find behind their poetic sheen the same pre-suppositions, interests and conclusions as those familiar to me as my own … Your deep grasp of the truths of the unconscious … the way you take to pieces the social conventions of our society, and the extent to which your thoughts are preoccupied with the polarity of love and death; all that moves me with an uncanny feeling of familiarity. So the impression has been borne in on me that you know through intuition – really from a delicate self-observation – everything that I have discovered in other people by laborious work. Indeed I believe that fundamentally you are an explorer of the depths, as honestly impartial and unperturbed as ever anyone was, and that had you not been so your artistic gifts, your mastery of language, and your creativeness would have had free play and made you into something pleasing to the multitude.[16]

If Freud and Hazlitt had lived at the same time might such a letter have been written to Hazlitt?

Chapter 5

William Hazlitt and Ronald Fairbairn

Such reasoning would be true, if man were a simple animal or a logical machine, and all his faculties and impulses were in strict unison; instead of which they are eternally at variance, and no one hates or takes part against himself more heartily or heroically than does the same individual. Does he not pass sentence on his own conduct? Is not his conscience both judge and accuser? What else is the meaning of all our resolutions against ourselves, as well as of our exhortations to others?[1]

You teach your child to speak your language. Your gift is invaluable. Within a few short years from rudimentary sounds to the sophistication of complex words and sentences, the most thorough means of human expression and communication has been born. Yet having taught her, you are not the owner of her imagination, and cannot lay claim to the creative uses she makes of what you have given her. She may turn pages of the dictionary that have been unopened by you and find new words. She may even invent them. In the fullness of her life, if her unique individuality finds expression, you will hear a new voice that has never before spoken in this way. But however independent and creative she may become, and a mistress of her own thoughts, she will always need to hold your hand. If she has imbibed your desire for truth she will remain always in touch with you. If you have schooled her to always search within her self and be attentive to the world of others she will surpass you and always be your pupil.

Freud taught us a new language of the mind. His words have been a source of inspiration to many people. The objects of his enquiry and the aspects of our human condition which concerned him and which he consistently addressed throughout his life remain as relevant today as they were in his time. He enabled human character to be examined and understood in a systematic fashion through the process of psychoanalysis. But while there is a universality to the human dilemmas he explored, the form of his conceptualisation is dated and bears the distinctive marks of the scientific discourse of his day. If psychoanalysis endeavours to express timeless and universal human truths then it cannot be encased forever within one particular theoretical structure.

One of the people within the Freudian tradition who took up the baton and sought to rethink Freud's ideas and come up with a new language was the Scottish psychoanalyst Ronald Fairbairn. Fairbairn is the psychoanalytic thinker with whom Hazlitt has the greatest affinity. He was born in Edinburgh in 1889 and graduated from Edinburgh University in 1911 with an honours degree in philosophy. He was interested in becoming a lawyer but wanted to pursue further study. He read theology and Hellenistic Greek as a post-graduate student at Kiel and Strasbourg in Germany and at Manchester, England. The First World War began when he completed his studies and he spent the next years on active military service in Palestine. He changed his ideas about what he wanted to spend his life doing and decided to become a psychotherapist. He had visited hospitals for 'nerve shaken' officers and the hysterical injuries or war neuroses which he witnessed made an indelible impression on him. He returned to Edinburgh University to study medicine, qualifying in 1923. He worked at the Royal Edinburgh Psychiatric hospital. In 1921 he began a personal analysis and in 1924 began working in private practice as a psychotherapist. From 1927 to 1935 he was a lecturer in psychology and philosophy at Edinburgh University and he also worked as a psychiatrist at the University Psychological Clinic for Children. He became a member of the British Psychoanalytical Society in 1931. His main writings appeared during the 1940s and 1950s when in the relative professional isolation of Edinburgh he examined Freud's ideas and in the light of his personal and clinical experience rewrote the textbooks. His essential papers were collected in book form and published in 1952 under the title *Psychoanalytic Studies of the Personality*. He died in 1964.

Freud believed that the fundamental motivating principles of the human being were the achievement of pleasure and the avoidance of pain. He developed a theory of drives and instinctual energy upon which he constructed a psychology. In early life the human child is geared to seek pleasure. The pleasure principle governs his life. Freud outlined the details of his theory of development and the child's movement through oral, anal and phallic phases. The infant sucks at the breast not only to get food but because it is pleasurable. The mouth is an erotogenic zone as also are the anus and the genitals, each in a developmental sense progressively important, each a bodily location of pleasurable sensation.

It was Fairbairn who most directly and consistently challenged Freud's conceptualisation and sought to replace a theory of instincts or drives with a theory based on the need for relationships with other human beings. In his view man is primarily a social animal and from the beginning seeks to establish and maintain relationships that not only provide for bodily needs but simultaneously satisfy emotional needs. The central driving force in any individual's development from the beginning is the need for human companionship and therefore the need not only to be loved but also to love.

Fairbairn took issue with Freud's theory of development and suggested that it is a rather introverted way of conceiving of growth, that it only considered one side and was centred on the body of the infant and their various bodily functions. Fairbairn began by asserting that a person can only be properly thought of, particularly in relation to development, in terms of their constant interaction with the human environment. Where is the body of the other, the mother, the object which relates to the subject? Fairbairn asked why not think of a breast phase, a faeces phase, a genital phase? This would form the basis of a theory which was founded on the relationship between the child and its mother, the self and the other, the subject and the object. Fairbairn said that the concept of erotogenic zones with the object as the means of providing libidinal pleasure was to 'put the cart before the horse'. He believed that the erotogenic zone was simply to be regarded as the path of least resistance to the object.

Fairbairn believed that the infant was 'object seeking' from the beginning. He posed the question, Why does the infant suck its thumb? Is it because the mouth is an erotogenic zone and pleasure is the aim? In his scheme the answer is: Because the thumb is a substitute for the mother's breast. The thumb sucking is a technique for dealing with the absence of the breast, or may be a way of dealing with an unsatisfactory relationship. Pleasure provided a sign-post to the object. Auto-erotic psycho-sexuality constitutes a default or failure in the mother/infant relationship. In his words 'Auto-eroticism is a technique whereby the person seeks not only to provide for himself what he can't get from the object, but also to provide himself an object he cannot obtain.' When things go wrong, when there is a failure to establish good, productive, satisfying and creative relationships with other people, we fall back onto ourselves.

If you walk through the bushland around Sydney and listen to the birdsong you may hear a call which sounds like a whiplash. It is the mating call of the whip bird. It is a long whistle followed by a brisk cracking sound. The male calls with a long whistle and the female answers with the crackle. However there is a twist to the story. Sometimes the male gets no reply. In the absence of a female response he adds the cracking sound and plays both parts. The listener cannot tell whether the sound is a product of one or two birds. This captures the human dilemma which Fairbairn was addressing. What happens when there is no human response, when you call out and there is no answer? The infant who is not responded to may supply their own response. In the absence of another person it may turn to its own body.

In his book *Psychoanalytic Studies of the Personality* Fairbairn[2] stated that a person created their own identity based on the meaning derived from relationships. If striving after pleasure became central in a person's life, this fact led to deterioration in the relationships between human beings. It led to people being used in an essentially selfish manner. The other is not valued as a person who enriches your life. There is no true mutuality and relationships are shallow and do not provide any deep or lasting satisfaction.

If we turn to Hazlitt we find that in his psychology he firmly rejected the notion of people as isolated individuals acting from a pleasure principle. He disagreed with Hobbes, Locke and Hartley, who he said reduced all 'thought to sensation, all morality into the love of pleasure, and all action into mechanical impulse'. (This mechanistic conception of the mind encouraged a self-centred, egotistical way of life: people who lived solely for themselves.) Hazlitt's first attempt to organise his ideas was in the *Essay on the Principles of Human Action*[3] (hereafter referred to as the *Essay*). This was also his first published work and it fell into oblivion shortly after publication when it was for the most part met with indifference and hostility. One reviewer described it as 'impious and illiterate'. Hazlitt always believed it was one of his most important works although he admitted it was 'tough and dry'.

There is a parallel between Hazlitt's debate with the philosophy and psychology of his day and Ronald Fairbairn's engagement with Freud's psychology. If I tune in to Hazlitt's ideas with a psychoanalytic ear I hear much that is familiar. The essentials of Fairbairn's scheme are that we originally seek another person and a relationship *with* another, that we are essentially social animals motivated by our desire and need for human attachment. Hazlitt argued that a person is most fully human when he goes out from himself and enters into the other. To create a great work of art or to engage in a great moral act involves losing a sense of one's 'personal identity in some object dearer to us than ourselves'. As Elisabeth Schneider says 'For [Hazlitt] the impossible is to be achieved not through assimilation of all *other* into the *self*, but through the projecting of *self* into all *other*.' [4]

Let us listen to what he wrote:

The prevailing doctrine of modern systems of morals and metaphysics, [state] that man is purely a sensual and selfish animal, governed solely by a regard either to his immediate gratification or future interest. This we mean to oppose with all our might, whenever we meet with it. We are, however, less disposed to quarrel with it, as it is opposed to reason and philosophy, than as it interferes with common sense and observation. If the absurdity in question had been confined to the schools, we should not have gone out of our way to meddle with it: but it has gone abroad in the world, has crept into ladies boudoirs, is entered in the commonplace book of beaux, is in the mouth of the learned and ignorant, and forms a part of popular opinion. It is perpetually applied as a false measure of the characters and conduct of men in the common affairs of the world, and it is therefore our business to rectify it, if we can. In fact, whoever sets out on the idea of reducing all our motives and actions to a simple principle, must either take a very narrow and superficial view of human nature, or make a very perverse use of his understanding in reasoning on what he sees. The frame of our minds, like that of our body, is exceedingly complicated. Besides mere sensibility to pleasure and pain, there are other original independent principles, necessarily interwoven with the nature of man as an active and intelligent being, and which, blended together in different proportions, give form and colour to our lives.[5]

Hazlitt is writing here in 1815 with a determination to rectify what he believed were false principles. The frame of our minds is exceedingly complicated. It is reductionism to build a psychology on a simple principle, and erroneous because you end up with a false measure by which the character and conduct of people are to be judged. It was to establish a true measure that Hazlitt wrote the *Essay*. His clear intention was 'to show that the human mind is naturally disinterested, or that it is naturally interested in the welfare of others in the same way, and from the same direct motives, by which we are impelled to the pursuit of our own interest.'[6]

He goes on to say that 'I could not love myself, if I were not capable of loving others. Self-love, used in this sense, is in its fundamental principle the same with disinterested benevolence.'[7] and 'It is a great folly to think of deducing our desire of happiness and fear of pain from a principle of self-love ... this sort of attachment to self could signify nothing more than a foolish complacency in our own idea, an idle dotage, and idolatry of our own abstract being.'[8] He goes on to assert that 'it is plain there must be something in the nature of the objects themselves which of itself determines the mind to consider them as desirable, or the contrary, previously to any reference of them to ourselves. They are not converted into good and evil by being impressed on our minds, but they effect our minds in a certain manner because they are essentially good or evil.'[9]

Hazlitt in his objection to the 'Modern Philosophy' and Fairbairn in his disagreement with Freud are in fact suggesting a fundamentally different view of human motivation, human meaning, and human values. Man is not part of a closed system characterised by entropy, but is a social organism interacting with his environment and being altered by it. Man is not seeking a state of equilibrium or homeostasis. Life is ongoing because there is a constant need for adaptation involving self-transformation and self-maintenance and it is through his social environment that man not only maintains himself but maximises his creativity.

What happens when things go wrong? In Fairbairn's scheme we fall back onto ourselves. Like the whip bird we ask the question and we supply the answer. We develop an inward-looking self-sufficiency. This happens because there has been a failure to establish good, productive, satisfying and creative relationships with other people. Fairbairn drew on a new set of ideas as the foundations of an inter-personal psychology.

Fairbairn believed there was a unified ego or self from birth which seeks relationships with others. The primary object that is sought is the mother as a whole person. The infant feels the need to be recognised, accepted and responded to as a unique autonomous person. It is not the mother's intelligence nor the extent of her knowledge of child development which was the most important factor. Rather it was higher capacity to convey to the child that she loves them 'by spontaneous and genuine expressions of affection'. If this does not happen there is 'a situation of emotional frustration in which the child comes to feel that he is not really loved for himself as a person by his mother, and that his own love for his mother is not really valued and accepted by her.' Fairbairn then says that the child comes to regard his mother as bad in so far as she does not seem to love him; that the child comes to regard outward expressions of his love as bad, with the result that, in an attempt to keep his love as good as possible, he tends to retain his love inside him; that the child comes to feel that all love relationships are bad, or at least precarious.[10]

In explaining his ideas he provided illustrative material from a female patient who came to him for analysis. One day she told him a dream. The dream 'consisted of a brief scene in which she saw the figure of herself being viciously attacked by a well-known actress in a venerable building which had belonged to her family for generations. Her husband was looking on, but he seemed quite helpless and quite incapable of protecting her. After delivering the attack the actress turned away and resumed playing a stage part, which, as seemed to be implied, she had momentarily set aside in order to deliver the attack by way of interlude. The dreamer then found herself gazing at the figure of herself lying bleeding on the floor; but as she gazed, she noticed that this figure turned for an instant into that of a man. Thereafter the figure alternated between herself and this man until she eventually awoke in a state of anxiety.'[11]

In this dream story we have several characters, the dreamer herself, her husband, a well-known actress, and an unknown man. From the knowledge he already had about the woman's life and from the conversations which took place between them subsequent to the dream, Fairbairn provides us with a picture of the patient's life. The dreamer was married but felt very ambivalent about her husband. They had sexual difficulties and she was unable to achieve orgasm. The man in the dream wore a suit which her husband had recently bought. She had encouraged him to get it but when he went along for a fitting he took along 'one of his blonds', a women who worked in his office. 'The actress who delivered the attack belonged as much to the personality of the dreamer as did the figure of herself against whom the attack was delivered. In actual fact the figure of an actress was well suited to represent a certain aspect of herself; for she was essentially a shut-in and withdrawn personality who displayed very little genuine feeling towards others, but who had perfected the technique of presenting facades to a point at which they assumed a remarkable genuine appearance and achieved for her remarkable popularity.'[12]

In elaborating he explains that her imaginative life since childhood was very masochistic, but in the life of outer reality she had largely devoted herself to the playing of roles, good wife, mother, business woman, but her real personality was quite inaccessible to her husband and the good wife he knew was for the most part only the good actress. She never told him that she was inorgasmic and always pretended to achieve orgasm. Her frigidity represented not only an attack upon a loving part of herself, but also a hostile attitude towards her husband as a loving person. The dream displayed her hidden aggression to her husband, but also showed her aggressive attitude towards part of herself.

Of relevance in her life history was an event that recurred frequently and also a major trauma. As a child she used to watch her father getting dressed in his dressing room. Her mother disapproved of this and would object in an emotional and hysterical manner. The child had very mixed feeling about this, was excited but also afraid. She felt she was caught up within the tensions and difficulties that existed between the adult couple. Her father was in the army and there was a world war in progress and therefore constant fears for his safety. She was only five and apart from her natural curiosity about bodies there would have been many things in her mind, including wanting to keep her father alive. Her worst fears were realised when he was killed in action the following year. The dream uses these historical facts and Fairbairn shows how the person is still struggling with a sense of violence and viciousness.

An understanding of the internal divisions that occur within the personality as it struggles with itself was central to Fairbairn's psychology. (He spoke of schizoid states in the mind.)

To Hazlitt man was not a simple animal and his faculties were eternally at variance. 'No one hates or takes part against himself more heartily or heroically then does the same individual.' The hidden nature of this activity was captured when he wrote:

> The constantly tampering with the truth, the putting off the day of reckoning, the fear of looking our situation in the face, gives the mind a wandering and unsettled turn, makes our waking thoughts a troubled dream, or sometimes ends in madness, without any violent paroxysms, without any severe pang, without any *overt* act, but from that silent operation of the mind which preys internally upon itself, and works the decay of its powers the more fatally, because we dare not give it open and avowed scope.[13]

He is here describing the same situation which Fairbairn presented to us in the actress dream. So much took place in silence in that little girl's life and the inability of anyone in the family to find words for what was happening allowed the internal workings of the mind a life of their own. Those silent operations that prey internally upon the self. In the elaboration of his understanding Fairbairn explored the internal war between the different parts of the self. He takes up the question posed by Hazlitt. Fairbairn described the part of the person who accuses and hates himself as 'taking up an uncompromising hostile attitude' towards the other part. If this internal war is a serious one there remains little of an independent self able to take responsibility for its own life or able to creatively engage in productive relationships. Such a rudderless person gets easily entangled and taken over by other, powerful people.

In Shakespeare's *Troilus and Cressida* we find a character similar to Fairbairn's 'actress'. Cressida feels very mixed up and tries to explain her predicament to Troilus:

> I have a kind of self resides with you;
> But an unkind self, that itself will leave,
> To be another's fool. I would be gone:
> Where is my wit? I know not what I speak.
>   Act 3.2.138–141

In case we miss these points Shakespeare leaves clues around for us to pick up. In *Troilus and Cressida* most characters speak in verse, with the exception of Pandarus and Thersites, who always speak in prose. Cressida is the only character who speaks in both. She adapts to whoever she is with, she speaks prose with Pandarus, verse with Troilus, taking on the identity of whoever she is with. Despite her ambivalence Cressida and Troilus pledge their love but it is not long before he discovers her with another man. Consider Troilus' position as he struggles to believe what he is seeing. If we read with Fairbairn in mind we find a telling description of the same internal war.

> Within my soul there doth conduce a fight
> Of this strange nature that a thing inseparate
> Divides more wider than the sky and earth,
> And yet the spacious breadth of this division
> Admits no orifex for a point as subtle
> As Ariachne's broken woof to enter.
>   Act 5.2.144–150

These two different parts of the self that war with each other often are so separate that they are as far away from each other as the sky and earth, and yet they lie side by side within the same person, are as close as the threads which the perfect seamless weaver binds together. As Troilus continued to speak he described how the good and the bad, the love and hate are so close that in an instant one trips into the other, the idealised becomes the demonised. Love tied with the bonds of heaven becomes nothing more than greasy orts and scraps, despised relics, the remains of the dead.

One of Fairbairn's influences in thinking out his ideas was the French psychologist Pierre Janet. Janet wrote about a process of dissociation being set up in the mind, but conceived of this as a passive process, as if the various parts of the self just drifted away from each other. Fairbairn accepted Janet's observation but took issue with his explanation and posited an active agency in the mind. Let us turn to Hazlitt. He was very clear about a similar sense of agency. He wrote:

> The author of the Rime of the Ancient Mariner, (who sees further into such things than most people,) could not understand why I should bring a charge of wicked-ness against an infant before it could speak, merely for squalling and straining its lungs a little. If the child had been in pain or in fear, I should have said nothing, but it cried only to vent its passion and alarm the house, and I saw in its frantic screams and gestures that great baby, the world, tumbling about in its swaddling clothes, and tormenting itself and others for the last six thousand years! The plea of ignorance, of folly, of grossness, or selfishness makes nothing either way: it is the downright love of pain and mischief for the interest it excites, and the scope it gives to an abandoned will, that is the root of all the evil, and the original sin of human nature. There is a love of power in the mind independent of the love of good, and this love of power, when it comes to be opposed to the spirit of good, and is leagued with the spirit of evil to commit it with greediness, is wickedness. I know of no other definition of the term.[14]

I have suggested that specifically in the *Essay* and generally throughout his writings Hazlitt's thought runs parallel to Fairbairn's. Hazlitt's notion of disinterested identification matches Fairbairn's emphasis on an interpersonal psychology. Both subscribe to a belief in the mind as an active agency from birth and concur in their view of the internal divisions and splintering of the self.

We are about to move on to one of the most turbulent periods in Hazlitt's life when in 1820, at the age of 42, he fell madly in love with Sarah Walker, a girl half his age. This was a time when he was despised and rejected, when many of his friends turned against him. We will need to think about this period of his life and why he aroused such an extreme reaction. Did he reveal too much about a splintering of his mind, more than people could bear? As a conclusion to this chapter and an opening to the next I quote from a letter Hazlitt wrote to his friend P. G. Patmore. It is 1822 and he is returning by steamboat to London from Edinburgh where he had been trying to obtain a divorce from his wife Sarah Stoddart.

> A raging fire is in my heart, that never quits me. The steam-boat (which I foolishly ventured on board) seems like a prison-house, a sort of spectre-ship,

moving on through an infernal lake, without wind or tide, by some necromatic power – the splashing of the waves, the noise of the engine gives me no rest, night and day – no tree, no natural object varies the scene – but the abyss is before me, and all my peace lies weltering in it! I feel the eternity of punishment in this life; for I see no end of my woes … I am tossed about (backwards and forwards) by my passion, so as to become ridiculous. I can now understand how it is that mad people never remain in the same place – they are moving on forever, *from themselves.* [15]

Chapter 6

The New Pygmalion

I look at my collection of Hazlitt's writings as they stand side by side on my shelf. I tilt *Liber Amoris* on its spine and place it flat on my writing table. *Liber Amoris: The New Pygmalion.* A book of love; a man who loved a marble statue of a woman, and wanted the gods to make it human. As I try to order my impressions and my thoughts on this book and this period of Hazlitt's life, on what I can understand about him, what I can learn from him, I begin to hear the rumbling of discontent, the sharp sounds of condemnation, the ascending chorus of rebuke and distaste that not only greeted its publication in 1823 but has with occasional pauses rolled on into modern days. Brimley Johnson's words referred to in chapter one return to my mind. 'We think much and often of what he has written; little and seldom of the man himself ... he repels us.' I also think of Robert Louis Stevenson who refused to write a biography of Hazlitt because he found the contents of *Liber Amoris* so abhorrent. As I set my eyes on the book I realise that my experience is similar to many others, that the actual text of the book as written by Hazlitt is rarely able to stand on its own. A certain reputation has preceded it. It is shrouded in a mist so as to be barely visible. Readers who come to it through one of the biographies of Hazlitt will already be aware of the furore it caused. On most of the eight occasions that the book has been reprinted it has been accompanied by an introduction and an account of its history. What happens if we skip the introductions, leave them until later and read the text itself? We might imagine we live in 1823 and walk into a London bookshop and pick up the book. It is by an anonymous author. What will we find as we turn the pages and make space in our mind to read the text as a story?

The book we have picked up has a brief preface or 'Advertisement' as it is called. Here we read of a man's fatal attachment to a woman which led to his departure from Britain, and his hope of recovery while living in the Netherlands, where he died 'of disappointment preying on a sickly frame and a morbid state of mind'. We read that the publisher, a friend of the author, tried to persuade him to omit many things from the book because they were 'childish or redundant', but he insisted on their inclusion. This introductory piece ends with the words 'the names and circumstances are so far disguised, it is presumed, as to prevent any consequences resulting from the publication, farther than the amusement or sympathy of the reader.'

The bulk of part one consists of a series of dialogues between 'H' and 'S'. 'H' is of course Hazlitt and 'S' is Sarah Walker. The dialogues are recorded like scenes in a play. There are seven scenes called 'The Picture', 'The Invitation', 'The Message', 'The Flageolet', 'The Confession', 'The Quarrel' and 'The

Reconciliation'.

H is a lodger in S's family home. Her daily work includes bringing him his breakfast in the morning. The story opens in the first dialogue with H offering S a gift. It is a picture of a woman. He sees a strong likeness between S and the woman. S cannot see the likeness. H seems to be trying to make S fit the picture, suggesting that the likeness would be revealed if she wore the same dress or let her hair down over her shoulders to match the picture. The painting is a delicate copy of a Guido or a Raphael. It could be of a Madonna or a Magdalen or St Cecilia. In this dialogue H addresses S as 'Sarah', and 'my dear girl' and 'my sweetest'. She calls him 'Sir'. She is generally matter of fact and brief with her words. H's words to her speak for themselves. Here is a sample:

> If you are never to be mine, I shall not long be myself. I cannot go on as I am. My faculties leave me: I think of nothing, I have not feeling about any thing but thee: thy sweet image has taken possession of me, haunts me, and will drive me to distraction. Yet I could almost wish to go mad for thy sake: for then I might fancy that I had thy love in return, which I cannot live without.[1]

Her unresponsiveness to his desire and demands seem to only intensify his longing and he continues:

> thou art heavenly – fair, my love – like her from whom the picture was taken – the idol of the painter's heart, as thou art of mine! Shall I make a drawing of it altering the dress a little, to shew you how like it is?[2]

The conversation continues in this vein in subsequent meetings. He tells her that if she loved him…

> I should feel like a God! My face would change to a different expression: my whole form would undergo alteration. I was getting well, I was growing young in the sweet proofs of your friendship; you see how I droop and wither under your displeasure! Thou art divine, my love, and canst make me either more or less than mortal. Indeed I am thy creature, thy slave – I only wish to live for your sake – I would gladly die for you.[3]
>
> Your power over me is that of sovereign grace and beauty. When I am near thee nothing can harm me. Thou art an angel of light, shadowing me with thy softness. But when I let go thy hand, I stagger on a precipice: out of thy sight the world is dark to me and comfortless.[4]

In another scene H tells Sarah he sees something more complicated in her.

I once thoughts you were half inclined to be a prude, and I admired you as a pensive nun, devout and pure. I now think you are more than half a coquet, and I like you for your roguery. The truth is, I am in love with you my angel; and whatever you are, is to me the perfection of thy sex. I care not what thou art, while thou art still thyself. Smile but so, and turn my heart to what shape you please! [5]

Detecting some anxiety in her when she returns from visiting a relative H says:

Cruel girl! you look at this moment heavenly-soft, saint-like, or resembling some graceful marble statue, in the moon's ray! Sadness only heightens the elegance of your features. How can I escape from you, when every new occasion, even your cruelty and scorn, brings out some new charm. Nay, your rejection of me, by the way in which you do it, is only a new link added to my chain. [6]

Sarah tells him of a previous attachment and painful parting from a man of a higher status in life. Here she speaks some sixty-five words. There is only one other passage of equal length in all the scenes. This meeting called 'The Confession' ends with H saying, 'You are an angel, and I will spend my life, if you will let me, in paying you the homage that my heart feels towards you.' [7] In scene six, 'The Quarrel', H believes that Sarah has deceived him, that she has been playing with him and making their intimacies a matter of public jest with her family. He says he would give the world to believe that his suspicions of her unjust and says:

After what I thought and felt towards you, as little less than an angel, to have but a doubt cross my mind for an instant that you were what I dare not name – a common lodging-house decoy, a kissing convenience, that your lips were as common as the stairs. [8]

He calls her 'a young witch'. Sarah protests saying she has been consistent and that she never offered him anything more than friendship. They argue about this. He asks if she has two characters, 'one that you palm off on me, and another, your natural one, that you resume when you get out of the room, like an actress who throws aside her artificial part behind the scenes?' When she tells him she once loved another he grasps at this hoping that if she was capable of love she could love him. Their conversation:

H: I love you to distraction! You are the only woman that ever made me think she loved me, and that feeling was so new to me, and so delicious, that it will never from my heart. Thou wert to me a little tender flower, blooming in the wilderness of my life; and though thou should'st turn out a weed, I'll not fling thee from me, while I can help it. Wert thou all that I dread to think – wert thou a wretched wanderer in the street, covered with rags, disease, infamy, I'd clasp thee to my bosom, and live and die with thee, my love. Kiss, me thou little sorceress!

S: NEVER!

H.   Then go: but remember I cannot live without you – nor I will not.[9]

The final scene is called 'The Reconciliation'. H is still imploring Sarah to love him, saying that her repeated cruel rejection drives him 'almost to madness'. The scene concludes with Sarah telling him that her former lover bore a resemblance to the bronze figure of Buonaparte which sits on his mantle piece, his prized possession. The dialogue ceases and H narrates the final exchange between them. He gives her the statue and then she comes and kisses him. Here he is directly speaking to the reader, referring to his exultation at that moment and his wretched state at the time of writing.

For the most part their words seem to run in parallel tracts. Sarah is regularly stepping out of his way and he rarely seems to listen to what she is actually saying, as if he has constructed a 'Sarah' in his own mind and is constantly relating to that image rather than the real person before him.

Two letters, dated February and March 1822, written from Berwick, continue H's expression of love, hope and despair. He declares himself 'a very child in love'. To this is added a note that Sarah never replied to his letter. Part one concludes with letters from H to S dated February and March 1822. Finally there is a page of notes written by the author under the heading 'Written in a blank leaf of Endymion' and this section of the book concludes with a piece headed 'A Proposal of Love' which is in fact a quotation from Shakespeare's *Troilus and Cressida*.

Part Two is a collection of ten letters mostly written by H to C. P—, Esq. who is in London. They are written from various parts of Scotland as H travels to Edinburgh to seek a divorce from his wife in the hope of marrying S. They are usually begun with the words 'My Good Friend'. The letters tell of the tumult in the mind and heart of the writer about his relationship with S. The section also includes a letter from C. P. to H, the copy of a letter from S and some reflections by H called 'Perfect Love' and 'Unaltered Love'.

One: Relates the events of the reconciliation, but with flashes of anger emerging. H here states 'I have begun a book of our conversations (I mean mine and the statue's) which I call *Liber Amoris*.'

Two: 'I suspect her grievously of being an arrant jilt, to say no more – yet I love her dearly ... What is there in her but a pretty figure, and that you can't get a word out of her? ... Am I mad or a fool?' [10]

Three: 'Oh God! Can I bear after all to think of her so, or that I am scorned and made a sport of by the creature to whom I had given my whole heart? Thus has it been with me all my life; and so will it be to the end of it! If you should learn any thing, good or bad, tell me, I conjure you: I can bear any thing but this cruel suspense, if I knew she was a mere abandoned creature, I should try to forget her; but till I do know this, nothing can tear me from her, I have drunk in poison from her lips too long, alas! Mine do not poison again. I sit and indulge my grief by the hour together; my weakness grows upon me; and I have no hope left, unless I could lose my senses quite. To forget, ah! To forget – there would be something in that – to change to an idiot for some few years, and then to wake up a poor wretched man, to recollect my misery as past, and die!'

Four: H has reverted to desperation and desire for her. 'My heart has found a tongue in speaking to her and I have talked to her the divine language of love. Yet she says, she is insensible to it. Am I to believe her or you? You – for I wish it and wish it to madness.' [11]

Five: 'I cannot describe the weakness of mind to which she has reduced me. This state of suspense is like hanging in the air by a single thread that exhausts all your strength to keep hold of it; and yet if that fails you, you have nothing in the world else left to trust to. The truth is, I never had any pleasure, like love, with any one but her. Then how can I bear to part with her? Do you know I like to think of her best in her morning-gown and mob-cap – it is so she has oftenest come into my room and enchanted me! She was once ill, pale, and had lost all her freshness. I only adored her the more for it, and fell in love with the decay of her beauty. I could devour the little witch. If she had a plague spot on her, I could touch the infection: if she was in a burning fever, I could kiss her, and drink death as I have drunk life from her lips. When I press her hand, I enjoy perfect happiness and contentment of soul. It is not what she says or does – it is herself that I love. To be with her is to be at peace. I have no other wish or desire, the air about her is serene, blissful; and he who breathes it is like one of the Gods!' [12]

Six: 'But now Paradise barred its doors against me; I was driven from her presence, where rosy blushes and delicious sighs and all soft wishes dwelt, the outcast of nature and the scoff of love! I thought of the time when I was a little happy careless child, of my father's house, of my early lessons, of my brother's picture of me when a boy, of all that had since happened to me, and of the waste of years to come ... What is to be done? I cannot forget *her*; and I can no more find no other like what *she seemed*. I should wish you to call, if you can make an excuse, and see whether or no she is quite marble.'[13]

Seven: 'If it were not for my little boy, whose face I see struck blank at the news, looking through the world for pity and meeting with contempt instead, I should soon, I fear, settle the question by my death. That recollection is the only thought that brings my wandering reason to an anchor ... The whole is like a dream, an effect of enchantment; it torments me, and it drives me mad. I had conversed too long with abstracted truth to trust myself with the immortal thoughts of love ... I am in some sense proud that I can feel this dreadful passion – it gives me a kind of rank in the kingdom of love – but I could have wished it had been for an object that at least could have understood its value and pitied its excess.'[14]

Eight: 'Who is there so low as me? Who is there besides (I ask) after the homage I have paid her and the caresses she has lavished on me, so vile, so abhorrent to love, to whom such an indignity could have happened? ... I am now enclosed in a dungeon of despair. The sky is marble to my thoughts; nature is dead around me, as hope is within me ... Oh! cold, solitary, sepulchral breakfasts, compared with those which I promised myself with her; or which I made when she had been standing an hour by my side, my guardian-angel, my wife, my sister, my sweet friend, my Eve, my all; and had blest me with her seraph kisses! ... I am not mad, but my heart is so; and raves within me, fierce and untameable, like a panther in its den, and tries to get loose to its lost mate, and fawn on her hand, and bend lowly at her feet.'[15]

Nine: 'Wretched being that I am! I have thrown away my heart and soul upon an unfeeling girl; and my life (that might have been so happy, had she been what I thought her) will soon follow either voluntarily, or by the force of grief, remorse, and disappointment. I cannot get rid of the reflection for an instant, nor even seek relief from its galling pressure ... Demoniacal possessions. I see the young witch seated in another's lap, twining her serpent arms round him, her eye glancing and her cheeks on fire – why does not the hideous thought choke me? ... You see by this letter the way I am in, and I hope you will excuse it as the picture of a half-disordered mind. The least respite from my uneasiness (such as I had yesterday) only brings the contrary reflection back upon me, like a flood; and by letting me see the happiness I have lost, makes me feel, by contrast, more acutely what I am doomed to bear.'[16]

Ten: Here we can see that while he is caught up with Sarah he is nonetheless able to write. 'Dear Friend ... Do you know you would have been delighted with the effect of the Northern twilight on this romantic country as I rode along last night? The hills and groves and herds of cattle were seen reposing in the grey dawn of midnight, as in a moonlight without shadow. The whole wide canopy of Heaven shed its reflex light upon them, like a pure crystal mirror. No sharp points, no petty details, no hard contrasts – every object was seen softened yet distinct, in its simple outline and natural tones, transparent with an inward light, breathing its own mild lustre. The landscape altogether was like an airy piece of mosaic-work, or like one of Poussin's broad massy landscapes or Titian's lovely pastoral scenes. Is it not so, that poets see nature, veiled to the sight, but revealed to the soul in visionary grace and grandeur! I confess the sight touched me; and might have removed all sadness except mine.' [17] But he cannot keep his mind away from her for long. 'I wept myself almost blind, and I gazed at the broad golden sunset through my tears that fell in showers. As I trod the green mountain turf, oh! how I wished to be laid beneath it – in one grave with her – that I might sleep with her in that cold bed, my hand in hers, and my heart for ever still – while worms should taste her sweet body, that I had never tasted! There was a time when I could bear solitude; but it is too much for me at present. Now I am no sooner left to myself than I am lost in infinite space, and look round me in vain for support or comfort. She was my stay, my hope: without her hand to cling to, I stagger like an infant on the edge of a precipice. The universe without her is one wide, hollow abyss, in which my harassed thoughts can find no resting-place. I must break off here; for the *hysterica passio* comes upon me, and threatens to unhinge my reason.' [18]

Part Three consists of four longer letters by H to JSK. The letters flow into each other and are really one long story. They tell of the events which led to the conclusion of the relationship between H and S. As in the previous part they recount the torment and the tumult in H (and the discovery that she had a relationship with another man).

In the first letter H reflects on a conversation he had with JSK as they walked around Loch Lomond when they spoke of two types of loss – where there was an old mutual attachment and where the attachment was one-sided. H continues:

We considered together which was the most to be pitied, a disappointment in love where the attachment was mutual or one where there has been no return, and we both agreed, I think, that the former was best to be endured, and that to have the consciousness of it a companion for life was the least evil of the two, as there was a secret sweetness that took off the bitterness and the sting of regret, and 'the memory of what once had been' atoned, in some measure, and at intervals, for what 'never more could be.' In the other case, there was nothing to look back to with tender satisfaction, no redeeming trait, not even a possibility of turning it to good. It left behind it not cherished sighs, but stifled pangs. The galling sense of it did not bring moisture into the eyes, but dried up the heart ever after. One had been my fate, the other had been yours!

H tells of returning and seeing Sarah. Her words are as sparse as ever. Her resistance is taken as a sign that she has honourably held out to the end, but the frustration that we have seen signs of is about to ignite within him. He describes the scene:

All this time she was standing just outside the door, my hand in hers (would that they could have grown together!) she was dressed in a loose morning-gown, her hair curled beautifully; she stood with her profile to me, and looked down the whole time. No expression was ever more soft or perfect. Her whole attitude, her whole form, was dignity and bewitching grace. I said to her, 'You look like a queen, my love, adorned with your own graces!' I grew idolatrous, and would have kneeled to her. She made a movement, as if she was displeased. I tried to draw her towards me. She wouldn't. I then got up, and offered to kiss her at parting. I found she obstinately refused. This stung me to the quick. It was the first time in her life she had ever done so. I could bear it no longer. I gave way to all the fury of disappointed hope and jealous passion. I was made the dupe of trick and cunning, killed with cold, sullen scorn; and, after all the agony I had suffered, could obtain no explanation why I was subjected to it. I was still to be tantalised, tortured, made the cruel sport of one, for whom I would have sacrificed all. I tore the locket which contained her hair (and which I used to wear continually in my bosom, as the precious token of her dear regard) from my neck, and trampled it in pieces. I then dashed the little Buonaparte on the ground, and stamped upon it, as one of her instruments of mockery. I could not stay in the room; I could not leave it; my rage, my despair were uncontrollable. I shrieked curses on her name, and on her false love; and the scream I uttered (so pitiful and so piercing was it, that the sound of it terrified me) instantly brought the whole house, father, mother, lodgers and all, into the room. They thought I was destroying her and myself. I had gone into the bedroom, merely to hide away from myself, and as I came out of it, raging-mad with the new sense of present shame and lasting misery, Mrs. F— said, 'She's in there! He has got her in there!' thinking the cries had proceeded from her, and that I had been offering her violence. 'Oh! no,' I said, 'She's in no danger from me; I am not the person;' and tried to burst from this scene of degradation. The mother endeavoured to stop me, and said, 'For God's sake, don't go out, Mr.—! For God's sake, don't!' Her father, who was not, I believe, in the secret, and was therefore justly scandalised at such outrageous conduct, said angrily, 'Let him go! Why should he stay?' I however sprang down stairs, and as they called out to me,' 'What is it? – What has she done to you?' I answered, 'She has murdered me! – She has destroyed me for ever! – She has doomed my soul to perdition!' I rushed out of the house, thinking to quit it forever; but I was no sooner in the street, than the desolation and the darkness became greater, more intolerable; and the eddying violence of my passion drove me back to the source, from whence it sprung.[19]

A long discussion with Sarah and a certain calm was restored. Sarah is reported to be unwell and does not appear for some days. On hearing some consoling words from her sister Betsey he feels restored. He says:

I did not know how to contain myself; I was childish, wanton, drunk with pleasure. I continued in this state of delirium or dotage all that day and the next, talked incessantly, laughed at every thing, and was so extravagant, nobody could tell what was the matter with me. I murmured her name; I blest her; I folded her to my heart in delicious fondness; I called her by my own name; I worshipped her: I was mad for her. I told P— I should laugh in her face, if ever she pretended not to like me again. Her mother came in and said, she hoped I should excuse Sarah's coming up. 'Oh, Ma'am,' I said, 'I have no wish to see her; I feel her at my heart; she does not hate me after all, and I wish for nothing.' [20]

But after a week this collapses. S comes to his room and their long conversation leaves him desolate. He feels that she has smashed him to pieces just as he had smashed the Buonaparte.

He describes his state of mind:

My head reeled, my heart recoiled within me. I was stung with scorpions; my flesh crawled; I was choked with rage; her scorn scorched me like flames; her air (her heavenly air) withdrawn from me, stifled me, and left me gasping for breath and being. It was a fable. She started up in her own likeness, a serpent in place of a woman. She had fascinated, she had stung me, and had returned to her proper shape, gliding from me after inflicting the mortal wound, and instilling deadly poison into every pore; but her form lost none of its original brightness by the change of character, but was all glittering, beauteous, voluptuous grace. Seed of the serpent or of the woman, she was divine! I felt that she was a witch, and had bewitched me. Fate had enclosed me round about. I was transformed too, no longer human (any more than she, to whom I had knit myself) my feelings were marble; my blood was of molten lead; my thoughts on fire. I was taken out of myself, wrapt into another sphere, far from the light of day, of hope, of love. I had no natural affection left; she had slain me, but no other thing had power over me. Her arms embraced another; but her mock-embrace, the phantom of her love, still bound me, and I had not a wish to escape. [21]

Three of Part Three: He finds she has another man. He meets them in the street. He later meets the man, an ex-lodger, and they talk for four hours, and he finds that she has been doing the same with him as she did in his room, and this had been going on for three months before he went to Scotland. 'The murder was out'.

This seems to be the first time he is able to think of her and who she is in herself. When he now thinks of her duplicity and her indifference to him and 'her triumph in my suffering' and how he must have incurred her contempt, he is not overpowered, but can think of her and her state of mind. He wonders about his idealisation of her and the effect it might have had on her, that if she in fact did not have such an exalted opinion of herself, she could have perceived his idealisation of her as ironic or insulting. Hitherto he had virtually always seen her indoors. He remarks on how she seems different in a different place. But this signifies an ability in him to look at her through new eyes. He writes:

> My seeing her in the street has gone a good way to satisfy me. Her manner
> there explains her manner in-doors to be conscious and overdone; and
> besides, she looks but indifferently. She is diminutive in stature, and her
> measured step and timid air do not suit these public airings. I am afraid
> she will soon grow common to my imagination, as well as worthless in
> herself. Her image seems fast 'going into the wastes of time,' like a weed
> that the wave bears farther and farther from me. Alas! thou poor hapless
> weed, when I entirely lose sight of thee, and for ever, no flower will ever
> bloom on earth to glad my heart again![22]

The Facts of Hazlitt's Life

Let us now turn to William Hazlitt's life. By July 1820 he and his wife Sarah were
no longer living together and he moved into lodgings in Southampton Buildings,
Holborn. There he became infatuated with the daughter of his landlord. Her
name was Sarah Walker. Hazlitt was forty-two, Sarah was twenty. He sought
a divorce and as divorce law in Scotland was more liberal than in England he
and his wife agreed to pursue the matter in Edinburgh. He was required to live
there a specified amount of time. His wife also had to make an appearance in
Edinburgh. After much confusion, wrangling and waiting they eventually were
granted a divorce. Hazlitt's hopes that Sarah Walker would marry him were
dashed when he discovered she had another man. The whole episode proved to
be one of the most tortured in his life. In May 1823 he published a book drawing
on his experience of the love affair. It was called *Liber Amoris: or The New
Pygmalion*. Despite the anonymity of the author his identity was immediately
transparent. Hazlitt was too clever a man and the disguise of his identity too thin
and flimsy to lend much weight to the suggestion that concealment was high
on his agenda. The first part of the book is a record of what took place between
Hazlitt and Sarah. The person in part two to whom Hazlitt wrote was his friend
P. G. Patmore and the friend in part three was Sheridan Knowles.

Reactions to *Liber Amoris*

The majority of those who read *Liber Amoris* on its publication were scandalised.
Hazlitt's revelations about his innermost thoughts and feelings during the affair
made him easy fodder for his critics. The more vitriolic arm of the Tory press
had long had Hazlitt in their sights. As I sketched in chapter 2, England at
this time was a repressive place and the Establishment had much to fear from
its critics. Hazlitt was no stranger to political controversy and was adept at
defending himself when such battles would rage from time to time. In 1818

he had successfully sued the most notorious right-wing organ, *Blackwoods*, for slander and they settled out of court paying him damages.

Nonetheless many of his friends believed he had gone too far in writing *Liber Amoris*. His son found the whole incident in his father's life painful and embarrassing. When he published *Literary Remains* (1836) he wrote 'my father had fallen into an infatuation which he has himself illustrated in glowing and eloquent language in a regretted publication called *Liber Amoris*. The subject is a painful one and admits of but one cheerful consolation – that my father's name and character were but momentarily dimmed by what indeed was but a momentary delusion'.[23] Even though the affair was an affair of the heart and of the mind, nevertheless the shock was too much to bear. In the decades that followed the publication, indeed even in modern times, the book has remained controversial and troublesome. We might follow a trail of its fortunes by glancing at a sample of reviews over the past two centuries. We can begin with some of the first reviews of 1823.

> Silly Billy has produced a record of vulgarity and nastiness which reveal 'Pyg' in all the nakedness of his conceit, selfishness, slavering sensuality, filthy profligacy, and howling idiotcy; the indecent trash is a display of silliness, cant, nonsense, bad English, obscenity. The conversations are indecent and childish, the letters common-place; the besotted cockney has written callous blasphemy, abominable gabble, and grossness and blackguardism. The book displays the blind and besotted bestiality of a dirty nature.[24]

> *Liber Amoris,* is the tale of a cockney's stupidity and folly, is filled with degraded practical sensuality, inveterate ignorance and depraved principle. Hazlitt is himself the hero of the book, which is the story of his attempt to seduce an innocent young girl whose honour should be defended. He is a disappointed dotard and an impotent sensualist whose folly and idiotism are revealed in the work.[25]

However, despite the above views being in the majority, there were also at the time a few of the opinion that the book contained more than filthy profligacy. An anonymous reviewer in the *Times* wrote:

> The book is an able delineation of a man under the influence of a degrading infatuation. The author serves the cause of sound sense and rational affection by describing the terrible impulses of self-will so as to excite pain and disgust. The painting of the drivelling imbecility and impotent dotage of the lover is morally instructive.[26]

In 1881, J. A. Noble recognised something of psychological interest in the book.

He described it as:

> A strange study in the morbid psychology of genius which is a contribution to
> pathology rather than to biography. The book is written with reckless unreserve
> and even a passionate disregard to grammar. But though the book is the outcome
> of erotic mania, it is worth reading because it assists one in understanding human
> nature and the strengths and weaknesses of Hazlitt.[27]

Richard Le Gallienne, in his introductory comments to a new edition of the
work (1893, 1894), wrote that:

> it is impossible not to feel that no man of forty should be able to mistake a woman
> for a goddess or an angel, and he should certainly never quote Milton or any great
> poet to her. It is unnatural, uncanny, in the bearded man. Naiveté is charming up
> to twenty, but the naiveté of middle-age is unattractive, and the *Liber Amoris* is
> full of that unattractive quality, – much like the naiveté we sometimes find in the
> poetical effusions of criminals.[28]

He adds that 'it is in fact not as literature, but as a document of madness, that
the book has its value.' [29]

He is rather worried that a new reader might pick up this book having never
read anything else by Hazlitt and turn away in disgust.

> To those who know the Hazlitt of the glorious essays … the *Liber Amoris* may
> be entrusted without fear. They will know where to place it, in a very subsidiary
> relation indeed to the Hazlitt beloved of all honest men who love virile English.
> It is but as a literary curiosity, a document of nympholepsy, a biographical
> appendix, that the *Liber Amoris* has any value – unless one sees in the literal tone
> of its opening conversations a naive promise of modern realism.[30]

In response to Le Gallienne's publication the range of reviewers seems to have
hardly changed.

> It is unfair to Hazlitt to remove *Liber Amoris* from its happy obscurity; it is dull
> reading and its interest is purely pathological. Any cleanly-minded lay reader will
> peruse it only in satisfaction of an unholy curiosity. [31]

But again some see beyond this moral indignation. '*Liber Amoris* … will be
of interest to students of morbid psychology and pathology.'[32] However over
time the shock was giving way to more thoughtful and reasoned criticisms of the
work. By 1916, nearly a hundred years after its publication, P. P. Howe wrote as
follows:

Too often in examinations of *Liber Amoris* biographical considerations have obscured aesthetic ones; the book is a perfectly deliberate and a highly characteristic work of art, not an embarrassment or a scandal. Viewed as a work of fiction, it manifests a very high degree of art. Hazlitt published the book not only to release an intolerable oppression, but because he had something to say, and he does so by retaining a measure of mental detachment throughout. *Liber Amoris* is not the least of his contributions to our knowledge of the heart of man. [33]

Howe's words point us in a new direction. They are like a new signpost such as we find when we travel near a coastline or places of scenic beauty. An alternative is available. Howe suggests we think of this as a work of art as well as a record of events in a life. But few seem to take notice and despite the openings offered by Howe, many biographers and commentators in the early part of the twentieth century remain within a narrow furrow of thought. They may be less moralistic but they consider *Liber Amoris* primarily as part of the diary of a life. Many pass over it with little or no comment, and therefore no new understanding is reached. The attitudes may seem new, but it is merely a change of clothing, a dressing up of the old. There is no new substance. For instance, to Catherine Macdonald Maclean, Hazlitt has 'a weakness' instead of being a filthy profligate. Hesketh Pearson's biography of Hazlitt, significantly called *A Fool in Love*, spends a considerable amount of time on Hazlitt's relationship with Sarah Walker, almost seeing his whole life through it, and yet moves in ever-decreasing circles, providing fewer and fewer insights as the author ploughs through his script. J. B. Priestley wrote of the affair as slipping 'from tragedy into squalid farce', and that it 'had almost made a maniac' out of Hazlitt.[34] Herschel Baker, who described Pearson's book as 'lurid', wrote about the episode under the heading 'A Mind Diseased' and described Hazlitt's relationship with Sarah Walker as 'a shabby liaison' and 'a sad farce.'[35]

Modern Criticism

In 1948 Charles Morgan wrote an introduction to a new edition of *Liber Amoris* and placed the work within a literary tradition that encompassed Montaigne's *Essays,* Shakespeare's *Sonnets* and Stendhal's *De L'Amour.* He believed these writers possessed an understanding of what took place between Hazlitt and Sarah Walker. I will explore Standhal's contribution in chapter 7. Morgan outlined the kernel of that understanding when he wrote quoting Montaigne. The central insight was

That we project our own imagining of Love on to her whom we say we love. We re-create her in an ideal shape – Hazlitt called Miss Walker 'the statue' – and worship her in that shape, and struggle to bring the statue to life. 'Like the passion of love,' said Montaigne, 'that lends beauties and graces to the person it does embrace; and that makes those who are caught with it, with a depraved and corrupt judgement, consider the thing they love other and more perfect than it is.[36]

Morgan believed that Hazlitt went further than Montaigne and Stendhal in exposing the process by which this projection takes place, that the subject who projects is not a blind fool, and can observe what is happening to him. 'Hazlitt,' he said, 'made no attempt to dignify his obsession. His division of mind between knowledge of Miss Walker's inadequacy and passionate exaltation of the ideal she represented is made plain in his terrible alternation of blame and praise, of angry distrust and wild confidence, of sickening triviality and high romance.' [37]

Morgan speculated on who Sarah was in herself and believed her opaqueness as a character was a weakness of the book, rightly pointing out that Hazlitt did not get into her mind. He went on to say that 'this very one-sidedness, this extreme subjectivity, gives it rare value as a document written at white-heat by a man of genius at the height of passionate obsession.'[38] Morgan's observations of Hazlitt's mind might suggest that he had Fairbairn's texts available to him (though I have no knowledge of this) when he wrote the following: 'He saw the woman and the goddess at the same time; was agonizingly aware both of the distinction between them on one plane of his consciousness and of their identity on another plane; was unceasingly observant of his self-division; was the sane, unsparing analyst of his own madness, and, therefore, racked.' [39] In Morgan's assessment of the Victorian mind, which condemned and could not understand Hazlitt, he pointed to their 'refusal to recognise that it is possible to respect and not respect at the same time, to despise and worship, to be mean and generous, cruel and kind, a sensual slave and a true lover, not only in turns but *at the same time*'.[40]

The writer and critic Cyril Connolly wrote a short essay on *Liber Amoris* in 1954 stating that it was an account of 'the most unfortunate love story in literature', that 'there is nothing like it in the language'. When he offers an explanation as to why Hazlitt became infatuated with Sarah Walker, this is what he had to say:

> There must have been a manic-depressive streak in him and I believe that the transition from depression to mania (cf. Goethe) is generally accompanied by falling in love which is, perhaps, provoked by glandular disturbance. Sally Walker was like a cancer of the soul to Hazlitt, an obsessional growth on the spirit set in motion through his sexual repression and last middle-aged clutching at innocence and youth. She attacked him in his weak spot as an insect paralyses

a grub, he was in the grip of a disease that had seized on a centre of retarded adolescence.[41]

In Connolly's opinion the book should be considered as something 'between a work of art and a case history'. This is a valuable point that allows the work to be approached from a broader perspective. However, the piece just quoted places so many things in the reader's mind at the same time that it is hard to see how any advancement in knowledge has taken place. The assertion that 'there must have been a manic-depressive streak in him' seems like a hastily erected hypothesis, using some borrowed psychiatric jargon which once put in place requires some swift scaffolding to hold it up. This is supplied by the remainder of the first sentence: 'I believe that the transition from depression to mania is generally accompanied by falling in love'; and this is followed by the suggestion (using the word 'perhaps') that manic depression is caused by a glandular disturbance. We are then treated to a succession of disease images: Sarah is 'a cancer of the soul', 'a growth on the spirit', an 'insect' paralysing a 'grub'. These extravagant metaphors act to create further obfuscation instead of providing clarification.

Later in the piece Connolly takes us to an important place when he suggests that many people have been repelled by *Liber Amoris* because they see a brilliant mind made helpless by adolescent lust. Hazlitt he says is 'unmanned by it, he is no longer master of himself and this morbidity is something that, like jealousy, we cannot forgive in other people because we so dread it for ourselves.' He also said that 'few, beside de Quincey, could appreciate the exquisite prose–poetry or the disturbing transitions from subjective to objective in this forerunner of modern psychology'.[42]

The third major contributor to a modern understanding of *Liber Amoris* is Gerald Lahey who in 1980 edited a new edition of the book. He argues that *Liber Amoris* should be considered among the unique works of English literature, alongside *Wuthering Heights, Moby Dick, Tristram Shandy* and others, suggesting it should be read as 'the love confession of a given historical moment, a specifically "Romantic" narrative expressing a notable phase of the temperament or imaginative sensibility of its period.'[43] A crucial arm of Lahey's thesis is that '*Liber Amoris* is a parable of the entire Romantic period trying to come to terms with its own flawed visionary conception of reality.[44] He points to the interest which the Romantic poets Wordsworth, Coleridge and Keats had in projective mental processes. They could poetically explore projective processes through the use of some object or objects in the natural world. Coleridge used the *Rime* to convey how man's destiny is caught up in the power of the Albatross that 'made the breeze to blow' and 'brought the fog and mist'. Keats used the nightingale in a similar way. Hazlitt projectively engaged a human object, Sarah Walker. For Keats it is 'youth' that 'grows pale and spectre thin'. With Hazlitt it is himself – 'I am grown spectral.'

Lahey suggests that Hazlitt's mind regressed to a mythic mode of viewing life, in particular to the Judeo-Christian mythology of his father, and he cites the many Biblical allusions in *Liber Amoris*. He believes that Hazlitt went back to his pre-rational days, that his imagination was fed by old 'types and shadows'. 'Here,' claims Lahey, 'Hazlitt was to find a key to the wild disorder of his interior being.'

Having moved us into this area Lahey seems to think he has provided an explanation of Hazlitt's state of mind. The remainder of his treatment of the subject anchors us to this point. Hazlitt, we are told has become a Fatalistic Calvinist. We are also told 'that Hazlitt at this hour felt a mysterious and compassionate Providence was preparing to crown his latter days with a new bliss cannot be doubted. The visionary luxuries of the 23rd Psalm floated before his eyes. He truly felt that the Lord was preparing a rich table for him to be feasted in the presence of his Tory enemies and was about to anoint his head with fragrant oils'. [45]

Lahey dismissed Cyril Connolly's suggestion of a manic-depressive streak in Hazlitt on the grounds that in manic-depression the patient while in one state of mind does not remember the other and as Hazlitt clearly did the thesis is flawed. Connolly's suggestion of a glandular disturbance is also treated with dismissiveness. Lahey discredits what he refers to as 'the jargon of literary psychology' [46] It is not really clear who or what he has in his sights. (Connolly is one candidate.) Is he claiming that a psychologically minded person, indeed a professional in his field, has no right to think and speculate and speak on these issues? I am reminded again of Kinnaird's comments quoted in the opening chapter, when he stated that 'our memory of Hazlitt will always be there reminding us that literature and criticism, whatever else they may be, end in the act of reading, in a dialogue that ensues; and he reminds us that these selves have brought themselves to write and read in order to know and judge, not "art" or "reality" or "the modern self," but themselves.' [47]

In 1985 Michael Neve introduced a new edition of *Liber Amoris*. The publication seems to have taken place without an awareness of Lahey's edition five years earlier. Neve describes *Liber Amoris* as 'a subtle, yet direct and powerful meditation on the philosophical ludicrousness of love itself. Through conversation, letters to friends about conversations (and sightings), through the use of literary asides, Hazlitt composes an exquisite, finished picture of driven desire, a desire that, with Freudian exactness, ends up without even an obscure object.' [48] Neve's publication is a very valuable contribution, not only for the brief but highly condensed introduction, but also for his re-publication of Le Gallienne's 1894 introduction and the addition of many valuable appendices.

There is much to learn from the thought which Morgan, Connolly, Lahey and Neve have brought to bear on this work. Morgan has taken us firmly out of the Victorian prejudices and pointed to the fact that Hazlitt's state of mind was not so strange and unique after all, that Montaigne and Shakespeare knew about it and described it well, and that Stendhal not only knew about it but tried to understand and explain its internal workings. While Connolly struggled to conceptualise the issues he nonetheless spelt out something important in bold letters. He attended to how we are disturbed by seeing a great mind losing control because we all fear the same happening to ourselves. While I remain unconvinced by Lahey's assertion that *Liber Amoris* is 'a parable of the entire Romantic period trying to come to terms with its own flawed visionary conception of reality'[49], I do think he was taking us in the right direction when he described Hazlitt as regressing to a world shaped by his father's religious mythology. Perhaps he has taken us to a valuable site and we need to probe deeper into his assertions.

Chapter 7

On the Edge of a Precipice

> My love is as a fever, longing still
> For that which longer nurseth the disease,
> Feeding on that which doth preserve the ill,
> The uncertain sickly appetite to please.
> My reason, the physician to my love,
> Angry that his prescriptions are not kept,
> Hath left me, and I desperate now approve
> Desire is death, which physic did except.
> Past cure I am, now reason is past care,
> And frantic-mad with evermore unrest;
> My thoughts and my discourse as madmen's are,
> At random from the truth vainly express'd;
>   For I have sworn thee fair and thought thee bright,
>   Who art as black as hell, as dark as night
>
> Sonnet 147

To indulge in ridicule usually creates a blind spot in our minds leaving us unable to see something of importance. A chorus of condemnation deafens itself to the pain and suffering of its victim. Calling Hazlitt a pig seemed to have left those critics devoid of any ability to ask a basic question as to why Hazlitt called himself a new version of Pygmalion. Pygmalion was a legendary figure in classical mythology who resided in Cyprus. He had problems in his relations with women and bitterly resolved to have little to do with them and remain unmarried. He was a sculptor of exceptional talent and artistry and he carved a statue of a woman so exquisitely that it convincingly resembled a live person. He began to admire his own work of art and he saw in it an instance of the ideal. His suppression of his desire for companionship, of a loving contact with a woman, of the need to love and to be loved, were unsuccessful, for having consciously sought to be rid of them by an act of will, they unconsciously returned. Having idealised his art the boundaries between a statue and a real person began to become blurred to him. He began to treat the statue as if it were real, caressing it, giving it gifts of jewels and beautiful clothes and soon he was talking to 'her' if she were his wife.

At a sacred festival he asked the gods to make his statue become his wife. Venus the goddess of love intervened and granted his wish. On his return home he kissed his statue and found the lips warm. Soon her eyes opened. She was alive and she fell in love with Pygmalion.

It is improbable that such a discursive writer as Hazlitt would accidentally describe himself as a Pygmalion. He published the book when he had become only too aware that he made Sarah out of his own desire, fashioned her from the particles of his own need.

Part of the outrage of 1823 towards *Liber Amoris* was politically motivated. Hazlitt was a marked man for the Tory press and they had their field-day with him. There was also the condemnation which stemmed from moral outrage, from the offence caused to the sensibilities of the Victorians. Le Gallienne's comments on the unattractiveness of the man idealising a young woman illustrate this position. Was the fear on reading *Liber Amoris* merely that of the man of forty giving in to adolescent lust, behaving like a youth? We hear of Hazlitt being 'unmanned', of the values of 'virile England' being threatened.

But to define the issue in terms of an offence to social, political and sexual mores is an incomplete statement of the concern in question. This moral indignation about sexuality was the first set of ripples set in motion by *Liber Amoris*. I suspect that the fear was in fact a much greater one. Clothing it in terms of sex allowed an eruption of hatred and condemnation, and the tendency to expel the unclean from decent society. Bryan Procter said, 'To this girl he gave all his valuable time, all his wealth of thought, and all the loving frenzy of his heart. For a while I think that on this point *he was substantially insane* – certainly beyond self-control. To him she was a being full of witchery, full of grace, with all the capacity of tenderness, the retiring coquetry, which had also brought others to her, invested her in his sight with the attractions of a divinity'.[1] (my italics) Procter dared to use the term 'insane', but was he frightened by his brashness and then pulled back by adding the statement about self-control? If we look again at the sample of reviewers of *Liber Amoris* over the years we note tentative use of the terms 'madness' and 'insane'. Noble in 1881 – 'a contribution to pathology rather than biography'; Le Gallienne in 1893 – 'a document of madness'; Connolly in 1956 was talking of manic-depression. Lahey pulls back from the usage of terms that would place Hazlitt in that category, but instead understands Hazlitt as regressing to some archaic world of his father's religious beliefs. Perhaps some would be more comfortable with the term 'breakdown' rather than 'mad' even though Hazlitt himself used the term 'mad' many times to describe himself. Perhaps there is a place for both if they help us to understand not just Hazlitt but what happens to the mind when such a breakdown occurs. Perhaps it is time to accept *Liber Amoris* into the canon of psychology text books used for the education of personal breakdown.

The inner turmoil which Hazlitt bore witness to was familiar to Shakespeare, Montaigne, Freud, Fairbairn, Steele and Bowlby. Hazlitt's suffering is not met with blame. The greatness of such people is measured by their ability to go beyond such simplistic meting out of punishment or abuse and instead they speak and think of responsibility. They all know that however damaging the evil may be that others direct at us, the evil we do unto ourselves is equally dangerous. Attention is directed to the nature of falling in love, particularly falling in love at first sight as Hazlitt did with Sarah. What happens when one person looks at another, and regardless of the actual qualities of that person, they see a perfect being, someone almost supernatural, a god? Interest is directed to *why* this takes place, and extends to *how* it takes place, exploring the nature of idealisation and the projective processes involved as evidenced by Sarah's words, 'You sit and fancy things out of your head, and lay them to my charge.'

Charles Morgan pointed us to Stendhal, and in particular to his book *De l'Amour* published in 1822. *De l'Amour* tells the story of how Stendhal fell madly in love with Mathilde Viscontini Dembrowski. They met when Stendhal was thirty-five and Metilde, as he called her, was twenty-eight. She had two sons and was separated from her husband. Their actual relationship had a formal distance about it and no real mutual intimacy ever developed between them. But Stendhal was infatuated with Metilde and became pre-occupied with her, his obsession being in many ways similar to Hazlitt's. However, Stendhal's text of *De l'Amour* is very different from Hazlitt's *Liber Amoris*. Rather than follow the story and lay out all the details of his infatuation the book was an attempt some time after the experience to explain not just what happened to him, but to develop some theory about obsessional love. In translation the text makes for very jagged reading, rather like an endless series of lists and statements. Of particular interest is the concept of crystallisation. This is how he described and explained it:

> At the salt mines of Salzburg, they throw a leafless wintry bough into one of the abandoned workings. Two or three months later they haul it out covered with a shining deposit of crystals. The smallest twig, no bigger than a tom-tit's claw, is studded with a galaxy of scintillating diamonds. The original branch is no longer recognisable. What I have called crystallisation is a mental process which draws from everything that happens new proofs of the perfection of the loved one.[2]

He gives an example of the crystallisation principle:

> A young woman learns that her cousin Edward, who is about to leave the Army, is a distinguished young man and is in love with her already because of what he has heard of her, even though they have never met; doubtless he wishes to meet her before declaring his love and asking for her hand. She sees a young stranger at church and hears him called Edward. She can think of no one else; she is in love. A later week the real Edward turns up, and he is not the stranger in the church.

She turns pale and of course will be utterly miserable for ever if she is made to marry him. [3]

In summary we might say that the book is dealing with the cause, the process and the outcome of the process of idealisation. As to the cause he says that the ideal breeding ground for love of this nature is 'the boredom of solitude'.[4] Love is also helped by misfortunes which precede it, for 'the imagination then recoils from the outside world which offers only sad pictures, and throws itself wholeheartedly into the task of crystallisation.[5]

In describing the process Stendhal writes that:

> Some people, over-fervent, or fervent by starts – loving on credit, if I may put it that way – will hurl themselves upon the experience instead of waiting for it to happen. Before the nature of an object can produce its proper sensation in them, they have blindly invested it from afar with imaginary charm which they conjure up inexhaustibly within themselves. As they come closer they see the experience not as it is, but as they have made it. They take delight in their own selves in the mistaken belief that they are enjoying the experience. But sooner or later they get tired of making the running and discover that the object of their adoration is *not returning the ball*; then their infatuation is dispelled, and the slight to their self-respect makes them react unfairly against the thing once overrated. [6]

We will return to Stendhal's thoughts later. To gather together enough information for our discussion I now need to turn to Hazlitt's use of a passage from *Troilus and Cressida*, which he placed at the end of Part One of *Liber Amoris*. It is one of no fewer than twenty references and allusions to Shakespeare that appear in the work. Its inclusion in Hazlitt's text has almost universally been passed over, rarely receiving more than a cursory acknowledgement. Cressida is trying to tell Troilus that she is not the ideal woman he thinks her to be. She says to him:

> Perchance, my lord, I show more craft than love;
> And fell so roundly to a large confession,
> To angle for your thoughts: but you are wise,
> Or else you love not, for to be wise and love
> Exceeds man's might; that dwells with gods above.
>
> Act 3.2, 143–147

Then follows the piece Hazlitt uses, which in the play is spoken by Troilus:

Oh! if I thought it could be in a woman
(As, if it can, I will presume in you)
To feed for aye her lamp and flames of love,
To keep her constancy in plight and youth,
Outliving beauties outward with a mind
That doth renew swifter than blood decays:
Or that persuasion could but thus convince me,
That my integrity and truth to you
Might be confronted with the match and weight
Of such a winnow'd purity in love –
How were I then uplifted! but, alas,
I am as true as truth's simplicity
And simpler than the infancy of truth.

Act 3.2, 148–160

Why did Hazlitt use the piece? He gave it the heading 'A proposal of Love' and adds the words 'given to her in our early acquaintance'. As he sat down to compile his text for publication and decided to insert this passage was he drawing our attention to something else? Was he suggesting we read the play and that our knowledge of *Troilus and Cressida* would enable us to understand his relationship with Sarah Walker? Five years earlier he had quoted the self-same piece in full in *Characters of Shakespeare's Plays.*

What would we make of Hazlitt's description of Shakespeare's Cressida? 'Her head is as light and fluttering as her heart.' 'It is the prettiest villain, she fetches her breath so short as a new-ta'en sparrow.' '[She] is a giddy girl, an unpractised jilt, who falls in love with Troilus, as she afterwards deserts him, from mere levity and thoughtlessness of temper. She may be wooed and won to anything and from anything, at a moment's warning.'[7]

Falling in love is falling into idealisation. It is a crystallisation of another person. All the suggestions so far point to some great need in the heart of the one who idealises as a driving force behind the idealisation – 'a boredom of solitude', a 'misfortune'. We can also see how projective processes operate, how the desire for the ideal seizes upon an object and bestows upon it qualities which it does not possess. We can further see how once set in motion this process is continually fed by a deep desire. Attempts by others to dissuade are brushed aside and reason once disposed of cannot be listened for.

Montaigne is keen to enter the debate at this point and after all he is the oldest and first of our group with most of his writings completed while Shakespeare was still a youth. He draws our attention to another part of this process, to the detrimental effect upon the person from whom the idealisation emerges. When Charles Morgan quoted Montaigne in his introduction to *Liber Amoris*, the piece was a sub-clause of a longer sentence. It would be instructive to read the whole paragraph in question. I place the piece Morgan quoted in italics. It is from the essay '*On Presumption*'.

> There is another kind of glory, which is to have too good an opinion of our own worth. It is an unthinking affection with which we flatter ourselves, and which presents us to ourselves as other than we are; *just as the passion of love lends beauties and charms to the object it embraces in such a way that the lover's judgement is troubled and distracted, and he finds the lady he loves other and more perfect than she is.* Yet I would not wish a man to be mistaken about himself out of fear of erring in this way, or think himself less than he is. The judgement should maintain its rights always and in all places; and it is reasonable that, here as elsewhere, he should see what truth sets before him. If it be a Caesar, let him boldly consider himself the greatest captain in the world.[8]

Montaigne understood that a depletion of the self occurs and the judgement is distracted, troubled, depraved and corrupted. He was aware of the damage which a person does to himself when he invests another with such qualities. Like an old-fashioned set of scales which has pans on each side, as one is more heavily weighted and goes down, the other being lighter goes up. Of Hazlitt, Procter wrote that 'his intellect was completely subdued by an insane passion.'[9] It is not unusual when one talks to a person who idealises another to hear them describe themselves as 'empty', 'lacking in something', or some such phrase. 'Stupid' is also a common word.

What would be turning over in Hazlitt's mind if he were a part of this discussion? Would he be in agreement with Bryan Procter that at this time he was substantially insane, that something within him had seriously broken down? Placed in the company of those who understand these states of mind, would he have been reminded of his letters to his mother and father from Hackney College telling of 'the nervous disorders' to which he was accustomed? Would he think of the depressive episodes to which he was prone?

At this point my attention turns to the latter part of the year 1807. Hazlitt is twenty-nine. He has become engaged to Sarah Stoddart whom he will marry in May of the following year. Before Christmas he became withdrawn and isolated himself in his lodgings. After some time his friends Charles Lamb and Joseph Hume became very concerned about him. They did not know how to deal with him. They concocted a story that he had committed suicide. This 'prank' took the form of a letter written by Lamb to Hume which they delivered to Hazlitt's lodgings. The letter read:

Last night Mr. H. a portrait-painter in Southampton Buildings, Holborn, put an end to his existence by cutting his throat in a shocking manner. It is supposed that he must have committed his purpose with a pallet-knife, as the edges of the cicatrice or wound were found besmeared with a yellow consistence, but the knife could not be found. The reasons of this rash act are not assigned; an unfortunate passion has been mentioned; but nothing certain is known. The deceased was subject to hypochondria, low spirits, but he had lately seemed better, having paid more than usual attention to his dress and person. Besides being a painter, he had written some pretty things in prose and verse.

Twelve days after receiving the letter Hazlitt wrote the following reply to Lamb and Hume. I will quote the letter at length as any summary or selections would fail to convey its essence.

The humble petition and remonstrance of William Hazlitt, now residing at No. 34, Southampton Buildings, in the parish of St. Ann's, Holborn, showing that he is not dead.

First, that he, the said W. Hazlitt, has regularly for the last month rang the bell at eleven at night, which was considered as a sign for the girl to warm the bed, and this being done, he has gone to bed, and slept soundly for the next twelve or fourteen hours.

Secondly, that every day about twelve or 1 o'clock he has got up, put on his clothes, drank his tea, and eat two plate-fulls of buttered toast, of which he had taken care to have the hard edges pared off as hurtful to the mouth and gums, and that he has then sat for some hours with his eyes steadfastly fixed upon the fire, like a person in a state of deep thought, but doing nothing.

Thirdly, that not a day has passed in which he has not eat and drank like other people. For instance, he has swallowed eight dozen of pills, nine boluses, and as many purgative draughts of a most unsavoury quality. What he has fed on with the most relish has been a mess of chicken-broth, and he has sent out once or twice for almonds and raisins. His general diet is soup-meagre with bread and milk for supper. That it is true that the petitioner has abstained both from gross feeding and from all kinds of intoxicating liquors; a circumstance, as he conceives, so far from denoting a natural decay and loss of his faculties, that on the contrary it shows more wisdom than he was always possessed of.

Fourthly, that in regard to decency he has been known to walk out at least once a week to get himself shaved.

Fifthly, that growing tired of his sedentary posture, he has occasionally got up from his chair and walked across the room (not as an *automaton* or dead man pulled with wires might be supposed to do, but with an inequality in his gait, resembling a limp.) At one time he turned the front of his great picture to the light, but finding the subject painful to him, he presently turned it to the wall again. Also, that he has attempted to read some of his own works, but has fallen asleep over them.

Sixthly, that the said W.H. has, it being Christmas time, received several invitations to entertainments and parties of pleasure, which he politely declined; but that on occasions he has generally about the hour of four in the afternoon been tormented with the apparition of a fat goose or a sirloin of beef.

Seventhly, that in compliment to the season, and to show a fellow-feeling with his absent guests, he has ordered a wine-glass and a decanter of water to be set upon the table, and has drank off a glass or two, making a show as it were port or sherry, but that he desisted from this practice after a few trials, not finding it answer.

Eighthly, be it known that the person, concerning whom such idle reports are prevalent, has actually within a given time written a number of love letters, and that a man must be dead indeed, if he is not alive when engaged in that agreeable employment. And lest it should be suggested that these epistles resemble Mrs. Rowe's *Letters from the Dead to the Living*, being just such vapid, lifeless compositions, it may be proper to state, by way of counteracting any such calumny, that they are full of nothing but ingenious conceits and *double entendres*, without a single *grave* remark from beginning to end. Farther that they had some life in them, he is assured by the quickness of the answers, which he received with that sort of pleading titillation and gentle palpitation common to flesh and blood, reading them with alternate smiles and sighs, and once letting fall a tear at a description given by the lady of the ruinous state of a cottage or tenement, which he hopes one day to call his own. That as it is possible he may not after all be able to defeat the arts of his calumniators, who may persuade the young lady before alluded to that the petitioner is a dead man, not able to go through the ordinary functions of life, that he has therefore formed divers plans for his future maintenance and creditable appearance in the world, as writing a tragedy, setting up as a quack doctor, or entering into holy orders.

Whereas it is scandalously and falsely asserted in a written paper circulated at the expense of the above-named W.H. that he has been heard to spout amorous verses, and sing licentious ditties and burthens of old songs with his latest breath a number of penny ballads and verses being also strewed about his room in an indecent manner, he begs leave to state that the only song he has once thought of late is the Cuckoo song, but that this has run a good deal in his head, and that he has often broken out into the following verse:

Mocks married men from tree to tree.

Also once, upon receiving some expressions of tender concern and anxious inquiries into the cause of his illness from a person that shall be nameless, he sung in a faint manner the following parody on two lines in the Beggar's Opera:

For on the pill that cures my dear
Depends poor Polly's life!

Lastly, as there are some appearances against him, and he is aware that almost everything goes by appearances, in case it should be determined that he is a dead man and that he must be buried against his will, he submits to this decision, but with two provisos, first, that he shall be allowed to appear as chief mourner at his own funeral, secondly that he shall have leave to appoint Joseph Hume Esq., of the Victualling Office his executor and administrator of his effects, as a man of prudence and discretion, well-looked on in the world, and the only person he knows, who will not be witty on the occasion.

A blank is here left which the modesty of the writer would not permit him to fill up. Perhaps he belonged to the class of *non-descripts* rather than any other. The opinion of the world was divided: some persons being inclined to regard him as a gentleman, and others looking upon him as a low fellow. It is hard to say whether he ought to be considered as an author, or a portrait-painter. It is certain that he never painted any pictures but those of persons he hired to sit for him, and though he wrote a number of books, it does not appear that they were ever read by any body.[10]

While some biographers allow this episode to possess a measure of seriousness many pass over it as insignificant. Ralph Wardle treats the whole of Hazlitt's letter and the depressive illness it depicts as a joke. Hazlitt is accepted as ill but it is seen in purely physical terms. Wardle sees nothing but flippancy and double entendres in the whole of Hazlitt's reply. The joke is seen as initiated by Lamb and Hazlitt is seen to heartily carry it on. There is no attempt to explore what might be going on in Lamb's mind. Lamb himself in 1795, at the age of twenty, was temporarily insane and spent some weeks confined in an asylum. The following year his sister Mary murdered their mother by stabbing her with a kitchen knife in a psychotic rage. She was certified insane and committed to an asylum. Three years later, after their father died, Mary was released into Charles's care. Neither ever married and they lived together for the rest of their life, with Mary requiring re-admission from time to time. Charles would die in 1834 and without him Mary sank into complete psychosis and remained so till she died thirteen years later.

From the time they met in 1803, Hazlitt and Lamb established a deep friendship. But friendships, however deep and abiding, can have their complications. I think Lamb and Hume were seriously worried about Hazlitt's emotional and mental health at the time. How do you handle such a condition in a friend? Why not go and talk to him? Insist on entry to his company? Hazlitt may have seen the humorous streak that ran through Lamb's letter and allowed it some moments of emergence in his reply. But a person unfamiliar with deep and depressive internal suffering could not have written that letter.

Grayling suggests that Hazlitt may have been suffering from a venereal disease contacted from a prostitute but admits that it is only speculation and that the question of Hazlitt's illness is an open one.[11] I read Hazlitt's letter as a serious account of his mental state at that time. If we turn to his letters to Patmore in *Liber Amoris* we find similar sentiments. In Letter Six he wrote:

> I have nothing but the blackness and the fiendishness of scorn around me – mocked by her (the false one) in whom I placed my hope, and who hardens herself against me! – I believe you thought me quite gay, vain, insolent, half mad, the night I left the house – no tongue can tell the heaviness of heart I felt at that moment. No footsteps ever fell more slow, more sad than mine...' [12]

And in Letter Seven:

> If the clock strikes, the sound jars me; a million of hours will not bring back peace to my breast. The light startles me; the darkness terrifies me. I seem falling into a pit, without a hand to help me. [13]

Hazlitt was prone to what we would call depressive episodes. If the cause of this illness is an open question we can consider it as a return of 'the nervous disorders' of his childhood. Silence was the family dictum in the face of deep emotional conflicts especially when a challenge to another was involved. To make sense of an emotional crisis it is as important to look forward in a person's life, as well as backwards. The concept of regression, a return to an earlier traumatic stage of life, can be required to carry too much weight. For example, we say of a man of thirty that he faced a crisis in his work when he was required to be more independent and the fear of failure and disapproval made him feel like a three year old, and then in effect be becomes as he was when three, anxious for his parents' approval. We also must look ahead – into the future and ask what new relationships on the path of life had this person come to? Where was he about to go? What new shape was he about to give his life? What new identity was he about to take on? With regards to falling in love in a manner similar to Hazlitt we can ask – why *at this time* in life does it happen to him? Why does he chase the ideal? What has he taken flight from? Why is the future so perilous that he takes refuge in the past? Why is reality so frightening that he gets lost in fantasy? A consequence of going backwards in time is that we are unable to move forwards. Part of the great tragedy of the person's life is that they cannot reap the benefits of maturity.

Hazlitt in the Christmas of 1807 was about to become a married man with the prospect of being a parent. Was he depressed because of what he was allowing himself to become? Was he facing the prospect of a lifelong relationship like his mother and father bound by duty and obedience? Can we read any of the accounts of the Hazlitts' in the USA and say that William senior really listened to Grace Loftus? And as we look at William senior and Grace and their children, which among them could establish and maintain a long relationship? Margaret we find at 65 writing with a bitterness, still smouldering with resentment. Seeing her words on the page and the hatred which has emerged she pulls back to a pious acceptance! And brother John in his early sixties, having broken up with his wife after many years of marriage, became an alcoholic and returned to the West Country where he was near his mother, eventually dying within a month of her.

Discussion

It is important to make a distinction between the falling in love that is being explored here and a very different phenomenon which often goes under the same name. Two people can on meeting feel an instant attraction, can indeed experience a 'falling in love at first sight'. But if it is more than an infatuation it must be subjected to thoughtful examination and the two people need to follow up with an honest knowing of each other then a deep and lasting friendship if compatibility may be found. The common belief that there is a Mr Right or a Ms Right out there, somewhere, and that one's happiness and fulfilment in life depends on somehow meeting up with that person is an instance of a belief in the ideal partner and a reliance on the idealisation I am speaking of. A closer examination will show it is premised on the belief that someone who has never met me actually knows me intimately, is waiting to meet me, already loves me, wants me and is eager to spend the rest of their life with me! The story Stendhal has told us about the young woman and her cousin Edward is an instance of this. A productive relationship is one where idealisation has given way to reality, where the notion of a perfect person has been replaced by the belief in a good enough human being.

Before we go further into this issue let us ask the question – who was Sarah Walker? The accounts of *Liber Amoris* that I have given above may provide some sense of her but they all come from Hazlitt's pen. One person who actually met her, Bryan Procter, had this to say:

> I used to see this girl, Sarah Walker, at his lodgings, and could not account for the extravagant passion of her admirer. She was the daughter of the lodging-house-keeper. Her face was round and small, and her eyes were motionless, glassy, and without any speculation (apparently) in them. Her movements in walking were very remarkable, for I never observed her to make a step. She went onwards in a sort of wavy, sinuous manner, like the movement of a snake. She was silent, or uttered monosyllables only, and was very demure. Her steady, unmoving gaze

upon the person whom she was addressing was exceedingly unpleasant. The Germans would have extracted a romance from her, endowing her perhaps with some diabolic attribute.[14]

We have read above how in the final paragraph of *Liber Amoris,* Hazlitt had described her thus:

> My seeing her in the street has gone a good way to satisfy me. Her manner there explains her manner in-doors to be conscious and overdone; and besides, she looks but indifferently. She is diminutive in stature, and her measured step and timid air do not suit these public airings. I am afraid she will soon grow common to my imagination, as well as worthless in herself. Her image seems fast 'going into the wastes of time,' like a weed that the wave bears farther and farther from me. Alas! thou poor hapless weed, when I entirely lose sight of thee, and for ever, no flower will ever bloom on earth to glad my heart again![15]

Many biographers have attempted to assemble a picture of her. The Irish novelist Anne Haverty[16] has written a novel with Sarah as the heroine, speaking in the first person about herself, her life and about William Hazlitt. This is an imaginative portrait and lays no claim to fact.

In exploring the issue of falling in love, Richard O'Neill-Dean[17] has helped considerably by a re-definition of the problem. Rather than speaking of an individual falling in love, he writes about the person *falling into the need for love.* This shift enables us to broaden our terms of reference. There is less weight given to the manifestation of some idyllic beauty embodied in a person; less importance given to being caught up in some mutual bliss. There is more emphasis on the *need* for love, on the *nature* of that need and additionally on the *type* of love involved. We are not only examining the fate of someone who finds some person, crystallises them and is absorbed in awe of them. O'Neill-Dean requires us to move ourselves into a new position from which to look at the one for whom we have fallen. He requires us to quantify the type of love and the amount of love which is being asked for. 'Asking' is an inaccurate designation. There is a falling involved not unlike the sense of falling from a great height. Only some miracle can bring safety. In other words, the person who is falling is expecting great things from the other. The person who falls in love emotionally looks to some other to miraculously save them. Like many psychoanalytic thinkers O'Neill-Dean couples this process with an exploration of regression. There is a return to an earlier state of being. A blissful state of oneness with a mother is the most common manner in which this wonderful state is imagined.

It is common in many situations like this for the other person to go along with the demands and play the part assigned to them. If such a dovetailing does not take place, a relationship does not usually get established. If a relationship is established on that basis, if the very foundation of it consists of one being the saved and the other the saviour, it usually 'suits' both parties. The saviour for his or her own reason needs such an identity. Also any interference with this delicate balancing act, any change that may come from outside the relationship, or from within either party, can lead to its collapse. The basic flaw lies in the fact that it is an alliance based on only a part of each and not on the whole person.

While the delicate balancing act is kept in place, this 'precious' relationship is held together. It is, however, a very narrow relationship because the common, usually unconscious, understanding between the two is that vast areas of each person must not be brought into play. Here we have to say that neither of these people is actually relating to the other. But they are not just relating to a part of the other, they are also intensely relating to some ideal that resides within their own mind. Often these ideals are the remnants of lost relationships which were vital to the person's life and identity, and which have never been mourned. Now, like dead stars, they have become black holes, invisibly populating the galaxy of the mind, drawing all creative life into themselves.

These relationships are precarious because they are built on the past and no emotional maturation can take place. As the world changes about them, they cannot adapt. As their friends grow up and mature they stay the same. In these kinds of situation, a mild or moderate degree of force is exerted by the one who idealises the other. If he is placing some qualities into the other which the latter does not possess, he is forcing something into that person. While the delicate balancing act is kept in place any force involved must be strenuously disavowed. When this force becomes excessive it does great violence to the recipient. This is not pleasing flattery. It is a destruction of the person as they are in themselves. In fact, who they are in themselves becomes irrelevant. The projector places so much into the recipient that there is no room left. Such force, such violence is experienced as an obliteration. As in the movie *Play Misty for Me*, the life of the character played by Clint Eastwood becomes irrelevant to the projector. His life is her property. She is convinced that they are in love. This is solely based on her expectations and wishes, not on any love existing between them. When he does not love her she feels utterly betrayed and tries to kill him. Such serious consequences are not just the creation of Hollywood. We hear of the couple who were childhood sweethearts, then teenage lovers. On reaching adulthood she finds him possessive and oppressive and ends the relationship. He pursues her but she will not comply. Various possibilities fork out from this juncture. He may grow to accept his loss and mature. He may retire from any emotional engagement in life and moan away his existence, miserable unto death. He may stalk her and use various forms of force and manipulation to get her back. He may kill her. He may kill himself. The relationship was built on the premise outlined above. The childhood idealisation occupied such a pivotal place in his identity that no change can be tolerated. Relationships based on these premises that persist into middle age and beyond can accurately be described as hell on earth.

We have seen how Hazlitt when writing *Liber Amoris* placed a section called 'Unaltered Love' and 'Perfect Love' near the end of Part Two. He had written to Sarah and received a very formal reply. In the wake of her blankness and non-responsiveness he wrote the following piece. He quotes (inaccurately) a few lines from Shakespeare's sonnet 116 followed by his own thoughts on the subject of unaltered love.

> Love is not love that alteration finds:
> Oh no! it is an ever-fixed mark,
> That looks on tempests and is never shaken.
> Shall I not love her for herself alone, in spite of fickleness and folly?

> To love her for her regard to me, is not to love her, but myself. She has robbed me of herself: shall she also rob me of my love of her? Did I not live on her smile? Is it less sweet because it is withdrawn from me? Did I not adore her every grace? Does she bend less enchantingly, because she has turned from me to another? Is my love then in the power of fortune, or of her caprice? No, I will have it lasting as it is pure; and I will make a Goddess of her, and build a temple to her in my heart, and worship her on indestructible altars, and raise statues to her: and my homage shall be unblemished as her unrivalled symmetry of form; and when that fails, the memory of it shall survive; and my bosom shall be proof to scorn, as hers has been to pity; and I will pursue her with an unrelenting love, and sue to be her slave, and tend her steps without notice and without reward; and serve her living, and mourn for her when dead. And thus my love will have shewn itself superior to her hate; and I shall triumph and then die. This is my idea of the only true and heroic love! Such is mine for her. [18]

We can see how he is wrestling to keep her as a separate person. When he writes 'To love her for her regard for me, is not to love her, but myself' he is trying to see Sarah as her own person. But as he believes she has robbed him of herself and her love, he sets up his own version of her inside his mind.

This is followed by his piece on perfect love. He writes:

> Perfect love has this advantage in it, that it leaves the possessor of it nothing farther to desire. There is one object (at least) in which the soul finds absolute content, for which it seeks to live, or dares to die. The heart has as it were filled up the moulds of the imagination. The truth of passion keeps pace with and outvies the extravagance of mere language. There are no words so fine, no flattery so soft,

that there is not a sentiment beyond them, that it is impossible to express, at the bottom of the heart where true love is. What idle sounds the common phrases, *adorable creature, angel, divinity,* are? What a proud reflection it is to have a feeling answering to all these, rooted in the breast, unalterable, unutterable, to which all other feelings are light and vain! Perfect love reposes on the object of its choice, like the halcyon on the wave; and the air of heaven is around it. [19]

As Hazlitt is drawing on Shakespeare's Sonnet 116 it is timely to have it available in full. We can also use it as a counterpoint to Sonnet 147 with which I opened this chapter. Together they provide us with boundaries to our discussion, opposite ends of the spectrum, the bliss of endless and total love, the hell and madness of utter rejection.

> Let me not to the marriage of true minds
> Admit impediments. Love is not love
> Which alters when it alteration finds,
> Or bends with the remover to remove:
> O no! it is an ever-fixed mark
> That looks on tempests and is never shaken;
> It is the star to every wandering bark,
> Whose worth's unknown, although his height be taken.
> Love's not Time's fool, though rosy lips and cheeks
> Within his bending sickle's compass come:
> Love alters not with his brief hours and weeks,
> But bears it out even to the edge of doom.
> If this be error and upon me proved,
> I never writ, nor no man ever loved.

Mourning provides us with a context within which to place idealisation. The tendency to idealise is present within the mourning process. If a loss is adequately grieved we pass through the stage of idealisation. To get stuck within it means we are unable to mourn.

Let us turn now and ask the question: why did Hazlitt fall madly in love at this time? Lahey suggests that Hazlitt was expecting a victory over his Tory enemies and turned to Sarah in disappointment. Whilst Hazlitt would have wished for this I can see no evidence that he was, in fact, expecting it. Should we turn to the events of his life and ask what effect the break-up of his marriage and his family had on Hazlitt? This aspect of his life is also often passed over, indeed clouded by the Sarah Walker affair. Little information is available about the nature of the difficulties in the relationship. Indeed it is often impossible to tell from the outside of any relationship what, in fact, goes on inside it. Whatever their struggles were, Hazlitt and his wife managed after their divorce to remain on friendly terms, and Grayling has suggested that it was Sarah Stoddart whose sentiments appeared on Hazlitt's burial stone and it was she who paid for its erection.[20]

What has been generally ignored is that exactly one month before he first set eyes on Sarah Walker, Hazlitt's father died. This event has been afforded little significance in his life. Lahey makes no mention of it. Ralph Wardle states that the death of his father 'could hardly have caused him deep grief; the old man was eighty-four years old now and had grown increasingly feeble.'[21] Grayling seems to suspect a link when he writes: 'It might be pure coincidence, and there is no obvious connection between the two events, but the death of William senior marked the beginning of a Dantesque journey for Hazlitt into heaven and hell.'[22]

I think the death of one's father is a highly significant event in anyone's life. William senior died on 16 July 1820. On 16 August Sarah Walker comes into his room and he immediately falls madly in love with her. Might these events have a connection? Wardle is typical of many biographers who allocate considerable space to Hazlitt and his father at the beginning of their story yet pass over the death of this same important figure as insignificant. They tell of William's attachment to his father, scenes of his walking with his father through the New England countryside, of the little boy sitting at his father's feet in the pulpit in Weymouth. Will the values of virile England be threatened if a man in his forties grieves the loss of his father?

Because Hazlitt's movements during the weeks of his father's death are not accurately accounted for some biographers intent on retracing all his steps have spent much time trying to plot his movements. He did not get the news for about a week after the death and therefore was not at the funeral. The news was delivered by his niece, Mary, daughter of John. Some speculate on whether he went to Devon to spend time with his mother and sister and how long he remained there before his return to London. Little attention has been given to his internal movements, to where he was taken within himself by this event.

I read *Liber Amoris* as a book about grief. Stendhal wrote about 'recoiling from the outside world which offers only sad pictures' and he understood that idealisation can be caused by 'misfortunes which precede it'. Loss, separation, loneliness, abandonment and death continually jostle with each other for places in the text of *Liber Amoris*. 'I am now inclosed in a dungeon of despair. The sky is marble to my thoughts; nature is dead around me, as hope is within me … If it were not for my little boy, I should soon, I fear, settle the question by my death. That recollection is the only thought that brings my wandering reason to an anchor … I stagger like an infant on the edge of a precipice.'

Within the internal economy of a person's mind when grief too great to bear has presented itself, an internal 'about turn' takes place, an ideal, everlasting loving object is called up. The eyes of the soul must be fixed, even transfixed. He can't take his eyes off her. He needs such a love to save his life. If the slightest imperfection should present itself the whole edifice is in danger of collapse. A frenzy of activity will convert the flaw into a virtue. She is perfection again. Why must every waking minute and hour be consumed on her? I believe it is because if he looks back, the loss will have to be squarely looked in the face. A Pygmalion old or new cannot live happily ever after with his new love. There is no equality in the relationship. He has never understood and overcome his difficulties with women and so they are doomed.

Soon we will pick up the tread of Hazlitt's life and see what course it took after 1823. But the question needs to be asked, did he learn something, did he understand what happened to him? Was he aware of being caught in some idealisation? If we listen to some of his thoughts we may be able to find some answers.

A separation needs to be made about two sets of thoughts. To deal with the first we return again to sonnet 147:

> For I have sworn thee fair and thought thee bright,
> Who art as black as hell, as dark as night

Was Sarah as black as hell, as dark as night? Did Hazlitt think so? I think he was appalled by the blackness of her deceit. He was pained and shocked to find she had become interested in another man but it was the discovery that she had been two-timing him that was the more powerful blow. For months she had been coming to his room, allowing him to caress and kiss her and speak of marriage whilst at the same time she had been sitting on another lodger's lap and doing the same with him. When he wrote about this hypocrisy later in 1823 he said:

> The greatest hypocrite I ever knew was a little, demure, pretty, modest-looking girl, with eyes timidly cast upon the ground, and an air soft as enchantment; the only circumstance that could lead to a suspicion of her true character was a cold, sullen, watery, glazed look about the eyes, which she bent on vacancy, as if determined to avoid all explanation with yours. I might have spied in their glittering, motionless surface the rocks and quicksands that awaited me below![23]

Lending weight to a repeat of the process which Stendhal had described in his discussion of crystallisation Hazlitt wrote:

> I do not think that what is called Love at first sight is so great an absurdity as it is sometimes imagined to be. We generally make up our minds beforehand to the sort of person we should like, grave or gay, black, brown, or fair; with golden

tresses or with raven locks; – and when we meet with a complete example of the qualities we admire, the bargain is soon struck. We have never seen anything to come up to our newly discovered goddess before, but she is what we have been all our lives looking for. The idol we fall down and worship is an image familiar to our minds. It has been present to our waking thoughts, it has haunted us in our dreams, like some fairy vision. Oh thou, who, the first time I ever beheld thee, didst draw my soul into the circle of thy heavenly looks, and wave enchantment round me, do not think thy conquest less complete because it was instantaneous; for in that gentle form (as if another Imogen had entered) I saw all that I had ever loved of female grace, modesty, and sweetness![24]

So what happened to Hazlitt after 1823 and after the publication of *Liber Amoris*? Well, part of the story has already been told. His enemies made sport, the uncommitted were scandalised and found justification in ignoring him. A few knew exactly what he was writing about and breathed a sigh of relief that someone had the courage to express these human truths. In literary circles the shock waves continued through the decades. He is despised by people like Brimley Johnson; he is ignored by such learned men as Matthew Arnold.

But what of Hazlitt himself? What became of him? Many of the *Table Talk* essays were written during his contact with Sarah and, while in the torment of his madness, he continued to write the most sublime prose. While tossed backwards and forwards by his passion so as to become ridiculous, his pen continued to attest to his reputation as the Shakespeare prose writer of his country.

In October 1823 when he is remembering Keats, of whom he writes: 'His verses were like the breath of Spring, and many of his thoughts like flowers,' he is prompted to describe his own general state of mind and adds:

I look out of my window and see that a shower has just fallen: the fields look green after it, and a rosy cloud hangs over the brow of the hill; a lily expands its petals in the moisture, dressed in its lovely green and white; a shepherd-boy has just brought some pieces of turf with daisies and grass for his mistress to make a bed for her sky-lark, not doomed to dip his wings in the dappled dawn – my cloudy thoughts draw off, the storm of angry politics has blown over – Mr. Blackwood, I am yours – Mr. Croker, my service to you – Mr. T. Moore, I am alive and well – Really, it is wonderful how little the worse I am for fifteen years wear and tear, how I come upon my legs again on the ground of truth and nature, and 'look abroad into universality,' forgetting that there is any such person as myself in the world.'[25]

In quantitative terms more than half of his total literary output occurred after 16 August 1820 and in term of quality many have pointed to these later works as his masterpieces, *Table Talk, The Plain Speaker* and *The Spirit of the Age*. In Geoffrey

Keynes's classic collection of Hazlitt writings three-quarters of the essays were written during this period.[26]

Stanley Jones[27] believed the act of writing and publishing the book may have helped him to come to terms with what had happened. Like all his experience of life it was gathered into himself and shaped who he would be for the rest of his days.

There is nothing that helps a man in his conduct through life more than a knowledge of his own characteristic weaknesses (which, guarded against, become his strength), as there is nothing that tends more to the success of a man's talents than his knowing the limits of his faculties, which are thus concentrated on some practical object. One man can do but one thing. Universal pretensions end in nothing.[28]

Chapter 8

A Creative Imagination

The examination of Hazlitt's ideas on the creative imagination can ironically be best explored in his most unimaginatively written piece, that hard, dry, metaphysical choke-pear, the *Essay on the Principles of Human Action* (1805). Hazlitt believed the *Essay* was one of his most important pieces of writing. Much of his later writings can be seen as developments of ideas he wrestled with in that text.

Hazlitt alerted us to the need for hard thought and the necessity to avoid simplistic solutions when he wrote that:

> this mistaken notion of simplicity has been the general fault of all system-makers, who are so taken up with some favourite hypothesis or principle, that they make it the sole hinge on which every thing else turns, and forget that there is any other power really at work in the universe; all other causes being either set aside as false and nugatory, or else resolved into that one. There is another principle which has a deep foundation in nature that has also served to strengthen the same feeling; namely, that things never act alone, that almost every effect that can be mentioned is a compound result of a series of causes modifying one another, and that therefore the true cause of any thing is seldom to be looked for on the surface, or in the first distinct agent that presents itself. [1]

Hazlitt felt much in common with the philosophical tradition of British Empiricism, in that the construction of abstract and ingenious theories about human nature was to be distrusted. Careful and detailed reflection on ordinary human experience was an altogether more profitable way to proceed. Hazlitt's starting point in the *Essay* is with a notion of self. He takes issue with the idea of self as an essentially egotistical entity. Such an idea is he says:

> founded in a mere play of words, [and] could not have gained the assent of thinking men but for the force with which the idea of self habitually clings to the mind of every man, binding it with a spell, deadening its discriminating powers, and spreading the confused associations which belong only to past and present impressions over the whole of our imaginary existence. [2]

W. P. Albrecht has explored the elements in Hazlitt's thought in his book *Hazlitt and the Creative Imagination*. In teasing out this core element Albrecht writes:

> There is a confusion (a sophism) here between motive and mechanical reaction.

The above view makes them the same when in fact they are different; it reduces all of man's responses to self love. Voluntary action does not arise solely from one's desire to avoid pain or seek pleasure, but may be determined by the idea of 'good' in itself. Hazlitt directed us to think of the past, the present and the future. He suggested that while the mind may be thought of as being 'mechanical' in its relation to the past and the present, in so far as it has something prior to go on, it required the imagination to connect its present self with its future self. He says 'there must be something in the very idea of good, or evil, which naturally excites desire or aversion.' We seek the good of another person because the removal or avoidance of another's pain is a good in itself and recognised as such. The power of exciting desire 'inheres in the very nature of the object.' A sentiment of general benevolence can only arise from an habitual cultivation of the natural disposition of the mind to sympathise with the feelings of others by constantly taking an interest in those which we know, and imagining others that we do not know [whereas artificial] self-interest ... must be caused by a long narrowing of the mind to our own particular feelings and interests, and a voluntary insensibility to every thing which does not immediately concern ourselves.[3]

In other words when thinking of the past, the present and the future Hazlitt said that we are in touch with past feelings through our memory. There is a mechanical aspect to such activity because the events have already happened and we cannot change them. The present we know through consciousness. How do I know the future? It is through my imagination. His line of thought is that my future self does not, in fact, exist and I can only conceive of it by a projection into the future and through an act of imaginative identification with my past and present self. This he calls an act of sympathetic imagination.

The imagination, by means of which alone I can anticipate future objects, or be interested in them, must carry me out of myself into the feelings of others by one and the same process by which I am thrown forward as it were into my own future being, and interested in it, and ... I could not love myself, if I were not capable of loving others. Self-love, used in this sense, is in its fundamental principle the same with disinterested benevolence.[4]

Hazlitt is asserting that when you go out from your present self and into your future self the activity which takes place at this stage of human consciousness is worthy of study. Like a director who calls a halt to the movement in order to study a particular moment, he calls attention to an important human transaction. He asks us to look closely at this action of going into the future. This is a leap into the unknown. We imagine a new and different self. The degree of difference can span a wide spectrum from having a radically different personality to a minor desire to know how we will feel later in the day. It is the otherness he asks us to dwell on and here he deals his trump card. This otherness we hope for is logically the same as another actual person. It follows therefore that the capacity to think of our future self goes hand in hand with the capacity to think about others. When I read and think of his line of thought I hear an account of a psychological process and think of what he is saying in a psychological context.

He summarises his position when he writes that it is his intention in the *Essay*:

> To show that the human mind is naturally disinterested, or that it is naturally interested in the welfare of others in the same way, and from the same direct motives, by which we are impelled to the pursuit of our own interest … When I say therefore that the human mind is naturally benevolent, this does not refer to any innate abstract ideas of good in general, or to an instinctive desire of general, indefinite, unknown, good, but to the natural connection between the idea of happiness and the desire of it, independently of any particular attachment to the person who is to feel it.[5]

The actual desire of good is not inherent in the mind of man, because it requires to be brought out by certain accessory objects or ideas; but the disposition itself, or property of the mind, which makes him liable to be so affected by certain objects, is inherent in him and is a part of his nature. The love of my own particular good must precede that of the particular good of others, because I am acquainted with it first: the love of particular good must precede that of general good whether my own, or another's, or the general good of mankind, for the same reason.

A few of the more digestible morsels from the *Essay* allow Hazlitt to carry the argument forward:

> A person is more likely to prefer their own interest because they anticipate them "with greater warmth and present imagination". Because our own past can be so immediately present to us and have this presentness to the imagination ... the feelings of others can never be brought home to us in the same degree. It is chiefly from this greater readiness and certainty with which we can look forward into our own minds than into those of other men, that the strong and uneasy attachment to self … takes its rise; and not … from any natural hardness of the human heart … It is a great folly to think of deducing our desire of happiness and fear of pain from a principle of self-love … this sort of attachment to self could signify nothing more than a foolish complacency in our own idea, an idle dotage, and idolatry of our own abstract being … It is plain there must be something in the nature of the objects themselves which of itself determines the mind to consider them as desirable, or the contrary, previously to any reference of them to ourselves. They

are not converted into good and evil by being impressed on our minds, but they affect our minds in a certain manner because they are essentially good or evil … It has been said that *to feel is to think, "sentir est penser"*: I believe this to be true of the human mind, because the human mind is a thinking principle: it is natural to it to think: it cannot feel *without thinking*.[6]

Hazlitt believed that the mind was creative even in its simplest activities. While the mind depended on the senses it was not mechanically reacting to them. The mind is not a passive entity. The mind worked actively on sensation and created ideas and symbols. One faced the world in a uniquely personal way and came to know truth and reality in the act of constructing them.

At times in the *Essay* we come across passages where Hazlitt escapes the confines of rigorous expression and imaginatively catches hold of the ideas that move about in his mind. This occurs when he describes the internal workings of a dynamic mind:

> If from the top of a long barren hill I hear the distant whistle of a thrush which seems to come up from some warm woody shelter beyond the edge of the hill, this sound coming faint over the rocks with a mingled feeling of strangeness and joy, the idea of the place about me, and the imaginary one beyond will all be blended together in such a manner in my mind as to become inseparable.[7]

Hazlitt enlarged the role of the mind. It was not only free and creative but it provided in its own operations an important source of empirical data. He had no interest in 'the incorporeal and invisible forms of things'. Nor was he very interested in theoretical distinctions about abstract thought processes per se. Whilst he would happily contemplate and debate abstract ideas, he believed that the man who resided in that place was like the person with one leg or the bird with one wing. Hazlitt was concerned with the dynamic process of thought. His bent was always inclusive of the practical and empirical. For Hazlitt the mind worked on everything and every idea was the *product* and not the *object* of understanding. For him reality was never static. We can see his opposition to the Enlightenment's notion that nature and creation are static with man as a spectator. He espoused a dynamic understanding of nature with man as an active participant in the vital forces of the world. He conceived of a dynamic interplay between the general and the particular and the human faculty that provided that movement was the *imagination*. Truth did not reside in any one place but in a movement between different areas. Truth is a social phenomenon; it is discovered in conversation; it submits naturally to publicity. Interpersonal relationships and inter-subjectivity lie at the centre of Hazlitt's conception of the human interaction. But his conception of the mind and its creative activity is also inclusive of the intra-subjective. (The inter-subjective refers to activity, often unconscious, that takes place between two people. The intra-subjective refers to activity that takes place between different parts of the self.) To abstract something is to take part of the whole out from the whole, examine and understand it in a new way. From a multitude of associations we choose a few to cast in a new relationship with each other or with the whole. But what is this 'choice' he is talking about? It is not a conscious choice or selection. It occurs by unconscious choice and unconscious selection. He states that 'imagination to be perfect must be unconscious, at least in production'. The term he used to describe this process was 'elective affinity'. I shall quote a passage from his essay 'On Genius and Common Sense':

> Nature has a thousand aspects, and one man can only draw out one of them. Whoever does this, is a man of genius. One displays her force, another her refinement, one her power of harmony, another her suddenness of contrast, one her beauty of form, another her splendour of colour. Each does that for which he is best fitted by his particular genius, that is to say, by some quality of mind in which the object sinks deepest, where it finds the most cordial welcome, is perceived to its utmost extent, and where again it forces its way out from the fullness with which it has taken possession of the mind of the student. The imagination gives out what it has first absorbed by congeniality of temperament, what it has attracted and moulded into itself by elective affinity, as the loadstone draws and impregnates iron.[8]

Here we see how the imagination is not a simple picture-making faculty. It is 'that faculty which represents objects, not as they are in themselves, but as they are moulded by other thoughts and feelings, into an infinite variety of shapes and combinations of power'. The imagination is directed by emotion. The imagination is never static; it exists in a dynamic multiplying interplay of image, thought and emotion. Emotion harmonises sensory materials, for example, the poem that is spoken unites the sound effects with the visual images – as Hazlitt said, the 'music of language [answers to] the music of the mind'. Thus the imagination fuses 'the world of thought within us, with the world of sense outside us'.

★★★

As I sit in Hazlitt's company and consider the deep well of thought and the many ideas he has laid before me I am aware of the essentially social nature of his view of the mind. I am struck by his many references to childhood throughout the *Essay* and I recall and return to his views on the vital activity of the mind from birth. I wonder what he would say to a question about the place of the creative imagination in the inner world of the infant, with little past to speak of and whose life sits at the beginning of its future. I would again refer him back to Shakespeare who seems to me to deal with this issue of the reliance on the other person to know oneself and the creatively imaginative processes involved. Cassius puts the question to Brutus. 'Tell me, good Brutus, can you see your face?' To which he receives the reply, 'No, Cassius; for the eye sees not itself/but by reflection, by some other things.' (Act 1.2, 50–53).

But I would point Hazlitt to *Troilus and Cressida*, the play he described as desultory in its movement (although he never would have seen it performed), but which he believed also dealt with 'a prodigious number of fine things'. The passages I single out could be thought of as a continuation of the theme which Shakespeare introduced in *Julius Caesar*. We need to extract ourselves from the actual narrative and the characters of the play. Within the story of *Troilus and Cressida* the arch manipulator, the 'great dog-fox' Ulysses is manipulating Achilles to get him to fight Hector and is trying to tell Achilles that he will soon be forgotten if his deeds are not seen by others.

I listen to the exchanges between them with two additional things in mind; Hazlitt's views on the relationship with the other, and the position of the child as it looks into its mother's face. Ulysses is reading a book and he meets Achilles. Achilles asks him what he is reading. Ulysses replies:

> A strange fellow here
> Writes me that man, how dearly ever parted,
> How much in having, or without or in,
> Cannot make boast to have that which he hath,
> Nor feels not what he owes, but by reflection-
> As when his virtues, shining upon others,
> Heat them, and they retort that heat again
> To the first givers.

Now Achilles seems familiar with this whole notion of inter-subjectivity, that we know who we are through other people and that we require a relationship with someone else if we are to find out who we are. Achilles says:

> This is not strange, Ulysses.
> The beauty that is borne here in the face
> The bearer knows not, but commends itself
> To other's eyes. Nor doth the eye itself,
> That most pure spirit of sense, behold itself,
> Not going from itself; but eye to eye opposed
> Salutes each other with each other's form.
> For speculation turns not to itself
> Till it hath travelled and is mirrored there
> Where it may see itself. This is not strange at all.

Achilles is saying that we not only know what we are through being in the company of the other. He says:

> speculation turns not to itself
> Till it hath travelled and is mirrored there
> Where it may see itself.

He is saying that thought requires another mind to reflect it. Ulysses answers:

> I do not strain at the position
> It is familiar – but at the authors drift;
> Who in his circumstance expressly proves
> That no man is the lord of anything,
> Though in and of him there be much consisting,
> Till he communicate his parts to others.
> Nor doth he of himself know them for aught
> Till he behold them formed in th'applause
> Where they're extended – who, like an arch, reverb'rate
> The voice again; or, like a gate of steel
> Fronting the sun, receives and renders back
> His figure and his heat
>
> Act 3.3, 95–124

It is human emotions he is now talking about. They are 'formed in th'applause', they take shape with the other. They are added to by the response. And lest we are in any doubt about the fullness of the human contact indicated there is mention of the voice, of image, of touch, of heat, of human warmth. Life is lived through sympathetic identification with the other.

Turning from Shakespeare's work to Shakespeare himself we meet the person who in Hazlitt's opinion possessed a most creative imagination. Shakespeare 'saw every thing by intuition;' his mind was 'a dancing mind full of swift transitions and glancing lights. He made infinite excursions to the right and the left. He made the commonest matter-of-fact float in a freer element with the breath of imagination.' He compares Shakespeare's mind to Chaucer's, which he said was consecutive rather than discursive. Chaucer arrived at truth through a certain process.

> Chaucer had a great variety of powers but he could only do one thing at once. He set himself to work on a particular subject. His ideas were kept separate, labelled, ticketed and parcelled out in a set form, in pews and compartments by themselves. They did not play into one another's hands, they do not react upon one another as the blower's breath moulds the yielding glass. There is something hard and

dry in them. What is the most wonderful thing in Shakespeare's faculties is their excessive sociability, and how they gossiped and compared notes together. [9]

Chaucer's mind was like a great river, strong and full. Shakespeare's was like the sea agitated this way and that, lashed by furious storms, capable of pushing forward with great strength and of subsiding into the deepest calm. About Shakespeare Hazlitt adds:

> The striking peculiarity of Shakespeare's mind was its generic quality, its power of communication with all other minds – so that it contained a universe of thought and feeling within itself, and had no one peculiar bias, or exclusive excellence more than another. He was just like any other man, but that he was like all other men ... The passion in Shakespeare is of the same nature as his delineation of character ... The human soul is made the sport of fortune, the prey of adversity: it is stretched on the wheel of destiny, in restless ecstasy. The passions are in a state of projection.[10]

Hazlitt would describe Shakespeare's capacity not only to produce individual acts of imaginative expression but also his facility to gather and cohere whole groups of such associations. Sub-plots and minor characters are not separate in pews and compartments but they take up and reflect aspects of the main plots and project variations of the main characters. Taking Cymbaline as an example Hazlitt writes about:

> the affinity and harmony, like that we observe in the gradations of colour in a picture. The striking and powerful contrasts in which Shakespeare abounds could not escape observation; but the use he makes of the principle of analogy to reconcile the greatest diversities of character and to maintain the continuity of feeling ... the effect is rather felt than observed; and as the impression exists unconsciously in the mind of the reader, so it probably arose in the same manner in the mind of the author, not from design but from the force of natural association, a particular train of thought suggesting different inflections of the same predominant feeling, melting into, and strengthening one another, like chords in music.[11]

Here we have Hazlitt writing about Shakespeare. For our present purposes I would like to bring Hazlitt into the foreground and tune into what he said and the way he said it. Hazlitt never wrote a verse of poetry or any work of fiction, but to my ear and my mind, he is the most marvellous writer of prose. I hear and see and experience in his writings the painter, the author of the *Essay*, the poet and the man of the common people. The image of the blower's breath moulding the yielding glass wonderfully conveys the interplay of opposing forces and the tension of such dialogue. Shakespeare may have had a magic power over words but so had Hazlitt. His description of words and phrases as being like sparkles thrown off from an imagination, fired by the whirling rapidity of its own motion, is an exquisite example of such magic. We can see the Hazlitt that Coleridge described as 'a thinking, observant, original man ... [who] sends well-headed and well-feathered thoughts straight forwards to the mark with a twang of the bow-string' and that 'he says more than any man I ever knew ... that is his own in a way of his own'.[12]

Hazlitt referred to Chaucer's ideas as hard and dry and in the passages quoted compared him unfavourably to Shakespeare. Yet hard and dry are the words he used to describe the *Essay* and Hazlitt had a mind which was also capable of working like Chaucer. He could write with the coolness of a mountain stream but he could also produce words that seemed to emerge from the centre of a sand storm. His *Letter to William Gifford*[13] is one such example. To quote Macdonald Maclean:

> The *Letter* is naked rebuke, in which there is no attempt to disguise the hot indignation which prompted it. It is less like a cool green ribbon of prose than like a river that storms its way along, flecked here and there with dangerous looking reflections of colour, forming itself into rapids and pouring itself now and again into pools that hiss and sparkle as if warmed by subterranean or subaqueous fires and that send up at times a jet of angry steam or foam reaching half way to the stars.[14]

In dealing with Hazlitt's ideas on imagination and intuition it is important to include a note of caution or perhaps provide a more precise definition. If we juxtapose Hazlitt's notions of 'talent' and 'genius' the point will be made.
Talent uses freedom to play around with things, to explore, to juggle, to frolic and leap about. The talented person has swagger and can dazzle us with his brilliance, our breath is taken away by his ingenuity. Genius also relies on a freedom to play and explore. It may frolic but it never has a swagger. Genius realises, develops, extends. Instead of dazzling us it enlightens us with its progressive truth. Commenting on Byron's *Childe Harold's Pilgrimage* Hazlitt writes: 'There is here in every line an effort at brilliancy, and a successful effort; and yet, in the next, as if nothing had been tried, the same thing is attempted to be expressed again with the same labour or satisfaction of mind.' In Hazlitt's opinion Byron was putting his own stamp on nature. After reading Shakespeare we experience and know something new about ourselves and others. After reading Byron we have taken a wild and exotic journey but are essentially still in the same place. Hazlitt believed the work of the imagination was done mostly unconsciously. 'This intuitive perception of the hidden analogies of things, or, as it may be called, this instinct of imagination, is perhaps what stamps the

character of genius on the productions of art more than any other circumstance: for it works unconsciously, like nature and receives its impressions from a kind of inspiration.'[15] Hazlitt was critical of those criteria of emotionalism which are rooted solely in the individual and are neglectful of the larger reality beyond. So what can be placed under the heading of imagination can cause problems. Imagination is a human potential. It can be used creatively. But it can also be wasted.

'Sensibility' was the word Hazlitt often used to refer to an extreme subjectivity that he believed the talented egotistical person was prone to fall into. He called it a 'false and bastard kind of feeling'. What is of greatest importance is an excitement within one's self. It is as if the feeling itself is the end result of the engagement, as if the feeling is to be seen as a value, as the ultimate good to be indulged in. For Hazlitt the value of a feeling comes from its truth. He stressed the importance of balance, of a sense of proportion between the strength of the external stimulus and the quantity of emotional response evoked in us. To keep both sides of the scales in unison the subject requires a continuous relating with the object, a stable awareness of the other, a free floating attention. The difference in simple terms would be like this. In a conversation do we seem to listen to what someone is saying, but really take in nothing and are away in our own world? Or do we keep listening, remaining in touch, eager to hear the next thought, really wanting to hear more?

'Nature' in the Enlightenment was predominantly thought of as a fixed essence. Pope wrote of 'one clear, unchanged and universal light'. This was a predominantly static view. For Hazlitt, nature was a moving, changing permanence. He believed that great art imitated nature, but he did not envisage it as a type of photographic process. He distinguished between 'the actual appearance of Nature' as opposed to 'the progress of feelings [that such appearances] excite in us'. In line with his view of imagination, man is a participant in the world. Hazlitt is continually trying to break from traditional abstractions of nature. The concrete phenomena of everyday life interests him. How do we relate to ordinary everyday events and objects? It is nature 'not as an idea of nature existing solely in the mind, got from an infinite number of different objects, but which was never embodied in an individual instance.'

★★★

Disinterestedness and a sympathetic identification with others and with the common patterns of human experience are necessary prerequisites for true and lasting greatness. Hazlitt wrote, 'Those who have the largest hearts have the soundest understandings; and he is the truest philosopher who can forget himself', and 'Those evils that inflame the imagination and make the heart sick, ought not to leave the head cold. This is the very test and measure of the degree of the enormity [of an iniquity] that it involuntarily staggers and appals the mind'.[16] We can see that Hazlitt has moved quite a distance from the attitude that the imagination must always be dominated by reason, a belief that had held sway in the Enlightenment. Hobbes had called imagination the 'decaying sense' and Samuel Johnson referred to it as a 'licentious vagrant faculty unsusceptible of limitations and restraint.'

Hazlitt's essays would become the living expression of these principles that I have been outlining. The titles of his collections speak for themselves – *The Round Table, The Plain Speaker* and *Table Talk.* He would continually go out of himself and into the life and mind and character of the other person in disinterested identification. From here – a position of empathy – he tried to describe the truth. In this activity he could contemplate the life of the other person and from there have another vantage point to view his own life. To know another is to know one's self. This is indicative of his pluralistic conception of human truth and his perennial bias towards dialogue.

Thirteen years later when the forceps was well and truly gone from his writings, he provided an imaginative summary of the *Essay* in 'On Reason and Imagination':

Man is (so to speak) an endless and infinitely varied repetition: and if we know what one man feels, we so far know what a thousand feel in the sanctuary of their being. Our feeling of general humanity is at once an aggregate of a thousand different truths, and it is also the same truth a thousand times told. As is our perception of this original truth, the root of our imagination, so will the force and richness of the general impression proceeding from it be. The boundary of our sympathy is a circle which enlarges itself according to its propulsion from the centre – the heart. If we are imbued with a deep sense of individual weal or woe, we shall be awe-struck at the idea of humanity in general. If we know little of it but its abstract and common properties, without their particular application, their force or degree, we shall care just as little as we know either about the whole or the individuals, if we understand the texture and vital feeling, we then can fill up the outline, but we cannot supply the former from having the latter given. Moral and poetical truth is like expression in a picture – the one is not to be attained by smearing over a large canvas, nor the other by bestriding a vague topic ... But I defy any great tragic writer to despise that nature which he understands, or that heart which he has probed, with all its rich bleeding materials of joy and sorrow. The subject may not be a source of much triumph to him, from its alternate light and shade, but it can never become one of supercilious indifference. He must feel a strong reflex in it, corresponding to that which he has depicted in the characters of others. Indeed, the object and end of playing, 'both at the first and now, is to hold the mirror up to nature,' to enable us to feel for others as for ourselves, or to embody a distinct interest out of ourselves by the force of imagination and passion. This is summed up by the poet – 'To feel what others are, and know myself a man.'[17]

Chapter 9

Vanity

No one has ever yet seen through all the intricate folds and delicate involutions of our self-love, which is wrapped up in a set of smooth flimsy pretexts like some precious jewel in covers of silver paper.[1]

Hazlitt's interest in human character is of perennial value. We saw in Chapter 8 how he set out in the *Essay* to systematically examine the notion of self and its place as an essentially egotistical entity within philosophy. I believe there is a psychological accuracy and truth to his theory. In this chapter I will demonstrate how the ideas from the *Essay* acted like yeast in Hazlitt's writings. His words from *The Plain Speaker* quoted above will serve to remind us of the pivotal position he gave to the place of self-love and how the idea of self as an egotistical entity can cling to and deaden the mind. In his essay '*On Living to One's-Self*' he stated at the outset that when he wrote of living to one's self, he did not have an egotism in mind. 'Egotism', 'affectation' and 'vanity' are terms we find throughout his writings. He cited Sir Charles Grandison (a character in the novels of Samuel Richardson) who was described as 'living to himself'. Let us pick up on Hazlitt's words:

> The character I speak of [when I think of living to oneself] is as little an egotist as possible: [Grandison] was as much a one as possible. Some satirical critic has represented him in Elysium bowing over the faded hand of Lady Grandison – he ought to have been represented bowing over his own hand, for he never admired any one but himself, and was the God of his own idolatry.[2]

Hazlitt gave us an example of the least egotistical person he knew when he wrote about his friend Joseph Fawcett:

> I have heard [Fawcett] explain 'That is the most delicious feeling of all, to like what is excellent, no matter whose it is'. In this respect he practised what he preached ...There was no flaw or mist in the clear mirror of his mind. He was as open to impressions as he was strenuous in maintaining them. He did not care a rush whether a writer was old or new, in prose or in verse – 'what he wanted' he said 'was something to make him think'... He gave a cordial welcome to all sorts, provided they were the best in their kind. He was not fond of counterfeits or duplicates. His own style was laboured and artificial to a fault, while his character was frank and ingenuous in the extreme ... Men who have fewer native resources, and are obliged to apply oftener to the general stock, acquire by habit

a greater aptitude in appreciating what they owe to others. Their taste is not made a sacrifice to their egotism and vanity, and they enrich the soil of their minds with continual accessions of borrowed strength and beauty.[3]

Vanity posed a great danger to the creative imagination. A reaching out from oneself was central in Hazlitt's scheme and he was critical of many of his contemporaries who just wrote about themselves. 'Egotism,' he said, 'is an infirmity that perpetually grows upon a man, till at last he cannot bear to think of anything but himself, or even to suppose that others do.'[4]

He was also an astute observer of people. Although he was fulsome in his praise of Wordsworth's poetry Hazlitt observed what he considered a fatal flaw in the poet's character. Wordsworth, he said, 'was a genius who came to believe he was a genius'. He believed Wordsworth had become 'jealous of all excellence but his own. He does not even like to share his reputation with his subject; for he would have it all proceed from his own power and originality of mind ... He tolerates only what he himself creates ... He sees nothing but himself and the universe ... His egotism is in some respects a madness; for he scorns even the admiration of himself, thinking it a presumption in any one to suppose that he has taste or sense enough to understand him.'[5]

We could juxtapose these two men as examples of different types of people. Fawcett delighted in what was excellent regardless of who had produced it. Wordsworth sought to possess all excellence. His own considerable output and greatness was seen as the extremities of man's achievements. Fawcett was interested in how a work provoked him to think, how it stimulated his mind, how it challenged his powers. Wordsworth saw himself in need of no such stimulation; the mind of no other man was up to his standard. Nature, the bare trees and mountains, cannot think or answer back and so he entered into full communion with them. He made nature great by lending her his mind. Fawcett was always aware of his debt to others. He needed to apply often to the general stock and acquired a greater aptitude in appreciating what he owed to others. Now we arrive at a fork in the road with two paths which lead in different directions. One path leads to gratitude, the other to self-sufficiency. Wordsworth not only believed he possessed all understanding but that he is 'beyond all understanding'. He considered the admiration of many to be of little value because they are not capable of perceiving his true greatness. He is indebted to no one. Fawcett knew he was in need of others and was continually grateful for what he was given. The soil of his mind was enriched by the beauties and strengths of others. One type of mind sees it as a weakness to rely on others; the other believes it is a strength. Such reliance is not a weakness. Fawcett was not a soft touch. He was not fond of counterfeits or duplicates. He could listen hard and argue hard. He was a good critic.

What we are now led to consider is how knowledge is acquired. This leads us beyond the actual content of a person's mind and directs our attention to the manner in which knowledge is arrived at. The focus is on the mental attitude of the learner rather than on a technique of learning. Hazlitt returned again and again throughout his writings to consider this topic. Let us take a look at one passage where in outlining his attitude towards knowledge and its attainment he argued for a state of mental and emotional receptivity, a fostering of a contemplative dream-like state of mind, an openness to what others can teach us.

> This sort of dreaming existence is the best. He who quits it to go in search of realities generally barters repose for repeated disappointments and vain regrets. His time, thoughts, and feelings are no longer at his own disposal. From that instant he does not survey the objects of nature as they are in themselves, but looks asquint at them to see whether he cannot make them the instruments of his ambition, interest, or pleasure; for a candid, undesigned, undisguised simplicity of character, his views become jaundiced, sinister, and double: he takes no further interest in the great changes of the world but as he has a paltry share in producing them: instead of opening his senses, his understanding, and his heart to the resplendent fabric of the universe, he holds a crooked mirror before his face, in which he may admire his own person and pretensions, and just glance his eye aside to see whether others are not admiring him too. He no more exists in the impression which 'the fair variety of things' makes upon him, softened and subdued by habitual contemplation, but in the feverish sense of his own upstart self-importance. By aiming to fix, he is become the slave of opinion. He is a tool, a part of a machine that never stands still, and is sick and giddy with the ceaseless motion. He has no satisfaction but in the reflection of his own image in the public gaze – but in the repetition of his own name in the public ear. He is himself mixed up with and spoils everything.[6]

There are many ways in which vanity can express itself. A common one is in the attitude we take to the past. When Hazlitt set to work on a series of lectures about the writers of the 16th and 17th century, the Age of Elizabeth, he articulated another arm of his ideas on vanity. Many of the people he spoke and wrote about, (the lectures later appearing in book form), were considered to be out of date and out of fashion. He picks up the strand of thought described above in relation to Joseph Fawcett – he did not care a rush whether a writer was old or new, in prose or in verse. In his analysis of the neglect of those people he returns to the issue of vanity. His comments can be seen as a further examination of 'the intricate folds and delicate involutions of our self-love'.

There is not a lower ambition, a poorer way of thought, than that which would confine all excellence, or arrogate its final accomplishment to the present or modern times. We ordinarily speak and think of those who had the misfortune to write or live before us, as labouring under very singular privations and disadvantages in not having the benefits of those improvements which we have made, as buried in the grossest ignorance, or the slaves 'of poring pedantry;' and we make a cheap and infallible estimate of their progress in civilisation upon a graduated scale of perfectibility, calculated from the meridian of our own times … We are so dazzled with the gloss and novelty of modern discoveries, that we cannot take onto our mind's eye the vast expanse, the lengthened prospective of human intellect, and a cloud hangs over and conceals its loftiest monuments, if they are removed to a little distance from us – the cloud of our vanity and short-sightedness.[7]

Here he reiterates the principles that underlie the narcissistic position, here he paints pictures that offer clarity to our eyes. We are shown the clouds that hang over and conceal the loftiest monuments. This image in all its clarity is used like a mirror to show the blindness of the eye full of flaw and mist. Hazlitt is telling us that such self-elevation, such exalting of the present and looking down on the past is not an achievement but a tower of Babel, an inability to listen to and appreciate others.

Hazlitt suggests this vanity, this narcissism, the preoccupation with oneself and one's productions leads to blindness. It operates as a scotoma as we face our mirror image. He believed that 'the works of greatest genius are produced almost unconsciously, with an ignorance on the part of the persons themselves that they have done anything extraordinary'[8] and Shakespeare was his prime example because he was not dominated by vanity and produced great works because he could look outwards. His eyes were not bent upon himself. His eyes however needed to have been able to also look upon himself and to know himself as he really was. He needed to be acquainted with his own character. He needed outlook and in-look. Human truth can only be arrived at and exist between people, in the dialogue which takes place in human encounter, as we heard Shakespeare speak through Achilles:

> Nor doth the eye itself,
> That most pure spirit of sense, behold itself,
> Not going from itself; but eye to eye opposed
> Salutes each other with each other's form.

A modern psychoanalytic thinker who like Hazlitt has given considerable attention to vanity and its place in life is Neville Symington. Symington uses the modern language of narcissism but the phenomena which they address are the same. Not surprisingly Fairbairn has a significant place in the development of Symington's thought. If we want to understand the principles of human activity we need to look at the centre of relationships. Symington believes that all personal disorders flow from narcissism and he has coined the term the *lifegiver* to denote a quality that resides in the other. It is a quality in the other that a 'person seeks as an alternative to seeking itself.' Just as Hazlitt visualised a going out from one's narrow self-interest into the world of others so also Symington sees the internal choice of the *lifegiver* as fundamental to being emotionally alive.[9]

To the *Essay* was attached an appendix 'On Abstract Ideas'. It too was to remain a constant thread in Hazlitt's writings. He saw in many an abstractionism that set up a 'war with nature'. He makes his point when speaking of Sir Joshua Reynolds, that he was 'at the head of those who have maintained the supposition that nature or the universe of things was indeed the groundwork or foundation on which art rested; but that the superstructure rose above it, that it towered by degrees above the world of realities, and was suspended in the regions of thought alone … the glittering phantom that hovered round the head of the genuine artist.' Hazlitt is not an anti-abstractionist. He believed it to be a necessary part of thinking but it is a particular brand of abstractionism that he objected to. He sees it as another subtle form of egotism, and closely related to a belief in the possibility of arriving at a notion of perfection in thought leading to an idolatry of our own abstract being. We can see further into his thoughts on the subject if we examine the following passage:

> I have more satisfaction in my own thoughts than in dictating them to others: words are necessary to explain the impression of certain things upon me to the reader, but they rather weaken and draw a veil over than strengthen it to myself. However, I might say with the poet, 'My mind to me a kingdom is,' yet I have little ambition 'to set a throne or chair of state in the understandings of other men.' The ideas we cherish most, exist best in a kind of shadowy abstraction, 'Pure in the last recesses of the mind;' and derive neither force nor interest from being exposed to public view.[10]

In this passage Hazlitt refers to the poem of Sir Edward Dyer (1550–1607). It is worth hearing some more.

> My mind to me a kingdom is,
> Such present joys therein I find,
> That it excels all other bliss
> That earth affords or grows by kind:
> Though much I want which most would have,
> Yet still my mind forbids to crave.

Hazlitt's observations are offered within an exploration of the value of the written word in contrast to painting. He is pointing to the limitations of speech and leading us to the image beyond, which the great painter can evoke. Perhaps these sentiments lay behind his desire to be a painter and his once saying that all his vast amount of words could never fully express what a visual masterpiece of art can convey. This line of thought takes us into Hazlitt's deep well but we will soon emerge from it. Our final step comes by way of remembering Francis Bacon's edifice of learning. Hazlitt was not attracted by his hierarchical model. In his *Advancement of Learning* Bacon had stated:

> But yet the commandment of knowledge is yet higher than the commandment over the will; for it is as a commandment over the reason, belief, and understanding of man, which is the highest part of the mind, and giveth law to the will itself. For there is no power on earth which setteth up a throne, or chair of estate, in the spirits and souls of men, and in their cogitations, imaginations, opinions, and beliefs, but knowledge and learning.[11]

We can almost see the building blocks of a pyramid being put in place. Here, while he praises Bacon for his ability to describe the workings of intelligence, he nonetheless dissociates himself from Bacon's edifice. So the notion of some disembodied ideal of truth as a motivating force in human action is foreign to Hazlitt. He sought to expose the fallacy of the idea that progress and advancement in the arts and sciences was by and in itself, a move towards a notion of perfection. The point Hazlitt is labouring here concerns the human tendency to create false gods out of a piece of knowledge. Having acquired knowledge and understand something important we might all be inclined towards the belief that we are capable of understanding everything. We get carried away with a sense of our own importance and we don't know when to stop. This is another form of vanity. 'A man, by great labour and sagacity,' wrote Hazlitt, 'finds out one truth: but from the importunate craving of the mind to know all, he would fain persuade himself that this one truth includes all others. The 'importunate craving of the mind to know all' is akin to the desire to build a tower of Babel. It is a failure to accept the limitations of what we know. Hazlitt believed that 'such has been the error of almost all systems and system-makers, who lose the advantage of the conquests they have achieved by pushing them too far, and aiming at universal empire.' [12]

Every time we understand something we have moved into a place where new questions arise. The excitement which learning and knowing arouse can be confused with the knowing itself. 'Excitement' as defined here is similar to the notion of 'sensibility' as explored in Chapter 8. If we crave this excitement we are likely to see it as a good in itself. 'Though much I want which most would have/

Yet still my mind forbids to crave.' He is underlining the necessity of a constant return to a passive receptivity. A passive receptivity was a notion familiar to Shakespeare.

> Unthrifty loveliness, why dost thou spend
> Upon thyself thy beauty's legacy?
> Nature's bequest gives nothing but doth lend,
> And being frank she lends to those are free.
> Then, beauteous niggard, why dost thou abuse
> The bounteous largess given thee to give?
> Profitless usurer, why dost thou use
> So great a sum of sums, yet canst not live?
> For having traffic with thyself alone,
> Thou of thyself thy sweet self dost deceive.
> Then how, when nature calls thee to be gone,
> What acceptable audit canst thou leave?
>   Thy unused beauty must be tomb'd with thee,
>   Which, used, lives th' executor to be.
>
> Sonnet 4

Shakespeare provided us with numerous sonnets about love and life, between two people and within oneself. Ronald Fairbairn's outline of the many parts of the self, their relationships to each other and also the common psychoanalytic demarcation of inter-personal, inter-psychic and intra-psychic should slide with ease into these discussions. Sonnet 4 explicitly chides the person who will not have a child but it also takes us back to Hazlitt's words and help to uncover another intricate fold and delicate involution of self-love. It might be called a reluctance to develop and grow, a premature retirement from life, a Lear-like abdication of responsibility. 'For having traffic with thyself alone/Thou of thyself thy sweet self dost deceive/Then how, when nature calls thee to be gone/ What acceptable audit canst thou leave?/Thy unused beauty must be tomb'd with thee.' Hazlitt often railed against waste. I think many of his tirades against Wordsworth and Coleridge were directed at this sort of waste. If you have traffic with yourself alone you deceive yourself of your sweet self, you deprive yourself of your sweetness.

This all strikes a chord with Montaigne who once more reminds us of his essay 'On Presumption'.

> There is another sort of glory, which is the having too good an opinion of our own worth. 'Tis an inconsiderate affection with which we flatter ourselves, and that represents us to ourselves other than we truly are; like the passion of love, that lends beauties and graces to the object, and makes those who are caught by

it, with a depraved and corrupt judgment, consider the thing which they love other and more perfect than it is. I would not, nevertheless, for fear of failing on this side, that a man should not know himself aright, or think himself less than he is; the judgment ought in all things to maintain its rights; 'tis all the reason in the world he should discern in himself, as well as in others, what truth sets before him; if it be Caesar, let him boldly think himself the greatest captain in the world.[13]

Montaigne is outlining the dangers of having 'an inconsiderate affection' for and thereby flattering ourselves. His piece has many dimensions to it. Besides pointing to what we do with another person he is also describing what I have termed an intra-psychic process, when one part of us tells another part that we are something which we are not. However Montaigne does not wish to leave the matter there and in proceeding with the discussion picks up a theme that will point us to the next chapter on the art of criticism. Montaigne understood how trying to get the balance right can lead to overdoing things in another direction and topple into a false modesty. Fair judgement must be exercised. Truth is at stake and the truth that is in us or we see in others must be discerned and the judgement ought in all things to maintain its rights. If he be Caesar let him know his qualities.

Chapter 10

The Art of Criticism

I conceive that the mind, in the search after knowledge, very much resembles the truffle-hunter: the dog finds out, and is led to the spot where the object of his pursuit lies by the smell, but it is by his teeth and claws that he is able to remove the rubbish that hides it.[1]

Having outlined the workings of the creative imagination and the various forms of affectation and vanity which impede its workings I now wish to move directly into an examination of the art of criticism. I do so aware that the words 'critic' or 'criticism' seems to have an electric charge attached to them. In many aspects of life 'the critics' have acquired positions of great power and have been anointed as the high priests and priestesses. What will the critics say? Reputations hang in the balance; riches or poverty are to be decided upon; fame or oblivion beckons.

I do not wish to concentrate on an exploration of the specialised field of the professional critic. Nor is it my intention to place Hazlitt on the stage and ask him to account for his credentials as a critic of art, drama and literature. During his lifetime and since his death much valuable scholarship has been extended on that task. Rather I hope to extract from his thought some elements which can be put to everyday use and with this in mind wish to begin by diffusing the electric charge which has become attached to the word criticism. A simple dictionary definition refers us to the finding of fault in someone or something and this is the predominant use of the term in common parlance. However, I begin with the belief that the act of thinking and the processes involved require every person who uses their mind to be a good critic. Criticism lies within the very essence of thinking; its presence is a constant as we weigh up the value of what we read, write, see, hear, touch and taste. Criticism is to the mind what breathing is to the body. I also wish to rehabilitate the word 'judgement'.

If we look at how we arrive at knowing something, the process begins with sensing and experiencing, from which we move on to ask questions which usually lead to other questions. We explore, we intuit, we enquire. We look for coherence, we have hunches, we look for causes, we risk a hypothesis, we test, we invite the examination of others to arrive at a theory, at a piece of 'truth'. We judge something to be. We make a judgement. Judgement in this sense does not have a moralistic connotation. It does however have a morality – it is a morality of what is true. Morality in this sense usually leads to robustness, whereas moralising usually leads to rigidity. Perhaps the words judgement and criticism are interchangeable or usefully considered as twin cornerstones.

Fear of the critic allows him to be a law unto himself and the rules by which he lives and works are therefore not questioned. I draw a distinction between two different types of critic. One engages in what I will name 'lazy comment', the other in what I call, 'constructive analysis'. The vast amount of what passes under the name of criticism is nothing more than lazy comment. It is in plentiful supply and can be found in its abundance in all walks of life, so much so that constructive analysis can be hard to find.

Lazy comment is a complex entity which requires careful scrutiny. The lazy commentator needs to be unmasked because he often presents himself as benign and helpful. He will go out of his way to teach you the error of your ways, and would be offended by being named lazy. But if we persist in removing the disguise we find a very destructive character, and the essentials of his activity remain the same regardless of his place of operation. The lazy commentator is a reactor. He meets ideas and they bounce off him. His return can be so swift and executed with such skill (and cunning) that those in attendance stand in awe. The flashing lights, the sparkles of his intelligence inform us of his wit and brilliance. At times he dons another guise, slips into a different uniform and instead of being first on his feet he will be the last of the questioners. He may then appear to be the sage, who not only has gone to the heart of the matter but in extending the vast net of his mind draws in all those minions that have gone before him. We are treated to a double feast and we stagger and sway in admiration of the keenness of his intellect. A lazy commentator? Perish the thought!

Whether he speaks early or later in the piece the lazy commentator can have a detrimental effect, particularly if he is part of an on-going group. When for example question time at a public forum comes around those who might have an ordinary, good enough addition to make to the proceedings can easily remain silent fearing that their thoughts are but a tiny morsel compared with the feast which the lazy commentator is waiting to serve up. Aware of tensions of this kind, Hazlitt observed 'A man may be dexterous and able in explaining the grounds of his opinions, and yet may be a mere sophist, because he only sees one-half of a subject. Another may feel the whole weight of a question, nothing relating to it may be lost upon him, and yet he may be able to give no account of the manner in which it affects him, or to drag his reasons from their silent lurking-places.'[2] The lazy commentator often has a talented mind. I mean talent as I defined it in Chapter 8. It is linked with the freedom to play around with things, to explore, to juggle, to frolic and leap about the place, but the underlying motive is to dazzle us with brilliance, to take our breath away with ingenuity. There is no real interest in developing thought for its own sake or to enlighten others by progressing to a larger truth. 'Unthrifty loveliness, why dost thou spend/Upon thyself thy beauty's legacy?/Nature's bequest gives nothing but doth lend.' Hazlitt was familiar with the lazy commentator and drew attention to this type of critic in his essay 'On Criticism'. The aim of such a person, he wrote, is not to do justice to the author or the art but 'to do himself homage, and to show his acquaintance with all the topics and resources of criticism'.[3] What if we follow Montaigne who has advised that if we be a Caesar let us boldly think ourselves the greatest captain in the world? Lead, advance, progress. Such confident movement, based as it is on a true assessment and judgement of oneself, can invite a particular type of problem. So let us follow an instance when someone proclaims themselves a Caesar. All societies, cultures and countries have a name for this type of person who through their own efforts do well in life. In Australia he or she is called a Tall Poppy, named after the flower that stretches its head high above the sea of others. It is a curious fact that while the educational forces of a nation strenuously encourage advancement, once the person actually arrives at such a position they find life is not as simple as they thought. 'Cut down the tall poppy' has long rung out as a rallying cry, to such an extent that people now refer to it as a syndrome, the Tall Poppy Syndrome.

At face value it seems simple. Push them up, but as soon as they are up pull them down, just in case they get too big for their boots. But are we dealing with a simple issue or a complex set of issues? I think what travels under the heading of this cutting down of the tall poppy are in fact three distinct and different activities, which I call the friendly, the jealous and the envious.

'The friendly' is, as its name implies, motivated by a concern for the achievement and the achiever. It allows the Caesar to celebrate his glory, indeed it partakes in such celebrations. But it reminds him that he is also an ordinary man, that he is not great in everything and each man can only be a genius in one area. A playful pulling of the leg is the more usual currency of this concern. Relating to the genius as just an ordinary person is not far behind.

'The jealous' cutting down of an achievement has its origins in a different place. This person wants what the achiever has and feels reminded of his own failure. He is pained at his own lack of success and would prefer not to be reminded of it. Such jealousy does not usually arise from any great interest in the life of the achiever. The achiever has held up a mirror in which the jealous person sees himself. He does not want to look at himself and so may look away or try to ignore it. However, he does not set out to destroy the achiever and can let him carry on as long as he can find suitable distractions.

'The envious' position is quite a different beast, in a class of its own. It often goes under the name of jealousy but such an intermingling of the two is inaccurate. It is also unfair to the jealous person and does not do justice to his state of mind. The envious carries no remnants of friendship and will not allow Caesar to have his glory; indeed he will undermine it in every way he can. He cannot tolerate such advancement by another. It not only shows up his imperfection but it strikes at his very heart and exposes an inner poverty of soul, and he cannot let himself see such poverty. If he catches a glimpse of it he must quickly look away. Whatever exposes him to seeing more must be destroyed.

It is of course Shakespeare's Caesar who understands all too well the envy that drives Cassius. In speaking to Mark Antony about Cassius, Caesar sums up the workings of the envious mind with superb accuracy.

> ...I fear him not:
> Yet if my name were liable to fear,
> I do not know the man I should avoid
> So soon as that spare Cassius. He reads much;
> He is a great observer and he looks
> Quite through the deeds of men: he loves no plays,
> As thou dost, Antony; he hears no music;
> Seldom he smiles, and smiles in such a sort
> As if he mock'd himself and scorn'd his spirit
> That could be moved to smile at any thing.
> Such men as he be never at heart's ease
> Whiles they behold a greater than themselves,
> And therefore are they very dangerous.
>
> *Julius Caesar*, Act 1.2, 198–210

He is dangerous indeed. It is necessary to keep an eye on him, and important to inform oneself of the length he will go to destroy the achiever. Hazlitt's psychological perceptiveness extended to his awareness of the paranoia in the envious mind and the projective processes at work. Cassius may swim the Tiber and out-do Caesar in physical prowess and health, but he cannot rule an empire. Neither can he face his own inadequacy, and even his brother Brutus' contentment is something he sets out to undermine. 'It is' wrote Hazlitt 'the property of true genius to force the admiration even of enemies. No one was ever hated or envied for his powers of mind, if others were convinced of their real excellence. The jealousy and uneasiness produced in the mind by the display of superior talents almost always arises from a suspicion that there is some trick or deception in the case, and that we are imposed on by an appearance of what is not really there. True warmth and vigour communicate warmth and vigour; and we are no longer inclined to dispute the inspiration of the oracle when we feel the "presens Divus" in our own bosoms.'[4]

***

As we turn away from what constitutes a bad critic we now need to ask the question what type of mind makes a good critic? Let us turn to Edmund Grosse's introduction to the 1894 edition of Hazlitt's *Conversations of James Northcote* where we find him writing on Hazlitt's approach to art criticism. Grosse writes that when Hazlitt described a painting

> He aims at nothing more nor less than a spiritual reproduction of a physical
> impression. He describes, but with the design of producing, on the mental retina,
> an image which shall create a like enthusiasm on the mind as the sight of the
> picture does when the physical eye regards it. This is not quite the same thing as
> repeating the impression made on the physical eye, because the critic endeavours,
> by subtly heightening his effects, to compensate for the necessary absence of
> colour and form. William Hazlitt writes not so much for those who were about
> to see the picture, as for those who will never have the chance of seeing it, and his
> object is to give these latter as much pleasure as the former will presently enjoy.[5]

When Grosse outlined Hazlitt's method of art criticism he explained that in
his day most great works of art were in private collections and the public for
whom Hazlitt wrote would never have a chance of seeing them. Hazlitt was
compensating for this by the vividness of his descriptive writing. We might
therefore be led to think that, as this is no longer the case, we can put aside
Hazlitt's method, thinking it time-bound. This would be a mistake on two
counts. First, Hazlitt's commentaries on written works of literature and his
dramatic criticism are often as imaginatively vivid as his comments on the visual
work of art, and the general public had easy access to written works and to such
performances. Second, introspection was the internal power-house of Hazlitt's
criticism.

The internal psychological reverberations of a work of art occupy a pivotal
position in his mind. His order of priority is exemplified by his account of seeing
a Rembrandt for a second time, twenty years after his first sighting. 'The picture
was nothing to me', he wrote; 'it was the idea it suggested. The one hung in the
wall at Burleigh; the other was an heir-loom in my mind.'[6] But how did it hang
in his mind? In the *Essay* Hazlitt questioned whether the mind was 'a sort of
inner room where the images of external things, like pictures in a gallery, are
lodged safe and dry out of the reach of the turbulence of the senses.' This is not
a crusty and dusty place. We have seen Hazlitt crying in front of a Titian. The
Man in Black struck him 'like a blow'; pictures were 'full of life and energy …
the paint still seemed wet, it was bursting with expression.' When he saw the
Italian masters they spoke to him 'in the eternal silence of thought'. Everything
he speaks and writes can be seen as ripples coming from his inner experience.

Hazlitt's term 'gusto' finds its proper place here in his scheme of things. With
Heaney's poem in mind, in Chapter 1, I described Hazlitt as digging with his
pen, his hands in the soil of his words, his mind strenuously unearthing the good
thoughts. Gusto is 'power and passion defining any object.'[7] 'In art, in taste, in
life, in speech, you decide from feeling, and not from reason; that is, from the

impression of a number of things on the mind, which impression is true and well founded, though you may not be able to analyse or account for it in the several particulars.'[8]

Gusto is the strength of the feeling, the emotional engagement, the spontaneous excitement. These are the essential conduits through which we are in touch with our inner nature, our inner truth. There is no need for a moral superstructure which comes from above or outside. Nature is true and art of whatever kind that enables us to feel and know the truth of life is great. There are no high or low subjects for art. Smollet's novels and Hogarth's prints may present what is commonly classified as 'low life', but Hazlitt disposed of such hierarchies and created a level playing-field. He was not entering into an amoral sphere as far as human behaviour is concerned, but rather was asserting that all aspects of human life and living are fit subjects for expression, representation and engagement. Looked at in this way his interest is profoundly moral. What lies at the centre of the creative activity is the ability of the artist to remain true to his interaction with nature and for the critic to similarly interact with what he sets out to critique. All aspects of life and living require representation. What we are afraid of, what we are unable to artistically represent and imaginatively engage with, what we emotionally repress or suppress, to use Freud's language, becomes in fact our greatest enemy. Love and hate, good and evil, the attractive and the repellent, all must be known emotionally.   The ability to exercise good judgement is built upon an engagement with every aspect of life. If we disown some part of ourselves, if we place ourselves higher than human nature, if we react with disgust claiming that we could never imagine ourselves being like that in our wildest dreams, then we are liars. Our judgement will be faulty because we have set ourselves above our own nature.

If gusto is absent a vacancy is created. This space can be filled in different ways, but they all leave 'a dead weight upon the mind'. The lazy commentator does not have time for gusto. He may lose his spot if he is not swiftly off the mark. He has long relied on 'a system' which he has implanted into his mind. While those who hear him may be suitably impressed, the product he has to offer soon leaves others with a dead weight upon their mind. Hazlitt said the good critic should 'reflect the colours, the light and shade, the soul and body of the work.' It should impart the essence of a piece of art, should show what passion has been touched and what tone and movement the creator's mind imparts to his subject or receives from it, what imaginative interchange takes place between the reviewer, the author and the subject.

Perhaps yet again we can return to Heaney's poem. While his father digs in the garden below, the poet sits upstairs writing his poem. He knows about the hard graft, he knows how to write, he has a subtlety of mind. To move from the circumference to the centre of an issue requires a subtlety of mind, or a compass of soul capable of directing attention towards imperceptible objects. 'Coarse minds' said Hazlitt 'think all that is subtle, futile: that because it is not gross and obvious and palpable to the senses, it is therefore light and frivolous, and of no importance in the real affairs of life; thus making their own confined understandings the measure of truth, and supposing that whatever they do not distinctly perceive, is nothing.'[9] Hazlitt refers to Seneca's belief that subtle truths are those which have the least substance in them, and consequently approach nearest to non-entity. The most important truths are the most refined and subtle.' This was because,

> they must comprehend a great number of particulars, and instead of referring to any distinct or positive fact, must point out the combined effects of an extensive chain of causes, operating gradually, remotely, and collectively, and therefore imperceptibly. General principles are not the less true or important because from their nature they elude immediate observation; they are like the air, which is not the less necessary because we neither see nor feel it, or like that secret influence which binds the world together, and holds the planets in their orbit.'[10]

In spelling out the degree of difficulty which faces the person who attempts to capture and communicate these strands and their elusiveness, he further defined the subtlety of mind necessary for the critic. He says that

> It cannot be expected that abstract truths or profound observations should ever be placed in the same strong and dazzling points of view as natural objects and mere matters of fact. It is enough if they receive a reflex and borrowed lustre, like that which cheers the first dawn of morning where the effect of surprise and novelty gilds every object, and the joy of beholding another world gradually emerging out of the gloom of night, 'a new creation rescued from his reign,' fills the mind with a sober rapture.[11]

We can see from these descriptions of the mind of the critic that Hazlitt does not see himself as a guru or rule-maker laying out the norms and testing a piece of art with a yardstick. Just as we would lift our eyes from the page of printed text to watch the trees swaying in the wind and the blue skies beyond, our mind like our eyes must be involved in an altogether more profound enterprise. As we move from that simple rectangle of print, some inches from our face, to focus on objects many miles away, our eyes and brain perform the most intricate of operations. Hazlitt asks his reader for a mental and emotional exchange of similar intensity. It will now be self-evident that Hazlitt wrote as if he was talking to us. He was a great literary conversationalist. Dialogue is taken for granted; the sense of good talk is continually present. Hazlitt had little interest in speaking to those of a passive or lazy mind. We will not hear an exhaustive inventory from him. Instead he had the ability to suggest by implication. He will not lay his ideas out in a straight line, consecutively, in pews and compartments. Instead of contiguity we have contrast. Points are laid out as if they were on the circumference of a circle. We are required to take up a position and look around us. The mind will not grasp truth by clinging tightly to a single strand. He talked expecting a subtlety of mind which could delicately pick up the fine strands. He left space for the listeners' ideas and associations. The pictures he painted with his words carry the atmosphere of the scene. We cannot fill in by numbers. If he used only a few colours of the rainbow he expected us to imagine the presence of the others and fill the vacancies on the spectrum. How do we fill in? How do we receive? We must return to his notion of 'elective affinity' as explained in Chapter 8. But let Hazlitt now explain it himself:

> Nature has a thousand aspects, and one man can only draw out one of them. Whoever does this, is a man of genius. One displays her force, another her refinement, one her power of harmony, another her suddenness of contrast, one her beauty of form, another her splendour of colour. Each does that for which he is best fitted by his particular genius, that is to say, by some quality of mind in which the object sinks deepest, where it finds the most cordial welcome, is perceived to its utmost extent, and where again it forces its way out from the fullness with which it has taken possession of the mind of the student. The imagination gives out what it has first absorbed by congeniality of temperament, what it has attracted and moulded into itself by elective affinity, as the load stone draws and impregnates iron.[12]

We might understandably find ourselves in a profound contemplation of these fine issues, but as we get carried away admiring the beauty and dexterity of serve, Hazlitt, noted for his fine volley when playing fives, will take us by surprise, requiring us to play some basic shots. 'You need one other thing to play this game and that is courage!' Our eye is distracted. Hazlitt wins the point! He calls out in triumph. Then he sits to explain:

> One source of the unbendingness (which some call obstinacy) is that, though living much alone, I have never worshipped the Echo. I see plainly enough that black is not white, that the grass is green, that kings are not their subjects; and, in such self-evident cases, do think it necessary to collate my opinions with the received prejudices. In subtler questions, and matters that admit of doubt, as I do not impose my opinion on others without a reason, so I will not give up mine to them without a better reason; and a person calling me names, or giving himself airs of authority, does not convince me of his having taken more pains to find out the truth than I have, but the contrary … Both from disposition and habit, I can assume nothing in word, look, or manner. I cannot steal a march

upon public opinion in any way. My standing upright, speaking loud, entering a room gracefully, proves nothing; therefore I neglect these ordinary means of recommending myself to the good graces and admiration of strangers (and, as it appears, even of philosophers and friends). Why? Because I have other resources, or, at least, am absorbed in other studies and pursuits. Suppose this absorption to be extreme, and even morbid – that I have brooded over an idea till it has become a kind of substance in my brain, that I have reasons for a thing which I have found out with much labour and pains, and to which I can scarcely do justice without the utmost violence of exertion (and that only to a few persons) – is this a reason for my playing off out-of-the-way notions in all companies, wearing a prim and self-complacent air, as if I were 'the admired of all observers'? or is it not rather an argument (together with a want of animal spirit) why I should retire into myself and perhaps acquire a nervous and uneasy look, from a consciousness of the disproportion between the interest and conviction I feel on certain subjects, and my ability to communicate what weighs upon my mind to others? If my ideas, which I do not avouch, but suppose, lie below the surface, why am I to be always attempting to dazzle superficial people with them, or smiling, delighted at my own want of success?[13]

Is that all there is to say! No, but it is a start. It all points to having enough courage to have an independence of mind. It is a rare quality. Good criticism can only come from a mind which truly possesses and values independence. There are many counterfeits and the real thing deserves proper examination.

Chapter 11

Independence of Mind

The English psychoanalyst Ella Freeman Sharpe (1875–1947), whom I referred to briefly in chapter 1, told a story about a young girl, aged 15, who came to see her for professional advice. She was threatened with being expelled from her school. She horrified the school staff and her parents by writing a letter to her boyfriend which had explicit sexual references. The letter was intercepted by the staff at her school. Her parents believed she had no knowledge of sexuality and that her boyfriend had led her astray and filled her mind with things she ought not to know. The staff at the school wanted the whole matter cleared up. The girl's mother told Sharpe that she wanted her daughter's innocence to be restored and that her child should remain dutiful and obedient. The girl herself told Sharpe she had behaved badly and should never have written the letter. 'My father and mother think it was disgraceful,' she said, 'and so it was. I'm not going to think or do anything more my parents would not like.' Sharpe believed that success could not be judged by any of these desired outcomes. Success, she writes, 'will mean that the girl will not remain the obedient child in the parents' sense, but will become independent and unafraid and mistress of her own sexual thoughts'.[1]

This piece of writing provided the title of my book on Sharpe, *Mistress of Her Own Thoughts*.[2] She did not see the struggle to have a mind of one's own as the sole province of young people trying to find their way in the world. All adult living carries the constant temptation and tendency to fall back into some infantile way of reacting to conflict, opposition and stress. Sharpe wrote with candour and openness about her own self and the workings of her mind. To illustrate this, and her struggles as a psychoanalyst to retain independence, I will pick up another strand of the story.

Finding the girl extremely reluctant to engage in any discussions about the letter and about her interest in her sexuality, Sharpe decided that she could not go along with this denial and broached the question of masturbation. The girl, when in Sharpe's consulting room, had been ringing her hands nervously and Sharpe wondered aloud whether she also played with her body sexually. The girl objected very strongly and when she came the next day she said she had told her mother what the analyst was asking about and her mother was writing to have a meeting with her as soon as possible. Like Hazlitt, Sharpe allows us entry into her mind and tells us the following:

> After this hour I began to experience a feeling of discomfort. I found myself doubting the wisdom of so direct and early an interpretation of her symbolic

masturbation. My discomfort behoved me to watch my own mind. I found I was anticipating in fantasy the mother's visit. The girl had rejected my interpretation of masturbation. How should I justify myself if the child had told her mother of this? For the mother would certainly believe in her daughter's innocence … The parents' condemnation, which I imagined might be directed towards myself in these external circumstances, I recognised as the strictures of my own infantile super-ego. I detected, too, at another time, a reaction to the child's stubbornness … I caught myself thinking: 'It isn't *my* fault you have had to come, you should not have written that letter, then you wouldn't be coming to me!!!' Here I was caught out by my identification with the parent in condemning the child's sexual interest, i.e. at the mercy of the infantile super-ego condemnation of myself.[3]

If we read further into the detail of Sharpe's story we see how she fosters the girl's curiosity, working to enable her to think for herself, to be the mistress of her own thoughts. But, as Sharpe reveals to us, she as the psychoanalyst can suddenly feel like a naughty child. She imaginatively finds herself in the presence of the mother, being taken to account for her actions, expecting a fierce condemnation. She takes us into her own mind and describes the conversation which takes place between the different parts of herself. Her imagined response and her feelings in the face of the mother's visit she locates as her own 'infantile super-ego'. Then she describes how her mind can switch. She is suddenly the condemning parent, blaming the girl. 'It isn't *my* fault you have had to come, you should not have written that letter, then you wouldn't be coming to me.'

An intricate process of argumentation is taking place within her and Sharpe displays this activity for us to see. What we have been introduced to is the importance of understanding the inner workings of our own minds, together with the emotional fluctuations which take place in our hearts and the leaps which our imaginative powers engage in. Such an exposition demonstrates that independence of mind is primarily an internal characteristic, and that it is born from an inner freedom. It relies on a comprehensive knowledge of oneself which comes about through the exercise of critical judgement.

A distinction must be drawn between independence of mind and something else which is often called eclecticism. I think the term laissez-faire is more appropriate than 'eclecticism'. A laissez-faire approach could be summed up as: 'let's have a bit of this and a bit of that – what's the difference?' It is a conflation of points of view. In the name of tolerance, it proclaims that all opinion is of equal value. I do not believe all opinion is of equal value. If I arrive at a place of discussion, to talk and eat with friends, to discuss professional matters with colleagues, and on the way my life had been placed in serious jeopardy by a careless driver, indignation and rage may colour my opinion. If on the other hand it was my carelessness that had just endangered someone else, and I refuse to acknowledge the fact to myself, my guilt and the lie I tell myself will affect my opinion. Apart from such sudden storms, if I have neglected to inform myself on a subject, have done little reading and even less thinking, I will know little. If I have read and thought and brooded over the idea, I should have more to say. If I were to proclaim to myself that I always make the same contribution, that everything I have to say is always equally good, I have deluded myself. Those who engage with laissez-faireism delude us all.

I believe there is a central fear which underpins and supports the position we call laissez-faire. It is a fear and inability to damn, an apprehension about pruning. Strength is confused with destructiveness, the cruel inseparable from the robust. The host in the house of laissez-faireism always serves up an insipid meal. All its taste, gusto, vibrancy and jest have been neutered. It means to please all, to offend no one. Instead it induces a limpness and a languid state of mind. All heads nod in unison. But this is a false unity. What has disappeared is courage.

Let us turn back to Hazlitt. 'A man changes his opinion readily, he thinks it candour: it is levity of mind.'[4] 'One cause of my independence of opinion is, I believe, the liberty I give to others or the very diffidence and distrust of making converts.'[5] 'My opinions have been sometimes called singular: they are merely sincere. I say what I think: I think what I feel. I cannot help receiving certain impressions from things; and I have sufficient courage to declare (somewhat abruptly) what they are. This is the only singularity I am conscious of.'[6]

In this last piece Hazlitt was replying to his critics who suggested his opinions on plays were rather idiosyncratic, delivered off the top of his head. Hazlitt's reply emphasises the personal colour of his dramatic criticism. But again this is not an indication of some wildly spontaneous reaction. Hazlitt had a comprehensive method of reviewing plays. He would first of all read the text some time before he went to the performance. He would let the characters come alive in his mind and then he would observe the players. So he had a balance between collecting information and the personal use he made of that information. Out of all this experience he said what he thought and felt. It was not all there was to say on a subject, but it was what he had to say:

> To the want of a general reading, I plead guilty, and am sorry for it; but perhaps if I had read more, I might have thought less. As to my barrenness of invention, I have at least glanced over a number of subjects – painting, poetry, prose, plays, politics, parliamentary speakers, metaphysical lore, books, men, and things. There is some point, some fancy, some feeling, some taste shown in treating of these ... I have, then, given proofs of some talent, and of more honesty: if there is haste or want of method, there is no common-place, nor a line that licks the dust; and if I do not appear to more advantage, I at least appear such as I am.[7]

***

Those who profess independence of mind, but who are in fact counterfeits and duplicates, can arrive in different guises. One of the most common I shall name 'The Rebel with a Cause'. He is an ingenious fellow, usually quite clever. He seems to have an original mind and he has a knack of detecting the flaw in the work of great men. He will zoom in and uncover the mistake in all its nakedness. It matters not to him whether the fault was due to benign neglect, malicious intent, omission or straightforward inadequacy. In revealing it to the world he makes his name. He has pulled the god from his pedestal and in the exposure of the wrong has made a new contribution to understanding. He is hailed as the new liberator. The old truth is discarded and many who were formally its disciples now worship the new order.

Regardless of what following the new order attracts, it may be the case that a valid point has been made. It may be that a false god has been toppled. But where has our rebel gone? In the midst of the applause and the incantation of the new mantra we have failed to notice that the pedestal has not remained empty. While you have been watching the crowd you notice a movement in the corner of your eye. Our rebel has crawled onto the pedestal himself! Some of the crowd seem to be supporting his assent; at least they are cheering loudly and a few are giving him a leg up. The speed with which he makes himself comfortable gives one the impression he believes it has always been his rightful place. Having accused others of an assault on truth he now assaults it himself and believes himself immune to all criticism. If criticism comes his way he says, 'They will do anything to get back at me. Everything they say and think is motivated solely by a desire for revenge.'

If we cast our minds back to the exploration of envy and jealousy in the previous chapter we may observe that the greatest obstacle to independence of mind is envy. If we need our old-fashioned scales we might even draw up an exact equation. The greater the amount of envy, the less the quantity of independence. The more consumed a person is with envy, the less space there is within his soul for independence of mind.

My rebel with a cause would more properly be called a rebel with two causes. The first is the piece of truth which he discovered; the second is his own aggrandisement and, in the instance I have depicted, he has come to love the pedestal and himself more than the truth. The pursuit of liberty and independence of mind have been corrupted. Those who give a leg up to the new heir of the pedestal are an interesting study. They are usually caught up in a type of nodding mindlessness. They can tend to be lost in the crowd, swallowed up in the mob, their actions blending with the group, their passivity passed over in the din. What is it they cannot stop and look at? I think they cannot stand the sight of how they would have climbed up if the chance had come their way. They will install another rather than face the potential destructiveness of their own envy. They know they would destroy others if the opportunity arose but the guilt on facing such a tendency had better be lost in the action, silenced within the roar of the mob.

***

Hazlitt's formative influence on John Keats has been increasingly acknowledged in recent times by writers such as Walter Jackson Bate (1964), David Bromwich (1983), R. S. White (1987) and Andrew Motion (1997). The young 22-year-old Keats greatly admired the 40-year-old Hazlitt, once saying that Hazlitt was the only person who could teach him philosophy. As Walter Jackson Bate has pointed out, Keats had read Hazlitt's *Essay* and a copy of it was among his books when he died.[8] They first met in 1817 and for the rest of Keats' short life they were good friends, Hazlitt being quite protective of the young man when he was unjustly criticised. Keats and Hazlitt knew that independence of mind was reliant upon an inner freedom. In a letter to his brothers George and Thomas, Keats discussed his opinion of Dilke, whom he believed was not satisfied unless he had made his mind up on everything. He had to be certain and have no doubt. Keats wrote:

> Brown and Dilke walked with me back from the Christmas pantomime. I had not a dispute but a disquisition with Dilke, on various subjects: several things dovetailed in my mind, and at once it struck me what quality went to form a man of achievement especially in literature and which Shakespeare possessed so enormously – I mean *Negative Capability*, that is when man is capable of being in uncertainties, mysteries, doubts, without any irritable reaching after fact and reason – Coleridge, for instance, would let go by a fine isolated verisimilitude caught from the Penetralium of mystery, from being incapable of remaining content with half knowledge. This pursued through volumes would perhaps take us no further than this, that with a great poet the sense of beauty overcomes every other consideration, or rather obliterates all consideration.[9]

There are many echoes here of what I have already said about Hazlitt. When describing how a teacher should approach his task Hazlitt said 'Instead of taking for his motto, "I will lead you into all knowledge", he should be content to say, "I will show you a mystery"'.[10] But these views are not entirely novel and both Keats and Hazlitt were indebted to Francis Bacon who in 1605 wrote about the obstacles to learning in *The Advancement of Learning*:

> Another error is an impatience of doubt and haste to assertion without due and mature suspension of judgement. For the two ways of contemplation are not unlike the two ways of action commonly spoken of by the ancients: the one

plain and smooth in the beginning, and in the end impassable; the other rough and troublesome in the entrance, but, after a while, fair and even: so it is in contemplation; if a man will begin with certainties, he shall end in doubts; but if he will be content to begin with doubts, he shall end in certainties.[11]

Roy Park, with access to Hazlitt's own copy of Bacon's work, remarked that Hazlitt wrote in the margin 'all good'. [12]

This wise passiveness, this negative capability, this contentment to being in doubt, this willingness to lead someone to a mystery, is the same quality of which Ella Sharpe spoke when she described the position which a psychoanalyst takes up towards a patient. The psychoanalyst listens not just with her rational mind. She allows herself to be spontaneously affected and thereby find out what communication is taking place between two people. This is the same attitude of mind which is necessary whether one is in the company of a piece of art, a work of literature or a human being.

But if we are alert, we will notice that a discussion on these matters attracts another brand of affected individual, the one who presents as valuing this attitude when in fact they are merely seeing it as the latest fashion, an occasion for further adornment of their precious self. They can be hard to detect. They display receptivity while really they have embraced ignorance. This is a perversion, a decline into meaningless. The scaffolding of thought is presented as the building which it is intended to support. When we see through such people, we are left facing a shell with nothing inside, flying buttresses pointing to the heavens, arrogantly ignoring the space which they surround. Like all forms of vanity, it cannot see that which it has destroyed.

Perhaps we are at the point where we need to consider the relationship between wisdom and knowledge. Wisdom may be the state of mind where knowledge is appreciated as a good in itself. One is not driven to pass it on, but it can be contemplated in the sovereignty of one's mind. What is good and true and beautiful may find a public expression but the presenter is not driven by vanity or affectation and his own ego is always in the background. The transmission of knowledge is therefore not used as an adornment. This is not a position of detachment nor does it imply an impersonal method. Far from it. If good knowledge is actually taken in, it will have infused the person and will naturally flow through their veins.

We can draw another distinction between wisdom and knowledge if we compare art and pornography. In the *Portrait of the Artist as a Young Man*, James Joyce describes improper art or pornography and how it excites the kinetic emotions and has an immediate and instant effect. Good art goes beyond such an immediate effect. It requires contemplation. Its coherence exists not at the surface level and therefore time must be spent in its presence for its internal beauty to be apprehended.

The issue of what is good in itself is relevant here and we can turn again to *Troilus and Cressida* to find Shakespeare debating the same issue. The men of Troy are discussing whether to give Helen back to the Greeks and so end the protracted war. Following a long outline of his reasons Hector speaks to his young brother, Troilus, and says:

> HECTOR: Brother, she is not worth what she doth cost
> The holding.
> TROILUS: What is aught, but as 'tis valued?
> HECTOR: But value dwells not in particular will;
> It holds his estimate and dignity
> As well wherein 'tis precious of itself
> As in the prizer. 'Tis mad idolatry
> To make the service greater than the god;
> And the will dotes that is inclinable
> To what infectiously itself affects,
> Without some image of the affected merit.
>
> Act 2.2, 50–59

In this exchange Hector is challenging his brother's subjectivism, which is an echo of Hamlet's 'nothing either is good or bad, but thinking makes it so'. Shakespeare is pointing us beyond the mind and will of any particular individual, to a good that is precious in itself and contains a dignity of itself. To see the good as solely invested in your own person is to place yourself on the pedestal, it is making oneself into a god. This is a mad idolatry, it is a dotage of the will. Hazlitt was not a subjectivist and believed in an objective truth. In Hazlitt's scheme the wisdom of long experience acted as a counter-balance, preventing a slide into extreme subjectivism. Creativity acts 'not to show us what has never been but to point out what is before our eyes and under our feet, though we have no suspicion of its existence ... The form of truth not its essence varies with time and circumstance'. This reaching out from oneself was central in his scheme. Disinterestedness and a sympathetic identification with others and with the common patterns of human experience are necessary perquisites. 'Those who have the largest hearts have the soundest understandings; and he is the truest philosopher who can forget himself.' Throughout Hazlitt's writings there is this constant warning that when you have come to know a truth you must beware of the tendency to possess it, to grasp it tightly. 'The more we are convinced of the value of the prize, the less we shall be tempted to lay rash and violent hands on it.'[13] To do so is to strangle it. If your vanity is a law unto itself you will be prone to this mistake because to live creatively involves a constant struggle with internal and external destructive and restrictive forces. Human truth is not something to be possessed in the sovereignty of an individual mind. If we are only interested in that which has originated from our own mind, then we shall miss out on the most delicious thing of all – to enjoy what is excellent, no matter whom it belongs to. 'The mind', wrote Hazlitt, 'resembles a prism, which untwists the various rays of truth and displays them by different modes and in several parcels.' An attitude of wise receptivity, a disposition to use one's mind not to lead another into all knowledge but to 'show a mystery', emphasises that the expanding universe of human truth is a common enterprise.

Do we now find ourselves in an odd position? The definition of independence of mind we are moving towards reveals that such an independence is really another form of dependence. It is dependence on an appreciation of others and on a good which is greater than us. The dynamics here are reminiscent of Fairbairn. He did not perceive of human maturity as being determined by self-sufficiency. Human beings moved from immature dependency to mature dependency. We cannot go it alone in life. It is the mature need and use of, and reliance upon, others that is the hallmark of mental health and human satisfaction. Through a creative imagination we live in sympathetic identification with other people.

Chapter 12

Liberty, Equality, Fraternity

There can be no true superiority but what arises out of the presupposed ground of equality: there can be no improvement but from the free communication and comparing of ideas. Kings and nobles, for this reason, receive little benefit from society – where all is submission on one side, and condescension on the other. The mind strikes out truth by collision, as steel strikes fire from the flint![1]

True equality is the only true morality or true wisdom.[2]

If you lived in Chile during the 1980's while General Pinochet was in power, did you object to government abuse? If you were in South Africa in the same years, what voice did you find in the face of the government's treatment of its people? If you were in the Balkans during the 1990's what price did you put on freedom of speech? If you are living in Burma in the present day would you find the courage to speak for government by the people? If we make a comparison between the state of political freedom in these parts of the world how does it compare with the state of democracy in England during Hazlitt's life time? The list of abuses is a long one: Habeas Corpus regularly suspended; government troops slaughter peaceful protesters; criticism of state policies forbidden; the formation of any organisation to campaign for social and political change outlawed; the leaders of any such assembly open to charges of sedition and treason; offences punishable by transportation or death by hanging; journalists and newspaper proprietors systematically imprisoned; parliament so unrepresentative that some large cities have no MP; elitism so endemic that only those of a certain class have the right to vote. If commenting on the behaviour of royalty today met the same restrictions as in Hazlitt's times, Wormwood Scrubs gaol in London would have many of the proprietors and journalists of the English press as permanent residents!

To describe the decades which straddle the 18th and 19th centuries as the Age of Romanticism is a misnomer. We might indulge ourselves in the great literary productions of the time and taste the freedom which these literary minds gave expression to, but it was also a time of tyranny, of religious discrimination, of severe restrictions on freedom of expression in the political domain, and of a draconian penal system. If we were dressed in rags with the stench of a convict ship in our nostrils and our feet bolted to the floor by a sadistic sea captain, and were on our way to Van Diemen's Land for seven years, our offence being the theft of a loaf of bread snatched to feed our starving child, what name would be on our lips to describe the times in which we lived?

Who among us finds the courage to speak out in these situations and under these circumstances, when to stand up incurs the risk of having a halter placed around our neck? We cannot begin to understand Hazlitt's political views if we are unable to place ourselves in his times. The England in which Hazlitt lived as a young man accepted the slave trade and he was 29 before it was officially abolished. It also pursued its perceived colonial rights to the continent of Australia and despite the fact that Australian Aboriginals had, as we now know, lived in the land for at least 40,000 and perhaps 60,000 years, the land mass was regarded a *terra nullius*, an empty space belonging to no one. Not until 1967 were the original inhabitants given the right to vote, by kind permission of a white referendum.

People with a passing knowledge of Hazlitt often know two things about him: one is the 'scandal' of *Liber Amoris* and the other his reputation for political invective, the famous Hazlitt spleen. Being better informed about *Liber Amoris* offers the possibility of a more balanced view. Becoming better educated about his politics will enable us to make a more balanced judgement.

Our education on issues of politics and history is often best begun in our own times. I am therefore not going to provide a lengthy account of the events of his time as such a task would require the writing of many books of history. Baker[3] covers the ground well, providing detailed background to Hazlitt's life and times. Instead, I wish to proceed on different lines which take us firmly into our own times. I will look at Hazlitt from the beginning of the 21st century, aware that we have left behind a hundred years distinguished by extraordinary brutality being inflicted by human beings on their own kind. Not only can the number of those killed be counted in tens of millions but we seem to invent ever newer weapons of destruction and a great variety of political systems designed to enslave and exterminate. We also live in a world distinguished by its gross inequalities. Do we want to listen to people like Hazlitt when the richest 50 million people on our planet, mostly in North America and Europe, have the same income as 2.7 billion poor people, and the richest 1 per cent have the same wealth as the poorest 57 per cent?[4] Perhaps we need all the help we can get if we are to pursue an interest in social justice and equality. It might be suggested that we need a greater knowledge to foster a more civilised world, but the experience of Germany and its creation of one of the worst systems of atrocities in human history ought to council us to be wary about the sort of knowledge we are talking about. Here a nation which had been the bastion of civilisation disintegrated into the most vile tyranny. What has Hazlitt got to offer? He offered these words to his contemporaries; how applicable are they to our times?

> We find indeed that the most blind and bigoted belief is the most dogmatical; and
> that those ages and nations which are the most ignorant, are the most intolerant
> of a shadow of difference from their grossest creeds (for having no evidence to

adduce in their favour, they cannot afford to have them called in question), and are the most bent on writing the proofs of their faith in the blood of their enemies.[5]

To understand Hazlitt's political radicalism we need to call to mind the social and political conditions sketched out in chapter 2 and now take a closer look at the state of the press in his day. In discussing *Liber Amoris* I gave examples of the personal abuse of Hazlitt in 1823 when the book was published. In chapter 2 I drew attention to the British government's sponsorship and use of the press to attack those who opposed its policies. The *Quarterly Review* and the *New Monthly Magazine* were avowed reactionary organs of the government and I quoted from the latter in describing the treatment of Hazlitt and Leigh Hunt and the personal abuse heaped on them. But the most infamous publication of the day was *Blackwoods*. This magazine was founded in Edinburgh in April 1817 by William Blackwood. It was set up to oppose the principles of journals like the *Edinburgh Review* to which Hazlitt regularly contributed. Reading the scurrilous abuse of Hazlitt by its reporters John Wilson and John Gibson Lockhart would leave us reeling and likely to regard the worst excesses of present-day tabloid journalism as mild and insipid. Wilson and Lockhart grouped Hazlitt, Hunt and Keats into what they called 'The Cockney School'. Not only were the members of this school to be castigated for their liberal politics but their right to compose poetry and write literature was considered an impertinence. They were seen to belong to an upstart class of society whose members ought to leave such lofty pursuits to their betters, especially those with a formal education in the Classics. Are we likely to read the following in our daily newspaper? 'The day is perhaps not far distant when the Charlatan shall be stripped to the naked skin, and made to swallow his own vile prescriptions'. Hazlitt had a clear, pale complexion but Lockhart coined the phrase 'pimpled Hazlitt' and referred to pimpled essays and pimpled criticism. He is described as a 'Slang-whanger', 'an angry buffoon, an unprincipled blunderer'. Wilson called him 'that wild blackbill Hazlitt. He is a mere quack, a mere bookmaker; one of the sort that lounge in third-rate book shops and write third-rate books.' 'A small fetid, blear-eyed pug steeped in ignorance and malice to his very ribald lips.' Commenting on Blackwood's treatment of Hazlitt, a critic in 1854 wrote:

> Wilson and Lockhart bent all their young power against a writer whom in their hearts they admired and from whom both learned much. The first twenty five volumes of Blackwood's Magazine are disgraced by incessant, furious and scurrilous attacks upon the person, private character, talents, and moral and religious principles of Hazlitt, which future ages shall regard with wonder and disgust.[6]

A person of radical political opinion is often defined as someone who is against the existing order, the status quo and is desirous of making major changes. He is classified as being against the government and against all authority. When Hazlitt's radicalism is spoken of he is sometimes presented as some hot-head anarchist against all authority and all government, temporal and spiritual. This is a grave calumny and a perpetuation of a prejudice against him when he was alive. What is often confused is his hatred of the abuse of privileged power with hatred of all in power. Hazlitt was no anarchist. Clarification of his politics hinges on an extension of the ideas I presented in previous chapters. Rather than seek to abolish authority he campaigned against a false authority, against the social and political equivalent of the pedestal occupier, against those who believed it was their divine right to take up permanent residence over the people and those who made their ascent by trampling on the lives and rights of their fellow men. What are the constituent parts that make up Hazlitt's good political authority and the particular 'radicalism' which he professed?

At the age of 15 he wrote to his mother about a visit while on holiday in Liverpool to a certain gentleman's house. 'He is a very rich man, but – the man who is a well-wisher to slavery, is always a slave himself. The King, who wishes to enslave all mankind, is a slave to ambition. The man who wishes to enslave all mankind for his king is himself a slave to his king.'[7]

We might term this a precocious opinion in a 15-year-old but we can see that it is not the adoption of a mere slogan, but evidence of a sophisticated understanding of the complicated dynamics of political positions. Hazlitt was soon (after the writing of this letter) to go to Hackney College, where he would be encouraged to think for himself. This independence of mind meant that Hazlitt sometimes found himself in a small minority. He was no politician nor a party man and could be equally critical of those on his own side of politics as he could of his opponents. He saw the simple chanting of slogans as unlikely to advance one's cause. One's position and one's arguments required clarification and consistency and he was not slow to point out the gaps in his own side's case. A good cause will not be advanced by false and deficient reasoning. Both truth and expediency demand consistency. Better to find your own weaknesses than have them exposed by your opponents.

In 1827 he wrote:

> I have inveighed all my life against the insolence of the Tories, and for this I have the authority both of the Whigs and reformers; but then I have occasionally spoken against the imbecility of the Whigs, and the extravagance of the reformers, and thus have brought all three on my back, though two out of the three regularly agree with all I say of the third party.[8]

His appreciation of how groups and sects and parties operate and his challenge to the faithful to always account for themselves and be aware of their proximity to hypocrisy meant that he was often a lone voice and not a very popular one at that. He exposed the zealots in whatever form they appeared, whatever garments they donned. He expressed these opinions in the essay 'On Party Spirit' when he wrote:

> We may be intolerant even in advocating the cause of toleration, and so bent on making proselytes to freethinking as to allow no one to think freely but ourselves. The most boundless liberality in appearance may amount in reality to the most monstrous ostracism of opinion – not condemning this or that tenet, or standing up for this or that sect or party, but in a supercilious superiority to all sects and parties alike. And prescribing, in one sweeping clause, all arts, sciences, opinions, and pursuits but one's own.[9]

Besides pointing to this phenomenon and calling it by what it was, Hazlitt also offers an explanation for it. He saw at work an idealisation of the self. We find someone to hate because we cannot tolerate our own imperfections. Due to an inability to acknowledge and accept the conflicts and contradictions within oneself, one finds another to attack. This can be a subtle move performed in a conscious belief that one is pursuing a good, but in truth it is a narcissistic self-righteousness, 'a foil to our self-love'. Hazlitt knew there was a constant danger within groups of constructing an idealised set of beliefs and in politics, where one side must never say anything good about the other, this type of splitting is encouraged. This tendency was an extremely dangerous one and required constant vigilance, the task of sentinel being one he often set himself.

The well-meaning apostle of reform, the pious pursuer of change, can turn out to be a dangerous beast so full of his own sense of perfection that he can soon justify the diminishment of civil rights and thus takes his first step on the road to tyranny. This form of patriotism is false, loud and noisy and ever ready to usurp the name of patriot from another. For this reason continual honest self-criticism is essential. Hazlitt was a radical in that he believed people were not made to fit in to existing society, because political and social institutions were historical constructs. They had evolved in time to serve the needs of men. His main problem with the institutions of his day was the simple fact that they had evolved to serve the needs of the few. Those who defended these institutions as sacred, who called upon an Almighty to confer a stamp of approval were protecting their own interests. Those who protected the status quo, by instilling fear of anarchy if the existing order changed, were also safeguarding their privileged position. In claiming that radical change always led to a reign of terror they were being highly selective in their reading of history as many revolutions were achieved without anarchy or terror. These people were erecting false gods. Hazlitt saw the belief in *Jus Divinium*, the Divine Right of Kings, as a false god and he was determined to dislodge it. To Hazlitt the social order was made for man, and not just some men, but all men. His god or his good was equality, it alone deserving of a place on high; it is the guiding light, the true star of liberty. The Rev. Malthus (1798) said the poor should not be fed because illness and famine were nature's ways of controlling the population; he argued that if the poor and the sick were kept alive the country would be over-populated and we would all starve, because there was a limit to the amount of food that could be produced. When Hazlitt's pen was unsheathed he demolished Malthus' reasoning,[10] but as he wrote he could see not only the starving poor but Malthus himself lobbying members of parliament to abolish Poor Law relief.

Hazlitt relished the pure pleasures of art and literature and in the quiet chambers of his mind fed on their nourishment. He also took delight in the doings of everyday life and thrived on skirmishes fought with gusto. As he moved from one to the other, from thinker to doer, he carried an energy with him. Each renewed the other. In thought he could contemplate the good; in action he upheld it. Thus great literature did not sit at a great distance resplendent on its throne. It stands side by side with life. Hazlitt was one of the rare writers who could sustain this productive relationship. Nor was he like some street fighter or disorientated soldier on the field of battle who reaches out for the first weapon to defend himself or to attack his enemies. The tools of his trade had been fashioned in the furnace of his own mind.

He also had a good teacher, a great expert in the field of power and its abuse, whose understanding of strength, of weakness and of courage is always available to enlighten us. In *Julius Caesar*, Shakespeare, speaking through Cassius, articulates the problem of the powerful leader becoming more powerful when met by a weak opposition. In the drama from beginning to end Cassius is full of hatred and resentment towards Caesar and determined to bring him down, but he allows himself and us this brief episode of tenderness towards him. It is as if he, for a moment, can look at a different side of things before he turns away again, and, as is often the case with Shakespeare, we have to catch hold of these passing insights before they vanish from our sight.

> And why should Caesar be a tyrant then?
> Poor man, I know he would not be a wolf
> But that he sees the Romans are but sheep.
> He were no lion were not Romans hinds.
> Those that with haste will make a mighty fire
> Begin it with weak straws
>
> *Julius Caesar* 1.3, 103–8

Cassius understands that weakness can provoke, and the tyrant climbs up to power because others let him walk on their backs. We find more of this in Shakespeare's creation of the character of Richard II. Shakespeare understood the necessity of a measured response in the face of powerful forces and individuals. Richard uses his authority in a wild and arbitrary way to banish Bolingbrook and Mowbray. This and his equally capricious recall of the latter, is a recipe for disaster. A threatening enemy if allowed free reign will wreak havoc. Richard's weakness, his inability and failure to use his authority wisely, his exposure of himself to Bolingbrook, is experienced by the other as a provocation. Hazlitt understood all these ramifications of power. He understood the consequences of fawning to power and was not afraid to wield his powerful pen with a mighty ferocity when faced with a formidable opponent. We see all the principles outlined in chapters 8–11 in operation in Hazlitt's political works. He did not fight for the sake of fighting. He wrote in 1806:

> It is no part of courage to fight, to show that you are not afraid of fighting. Calm steady courage does not distrust itself ... Firmness and moderation seemed to be only not incompatible with each other but that the one is a necessary consequence of the other. On the other hand, meaness and pride are nearly always allied together. In common life we should think that a readiness to seize the first occasion of quarrel shewed a man to be either a bully or a coward; it would seem as if he was afraid that by deferring his resentment he should either want courage or opportunity for showing it another time ... Yet the great excuse for our going into the war was that by yielding anything to the demands of the enemy, we should soon lose all power of resistance, and crouch in abject submission at his feet. This is not a proud confidence in ourselves, but the mean dread of our own pusillanimity and want of firmness. It was to suppose that we had no security for our firmness but in the heat of our passions and in the infliction of mutual injuries.[11]

If we are to understand his position we need to see further than the duel in progress, whether it was with Malthus, Gifford or *Blackwoods*. Those who have examined the blistering exchanges which Hazlitt engaged in and recoiled in shock, horror or condemnation, have turned away prematurely and missed the point that Hazlitt fought because he had a broader and deeper vision of life. He fought because he had to defend what needed defending. The larger picture was always in his mind. Basic human values required defending and upholding. To be silent was to be a slave and pointed to an abdication of principle, a betrayal of the belief in sympathetic identification. Are men born slaves or free? Are equal rights available to all? These remained his constant touchstone, the measuring tool he applied to every instance of social and political conflict.

This is the context in which his quarrel with Wordsworth and Coleridge needs to be understood. The French Revolution signalled the dawn of a new age for Hazlitt, Wordsworth and Coleridge – 'Bliss was it in that dawn to be alive, But to be young was very heaven', wrote Wordsworth. Hazlitt was as shocked as Wordsworth and Coleridge by such excesses as the Reign of Terror but he saw beyond and did not renounce the original principles because some people had become zealots in their pursuit of those ideals. Commenting on the disrespect shown to Louis XVI during his trial, Hazlitt wrote 'The treatment of the Dauphin is another of those abominations which shew the extent of the revolutionary reaction at this period, when, to express their contempt for the old system, men fancied that nothing but *slang* was decent, and that everything but outrage was affectation. This is that true *low-life* of democracy, which feeling no respect for anything, can only exalt one side by degrading the other, and can allow no merit in an adversary, lest it should outweigh its own meanness and want of it.' [12]

Hazlitt's stinging criticism of the Lake Poets did not begin until after 1815. In the face of the appalling social and political conditions that followed the Napoleonic Wars, the Lake Poets either sided with the establishment, engaged in esoteric speculation or remained silent on these issues. Leigh Hunt summed up Coleridge's detachment from the real world when he wrote that Coleridge 'would persuade a deist that he was a Christian, and an atheist that he believed in God: all which would be very good, if the world could get by it, and not remain stationary; but meanwhile, millions are wretched with having too little to eat, and thousands with having too much; and these subtleties are like people talking in their sleep, when they should be up and helping.' [13] This pushed Hazlitt into his most strident and incisive writings and what is often remembered is Hazlitt's activity and not Wordsworth and Coleridge's passiveness. These were the years of Peterloo and the years when heroes of the Napoleonic wars, some of whom having joined the new army of the two million paupers, turned to petty crimes and were led to the gallows at Tynburn or transported to New South Wales. As we read in chapter 2, Wordsworth campaigned for the exploitative landlord Lowther against the liberal lawyer Brougham, who had defended the Hunts. To Hazlitt it did not make sense that someone who championed freedom of the mind and of the human imaginative spirit in poetry could allow the same human freedom to be politically abused and denied. The artist cannot exempt himself from his human and social responsibilities. Hazlitt remains disturbing to those who like their literature and their politics placed at a respectable distance from each other. He saw the yawning split in British society. To the left a culture of creativity and great learning; to the right a primitive political barbarism. He constantly challenged this dichotomy, this hypocrisy, and he would always keep in his sights those individuals who actively justified these affairs of the state.

While Hazlitt never felt close to Wordsworth, he had a greater affinity with Coleridge and the break with him was all the more painful. Coleridge was to

Hazlitt the only person he knew who answered to the name of genius. They had both come from Unitarian stock, and Hazlitt saw in him the potential of a great leader of reform. 'He talked on for ever; and you wished him to talk on for ever.' Hazlitt was both deeply saddened and infuriated by this waste and often when you read him raging against Coleridge, he seems to be almost biting his tongue and holding on to his grief. To Hazlitt, Wordsworth and Coleridge had a moral responsibility to uphold true equality. In his mind an artist who lives by freedom of mind has a social responsibility and has no right to ignore the world around him. Silence or a failure to act is an offence, a sin of omission. The nature of this moral dilemma is captured in the scene in *Troilus and Cressida* when Patroclus is saying to Achilles that he cannot sit idly by and leave the fight to others:

> ACHILLES: I see my reputation is at stake
> My fame is shrewdly gored.
> PATROCLUS: O, then, beware;
> Those wounds heal ill that men do give themselves.
> Omission to do what is necessary
> Seals a commission to a blank of danger;
> And danger, like an ague, subtly taints
> Even then when we sit idly in the sun.
>
> Act 3.3, 225–232

To sit on the fence when vital human values are being destroyed is read as tacit agreement with, and support of, those attacking such values. It gives them a blank cheque. You give them your signature and they can write what they will. In passivity you inflict damage on yourself and, because you are inclined to say to yourself that you have done nothing, you are blind to the consequences of your inaction.

Hazlitt, taking his political opponents to account for their political change of mind, cannot be compared to an instance where in a modern democracy a person gives up membership of one political party to join another, a move from left to right or right to left. In such a case the person continues to espouse the same basic principles of democracy which both sides of the political spectrum uphold. Hazlitt believed that Wordsworth and Coleridge had renounced basic principles, they were apostates, they had relinquished the common ground upon which all who believed in freedom stand. Lose that and all is lost!

In contemporary history and politics we have seen the equivalent in Nelson Mandela's attitude, which avoided years of a bloody transition of power in South Africa. In his autobiography Mandela said that as a youth he learned an invaluable lesson. It was common to engage in stick fights with other young men. This was a game as well as an education in combat. He found he was good at it and often got the upper hand. He went on to say that he learned how important it was never to humiliate someone whom you have vanquished, because to do so can lay the seeds for an even more formidable enemy in the future. I doubt if he could have led the transformation of South Africa if he had not learned that lesson. Perhaps this defines the difference between a strong leader and a great statesman. Also if we move on from seeking justice to exacting revenge by humiliation we diminish ourselves and are lesser human beings for it.

Hazlitt fought with his mind and his pen and always with robustness. When the stakes were high and the values he treasured were in danger of extinction a pugilistic fierceness could possess him. So in the heat of the battle how are we to distinguish the avenger from the seeker of justice? With difficulty! Hazlitt fought with a force equal to his opponents. He matched them, word for word, blow for blow and he did not recoil from delivering his punches with splendid invective. In full flight he was a fierce and furious fighter. But, like Mandela, he saw no reason to humiliate his opponent, his eyes always looking beyond to the victory of principle. Without a vision, without a view of the basic principles involved, he knew that people fell back into a desire for revenge. Hazlitt knew life too well and he knew his Shakespeare too well to miss the point that when we pursue revenge we set ourselves on a path of self-destruction. We are then caught in a cycle of destruction perpetuated. We are blinded by our revenge and our humiliated opponent is being fashioned into a creature just like ourselves. Who can see an end to it?

***

In the final years of his life Hazlitt set himself the task of writing his *Life of Napoleon* and eventually produced a mammoth four-volume work. This is not an easy read and one might be surprised that this text came from the same pen as the familiar essayist. It is packed with relentless detail and only occasionally are we suddenly interrupted from our mechanical thumbing of the pages by passages which remind us of the writer we are familiar with. Hazlitt, it has been said, worshipped Napoleon, regarded him as a hero, and would hear no wrong spoken about him. His *Life of Napoleon* has been described by some as hagiography. What truth is there in all this? The question is important because if Hazlitt regarded Napoleon as some god that could do no wrong then this would point to a contradiction in his own thought.

Certainly in his own essays, and from stories related by his friends and others, he passionately defended Napoleon and had the greatest admiration for him. But is this idealisation and does it mean that he placed Napoleon beyond criticism? Hazlitt himself seemed to have an awareness of such questions being asked of him and attempted to answer his critics. In the *Life* he wrote, 'it is true, I admired the man; but what chiefly attached me to him, was his being, as he had been long ago designated, "the child and champion of Liberty"'.[14] To Hazlitt the greatest social and political evil was the *Jus Divinum,* and the most precious good: that mankind was born free. Napoleon was to him the man at the head of the dispossessed, an arm of steel, the protector of freedom and a thorn in the side of kings. 'He stood (and he alone stood) between them and their natural prey. He kept off that last indignity and wrong offered to the whole people (and through them to the world) of being handed over like a herd of cattle to a particular family, and chained to the foot of a legitimate throne.' As to Napoleon's faults, Hazlitt wrote, 'He did many things wrong and foolish; but they were individual acts, and recoiled upon the head of the doer. They stood upon the ground of their own merits, and could not urge in their vindication "the right divine of kings to govern wrong". They were not precedents, they were not exempt from public censure and opinion. They were not softened by prescription, nor screened by prejudice, nor sanctioned by superstition, nor rendered formidable by a principle that imposed them as obligations on all future generations: either they were State-necessities extorted by the circumstances of the time, or violent acts of the will that carried their own condemnation in their bosom.'[15]

Hazlitt presents Napoleon as acting out of necessity in extending war beyond France, claiming he was not a free agent, that all the crowns of Europe were in effect out to destroy the Republic because its very existence was an implied threat to their rule, and so he could take the war to them or await destruction. 'France was in a state of siege; a citadel in which Freedom had hoisted the flag of revolt against the claims of hereditary right; and that in the midst of distractions and convulsions consequent on the sentence of ban and anathema passed upon it by the rest of Europe for having engaged in this noble struggle, required a military dictator to repress internal treachery and headstrong factions and repel external force.'

Hazlitt looks at the line of Napoleon's critics. The English, he says, set the example of liberty to the world but would now stifle it. Other European monarchs had vested interests in crushing the Republic. The Jacobins 'made the tree of liberty spout nothing but blood', and 'its paper advocates reduced it to a theory'. None of these had any right to criticise. The only group who were entitled to call Napoleon to account were the true friends of liberty and these, among whom Hazlitt counted himself, chose to be silent for two reasons. First, they are so small and without any political power and would be unable to carry out any changes they desired; and second, they accepted that as the stakes were too high Napoleon took the 'reins of government and held them with a tight hand' because 'there was but one alternative between him, and that slavery, which kills both the bodies and the souls of men.'[16]

Hazlitt was, in effect, very accepting of Napoleon's excesses and essentially thought of him as a benevolent despot. While others in his day and in ours would be more inclined to regard Napoleon as a malevolent one, Hazlitt saw the times and circumstances as justifying a military dictatorship both to 'repress internal treachery and headstrong factions and repel external force.' While he allows certain criticism of Napoleon, it is rather patchy, and it is therefore a puzzle to understand how the freedom of his critical faculties, so evident in many other areas of his life, became restricted.

It is a serious mistake to gather all one's enemies in one group and place them in the same corner. If we do this, how do we distinguish between a Richard II and Richard III? The same crown sits on both heads but the heads are very different. The upstart, boyish, weak pretender with his brain in the clouds is very much unlike the treacherous psychopath. We treat them in similar fashion at our own peril. It is a further misjudgement to impose a silence on all those who differ from us. Our most virulent enemies may be intent upon our destruction, but unless we exercise caution in our judgements we shall soon create an axis of evil, elevating ourselves to the throng of archangels and consigning all dissenters to the realm of the damned.

Finally, what good are our friends to us if they remain silent in the face of our excesses? Does moving in the same direction, walking side-by-side with someone, demand of us that we never cast at them a sideward glance? It is a great disservice to anyone to support them mindlessly. To switch off our capacity to think, to confuse support with blind faith, is akin to removing the net which provides safety in the event of the wayward step. Pushing one person forward into a position of sole leadership and placing on their shoulders the burden of the world is an abdication of our responsibility, of our part in shaping the future. Is it any wonder that they are soon up on the pedestal and adorning themselves with the laurels of absolute power? In protesting that Napoleon achieved power solely on his own merit, and was therefore the champion of a meritocracy and a despiser of inherited power, Hazlitt must pass over Napoleon's wish to establish a dynasty, and his naming of his 3-year-old son as his successor in 1814. Such a move to establish a new elite family makes one suspicious that, having dismantled the building blocks of *Jus Divinum*, the fragments are put to use as the foundation stones of a new pedestal. To exploit Montaigne's wisdom, even the greatest of people who emerge into positions of power at epoch-shaping moments of history, and whose influence will shape the fate of millions, need to be reminded of the fact that, although they sit on a throne, the backside they sit on is similar in all respects to the one used by the poor beggar whose place of rest is no more than a humble patch of earth.

To address Hazlitt in this way may seem strange because this is knowledge he has given evidence of possessing, and we hear an echo in our heads – but he knows all this! However, the evidence suggests that in relation to Napoleon he lost it.

There is always a value in examining what Hazlitt has to say about himself and if we look again at what he wrote we may find part of an answer. His central statement explaining what attached him to Napoleon was 'his being, as he had been long ago designated, the child and champion of Liberty'. He seems to have embedded the *person* of Napoleon with the *principle* of liberty and joined the two so forcibly that he could not tell them apart. It is my suspicion that something similar to what happened with Sarah Walker happened with Napoleon; in both cases did he fly like Icarus too near the sun and slip and fall to the ground?

Perhaps it is instructive to return to *Liber Amoris* because we will find that in the story Napoleon makes an appearance and perhaps has more than the walk-on part which is usually attributed to him. As I related in chapter 6, a bronze statue of Napoleon figures strongly in two parts of the story. On one occasion when Sarah seems more distracted than usual Hazlitt teases out of her that she is thinking of an old lover. She tells him that the old lover bore a resemblance to Hazlitt's prized possession, the little statue of Napoleon which stands on his mantelpiece. Hazlitt is elated by this news thinking that if she could love someone like that he was in with a chance. He gives her the statue and she then comes to him and kisses him. At another point Hazlitt gets into a great rage with Sarah. 'I could bear it no longer. I gave way to all the fury of disappointed hope and jealous passion … I was still to be tantalised, tortured, made the cruel sport of one, for whom I would have sacrificed all. I tore the locket which contained her hair (and which I used to wear continually in my bosom, as the precious token of her dear regard) from my neck, and trampled it in pieces. I then dashed the little Buonaparte on the ground, and stamped upon it, as one of her instruments of mockery.'[17]

What would have happened had he separated the person from the principle? What could he do with the information that, while Napoleon was increasing the liberties of the Jews in one part of his empire, he was at the same time slaughtering the Spanish peasants who objected to his regime? Given Hazlitt's instinct to rise in defence of the down-trodden, was he wary of allowing his latent disappointments with Napoleon to rise in his breast out of a fear that, as with Sarah, he might be overcome with passion and his hero might end up in pieces?

One of the perennial struggles for all people as individuals and as members of their society and culture is with the tendency to erect gods (of one sort or another). If we are suddenly without leadership in our lives we cannot wait and we will melt down our good and good-enough objects to construct our golden calf. It is perhaps very difficult to escape our proneness to erect them. Even those which we have painstakingly dismantled have a tendency to attempt unconsciously a reconstruction of themselves in some outpost of our minds. A healthy state exists when we can move in and out of identification with an ideal. We can all get trapped and linger too long. There are times when Hazlitt needs to be reminded of his own words that 'the mind strikes out truth by collision, as steel strikes fire from the flint', and his protection of Napoleon from steely criticism blinded him from the truth that his leader in many instances simply replaced one form of slavery with another; and his inability to scrutinise Napoleon's vanity, affectation and narcissism, and its destructive effect on the course of history, deprived the world of what might have been one of the great classics of biographical endeavour, a first class *Life of Napoleon Buonaparte.*

Chapter 13

On the Love of Words

There is a method of trying periods on the ear, or weighing them with the scales of the breath, without any articulate sound. Authors, as they write, may be said to 'hear a sound so fine, there's nothing lives 'twixt it and silence.'[1]

The first impressions I received on reading *Table Talk* pointed to Hazlitt's love of words, the depth and breath of his thought, the relevance of his writings to our present time. Time has a meaning for him which goes beyond any ordinary conception of the term. His references to the past are often thought of as nostalgia and his preference for 'old books' are seen as an indication of a literary conservatism. Such simplistic summation by-passes the richness of what is contained in his sense of time.

Hazlitt's prose has been the subject of extensive comment for generations. The latest in a long list of excellent books has come from the pen of Tom Paulin. In *The Day Star of Liberty: William Hazlitt's Radical Style*, Paulin's poetical mind draws out the magic of Hazlitt's prose;[2] his investigation of Edmund Burke's influence on Hazlitt is second to none. In seeking to explore the issue which my chapter title suggests I will not attempt to replicate the work of others. My aim is therefore a modest one, to convey some sense of what I hear in Hazlitt's words. When I read and listen to him, sometimes reading out aloud, I am often aware of the sounds within the words. They can be so fine as to dissolve into nothingness. Sometimes the music of his language echoes the meaning he is trying to convey. At times the sounds can be like a gentle breeze among the leaves, or they can trot with a contentment and purpose, or resemble the incessant banging of a drum, or tear through the landscape of thought challenging and cleansing everything in their path.

In 1826 Hazlitt and his wife travelled through Europe and on their journey from Sardinia to Florence they encountered a problem when custom officials eyed their luggage with suspicion. This is how Hazlitt described the incident:

> I had two trunks. One contained books. When it was unlocked, it was as if the lid of Pandora's box flew open. There could not have been a more sudden start or expression of surprise, had it been filled with cartridge-paper or gunpowder. Books were the corrosive sublimate that eat out despotism and priest-craft – the artillery that battered down castle and dungeon-walls – the ferrets that ferreted out abuses – the lynx-eyed guardians that tore off disguises – the scales that weighed right and wrong – the thumping make-weight thrown into the balance that made force and fraud, the sword and the cowl, kick the beam – the dread

of knaves, the scoff of fools, the balm and the consolation of the human mind – the salt of the earth – the future rulers of the world! A box full of them was a contempt to the constituted Authorities; and the names of mine were taken down with great care and secrecy … my box was afterwards corded and *leaded* with equal gravity and politeness, and it was not till I arrived at Turin that I found it was a prisoner of state, and would be forwarded to me anywhere I choose to mention, out of his Sardinian Majesty's dominions. I was startled to find myself within the smooth polished grasp of legitimate power, without suspecting it; and was glad to recover my trunk at Florence, with no other inconvenience than the expense of its carriage across the country.[3]

As we observe the scene of Hazlitt's trunk-full of books being examined by officials and described by him we are provided with his explanation of the place of the written word in human affairs. Here the might of the pen over the sword is given a new expression, a new gusto. A great hater of humbug and prostituted intelligence, of inequality and the abuse of power, he could wield his pen like a mighty rapier with devastating consequences to his opponents. But if books had a place in war they also were essential to peace, 'the balm and the consolation of the human mind, the salt of the earth, the future rulers of the world'. When the distresses of the people are being addressed and fundamental human rights are being upheld Hazlitt, as we have seen in the previous chapter, leads the charge and is not open to negotiation. Much of the rest of life's business, however, calls forth a different approach.

I knew a student of English Literature who was required to read the Bible in seven days. By contrast my Professor of Scripture, a scholar of Hebrew, Greek, Aramaic and Latin, once spent an hour lecturing on St. John's Gospel and did not move beyond, 'In the beginning was the Word,'. If anyone reads the Bible in seven days, with no time to pause and savour, how will he know if a story has been told well or badly, how will he relish the poetry of the psalms, how can he feel the lamentations of a people torn from their native soil, how can he take time to sing the Songs of Solomon, in what historical corridors can he wrestle with the mysteries of death and life? The lecturer caught up in tiny circles of detective investigation delights in the unfolding of meaning but he runs the risk of talking to an ever-diminishing audience.

If in our approach to Hazlitt we have been leading with our logical minds it is time to remove such faculties from their ascendant position. Unless we can allow his words to flow over us, unless we can meander with him and follow his bearings, unless we suspend our daily sense of time's measurement and allow a transportation to be effected, there will be many places to which he invites us which we will pass by ignorant of their existence. In February 1818 John Keats became critical of Wordsworth for confusing poetry and philosophy. He articulated his thoughts in a letter to John Hamilton Reynolds:

But, for the sake of a few imaginative or domestic passages, are we to be bullied into a certain Philosophy engendered in the whims of an Egotist – Every man has his speculations, but every man does not brood and peacock over them till he makes a false coinage and deceives himself. Many a man can travel to the very bourne of Heaven, and yet want confidence to put down his half-seeing ... We hate poetry that has a palpable design upon us – and if we do not agree, seems to put its hand in its breeches pocket. Poetry should be great and unobtrusive, a thing which enters into one's soul, and does not startle it or amaze it with itself, but with its subject. How beautiful are the retired flowers! how would they lose their beauty were they to throng into the highway crying out, 'admire me I am a violet! dote upon me I am a primrose!' ... we need not be teased with grandeur and merit when we can have them uncontaminated and unobtrusive.[4]

Apart from this passage showing us how Keats not only shared Hazlitt's views of Wordsworth's egotism and affectation, but also his understanding of vanity, Keats is making the point that poetry is not philosophy. Poetry cannot be didactic. Poetry cannot forcibly insist on itself. Its power is in its truth and beauty, not in its politics.

Let us return to that cold, wet, comfortless day in January 1798. Some 25 years after first meeting Coleridge, Hazlitt sat down to record the events of those days in what some regard as his most famous essay, 'My First Acquaintance With Poets'. Coleridge had journeyed to Shrewsbury to preach by way of testing the waters as there was a vacancy for a Unitarian minister and, as was the practice in those days, both congregation and prospective preacher had the opportunity to meet and see what they thought of each other. As Hazlitt's father was the minister in the neighbouring town of Wem, both interest and etiquette required that Coleridge would be invited to the Hazlitt household. I suspect also that Coleridge might have heard that the Rev. Hazlitt was not the easiest man in the world to get on with and had an interest in checking him out. In all events Coleridge spent the Tuesday night after preaching at the Hazlitt home. Hazlitt passed much of the evening's conversation between his father and the poet-preacher in shy, silent observation; Coleridge would later remark that he spent most of the evening looking at the top of Hazlitt's head.

We may wonder where Margaret was during this visit. Was she part of the talk? Did she sit at table with Coleridge and the rest of the family? She was the same age as Coleridge. We might recall her feelings about Wem and how she described it as 'a little, disagreeable market town where we could not see the green fields and scarcely the blue vault of heaven'. She was not adverse to good company. America was to her a place of 'the most agreeable and worthy friends'. As to the company she habitually had to keep, we have read her referring to her 'evil destiny' to be forced to tolerate 'the dullness, petty jealousies, and cabals of a little country town'. Her experience of the evening with Coleridge, if she was present has not been recorded.

The next morning a letter arrived from a patron, Mr Josiah Wedgwood, son of the famous potter, offering Coleridge a significant annuity to enable him to devote himself to the study of poetry and philosophy. To the disappointment of his hosts, he accepted this offer. Before leaving, Coleridge offered the young William an invitation to visit him at his home in Nether Stowey in Somerset some weeks hence. Filled with delight and perhaps unable to let his new-found inspiration depart easily, Hazlitt walked with Coleridge for six miles on his return journey. Much was talked about. Hazlitt now had the great man to himself and revelled in the opportunity. The forceps which Coleridge would speak of were, however, much in evidence and Hazlitt's conversation very much unlike a game of nine-pins. The subject of the natural disinterestedness of the human mind came up. Hazlitt takes up the story:

> I tried to explain my view of it to Coleridge, who listened with great willingness, but I did not succeed in making myself understood. I sat down to the task shortly afterwards for the twentieth time, got new pens and paper, determined to make clear work of it, wrote a few meagre sentences in the skeleton-style of a mathematical demonstration, stopped half-way down the second page; and after trying in vain to pump up any words, images, notions, apprehensions, facts or observations, from that gulf of abstraction in which I had plunged myself for four or five years preceding, gave up the attempt as labour in vain, and shed tears of helpless despondency on the blank unfinished paper.[5]

The natural disinterestedness of the human mind would form the foundation of Hazlitt's *Essay* which would eventually become his first published work in 1805. But relief from his pain and despondency would not arrive for some time and a few years later he would still complain of his inadequacy with words. The *Essay* had advanced no more than eight pages from eight years' work. Eventually he would be delivered of it but he would still serve a long apprenticeship before his own thoughts and ideas could emerge from him with fluency and ease. His description of himself as 'dumb, inarticulate, helpless, like a worm by the wayside' is therefore a true reflection on how he felt about his abilities at the time. He became the abridger and editor of other men's work and would write his *Grammar of the English Language* but we can see in his work as editor and his social and political publications of the time an emerging ability to express himself in the written word.

However there is another aspect to this dumbness which deserves some consideration. In chapter 8 I compared the thinking through of the content of the *Essay* to the sinking of a deep well in his mind from which he would regularly draw sustenance. Twelve months after meeting Coleridge and Wordsworth he 'met' Titian, Raphael, Guido, Domenichino and Caracci. 'I saw the soul speaking in the face … these mighty works and dreaded names that spoke to me in the eternal silence of thought.'[6]

In 1823 he looked back at his earlier struggles to find words and wrote 'I can write fast enough now. Am I better than I was then? Oh no! One truth discovered, one pang of regret at not being able to express it, is better than all the fluency and flippancy in the world. Would that I could go back to what I then was! Why can we not revive past times as we can revisit old places?'[7]

This points to a position more complex than a simple mastery of an inhibition where a victory is achieved and one passes on forever from one's difficulty. Hazlitt's psychology is more all-encompassing. We never jettison any part of our past into some black hole of psychic space. Everything we have been remains a part of our self. Rather than extinguishing our painful helplessness we acquire an additional skill in pleasurable helpfulness. Richard Steele understood this internal state of affairs. His strength and his weakness sat side by side within him. Anxiety could be 'sweet'. He could 'enjoy' the memory of past afflictions. He had put his suffering to good use. His weakness could be used as a strength. His capacity to understand others was enlarged and he could 'the better indulge myself in the softness of humanity'. The issue I deal with here could also be illustrated by the incident of an actor who broke down crying during rehearsals because the part he had to play had suddenly presented him with a painful and unresolved childhood trauma. A thoughtful director believed that proper attention there and then enabled a recovery. The actor was seen to have soon resolved his struggle and could get on with playing the part. In one sense this is true and a genuine advance is made. Perhaps great actors never quite leave such painful experiences behind, and at moments of supreme performance they are poised on a knife edge, a hair's breath from fear as they boldly move on. In this sense Hazlitt's dumbness was never far away and he grew not to be afraid of it. When he wrote about 'that undisturbed silence of the heart which alone is perfect eloquence' I believe he was addressing a way in which dumbness had undergone a transformation. As a painter he had learnt that the dumb can speak. The fear and apprehension which has accompanied an inhibition had been removed. Now when he needed to he could freely reside within it, even at times wish to be divested of all the need for talk and writing – a sort of dreaming existence is the best. My mind to me a kingdom is. And still my mind forbids to crave words and expression. The Hazlitt here is the one who wished he could be capable of painting one masterpiece and would swap all his words for such an achievement. It is the same Hazlitt who said that the study of history must go beyond the acquisition of details, facts and events. If we are to know people from bygone days we need to look them in the face, hence a study of portraiture had an indispensable place in his scheme of things. I think Hazlitt's dumbness was something he must have learned not to fight, nor battle with. He could hear a sound so fine there nothing lives 'twixt it and silence.

In his essay 'The Difference between Writing and Speaking', Hazlitt provides us with a window through which we can look into the mind of the writer:

> There are persons who in society, in public intercourse, feel no excitement,
>
>   'Dull as the lake that slumbers in the storm,'
>
> but who, when left alone, can lash themselves into a foam. They are never less alone than when alone. Mount them on a dinner-table, and they have nothing to say; shut them up in a room by themselves, and they are inspired. They are 'made fierce with dark keeping.' In revenge for being tongue-tied, a torrent of words flows from their pens, and the storm which was so long collecting comes down apace. It never rains but it pours. Is not this strange, unaccountable? Not at all so. They have a real interest, a real knowledge of the subject, and they cannot summon up all that interest, or bring all that knowledge to bear, while they have anything else to attend to. Till they can do justice to the feeling they have, they can do nothing. For this they look into their own minds, not in the faces of a gaping multitude. What they would say (if they could) does not lie at the orifices of the mouth ready for delivery, but is wrapped in the folds of the heart and registered in the chambers of the brain. In the sacred cause of truth that stirs them, they would put their whole strength, their whole being into requisition; and as it implies a greater effort to drag their words and ideas from their lurking places, so there is no end when they are once set in motion. The whole of a man's thoughts and feelings cannot lie on the surface, made up for use; but the whole must be a greater quantity, a mightier power, if they could be got at, layer under layer, and brought into play by the levers of imagination and reflection. Such a person sees farther and feels deeper than most others. He plucks up an argument by the roots, he tears out the very heart of his subject. He has more pride in conquering the difficulties of a question, than vanity in courting the favour of an audience. He wishes to satisfy himself before he pretends to enlighten the public. He takes an interest in things in the abstract more than by common consent. Nature is his mistress truth his idol. The contemplation of a pure idea is the ruling passion of his breast. The intervention of other people's notions, the being the immediate object of their censure or their praise, puts him out. What will tell, what will produce an effect, he cares little about; and therefore he produces the greatest. The personal is to him an impertinence; so he conceals himself and writes. Solitude 'becomes his glittering bride and airy thoughts his children'.[8]

Hazlitt is here introducing us to the various chambers of his own mind – those secret springs of action. What we can also observe is a certain fearlessness in such a writer. He has little interest in constantly looking at the gaping multitude to see if he is being well received or not. We are directed to the freedom which comes from an absence of vanity and affectation. This fearlessness is the freedom which is the domain of those who possess independence of mind.

Tasmanian writer Richard Flanagan takes us to a similar place. Commenting on the necessity to write he said, 'Words, words, words – I'd build a bonfire with the bastards if it would illuminate one moment of truth'. Pile up a heap of words. Set them on fire. We need their heat, their force, their power. This image is a dramatic one. A bonfire of words for one moment of truth! Hazlitt's imagery in the passage above is equally dramatic. The writer when locked away is unleashed. What has been gathering within him has broken loose. From the inner depths, the folds of the heart and the chambers of the brain come forth eruptions. Words and ideas take up a shape and emerge from their lurking places, and a mighty power is set in motion. The bonfire blazes. There is a volcanic torrent of words. The digging pen sets the world ablaze. Earth, air, fire and water – all the ancient elements of the world are in turmoil. The writer is plucking up an argument from its roots, tearing out the heart of a subject.

One could be led by all this display of elemental forces to think that the truth can only be seen and grasped and known by some grand realisation, a loud lashing by furious storms, a bolt from the blue, a Pauline conversion. But herein lies a curiosity. Most emotional truths that we grasp about ourselves exist in a delicate state. They are refined and not gross. They live in or near the borders of silence. They do not easily lend themselves to amplified expression. They need to be listened to with a wise passiveness through placing oneself in the borderland where you hear fine sounds and, perhaps if we cannot listen to our own heartbeat we will not be able to hear what is on offer. As we have already seen, Hazlitt believed that creativity acts 'not to show us what has never been seen but to point out what is before our eyes and under our feet'. The apprehending of some such important truth can lead to external changes, to alterations in our behaviour which could well be described as dramatic. There can be a tendency for this aspect of change to be the part which stands out and which attracts attention. The silent is swamped by the spoken. Perhaps it is more accurate to identify three stages: first, the turmoil and torment which Hazlitt describes as preceding the realization; second, that moment in the eternal silence of thought; and last, the manifest consequences.

***

If Hazlitt's love of words is in the ascendancy we may see him looking fondly at Steele, eyeing Montaigne, Shakespeare and others with a face full of gratitude. Speaking of the great works of literature he said, 'But to the works themselves, "worthy of all acceptation," and to the feelings they have always excited in me since I could distinguish a meaning in language, nothing shall ever prevent me from looking back with gratitude and triumph. To have lived in the cultivation of an intimacy with such works, and to have familiarly relished such names, is not to have lived quite in vain.' Describing his original experience on reading his old favourite writers he said, 'To what nameless ideas did they give rise, – with what airy delights I filled up the outline, as I hung in silence over the page! – Let me still recall them, that they may breathe fresh life into me, and that I may live that birthday of thought and romantic pleasure over again! Talk of the ideal ! This is the only true ideal – the heavenly tints of Fancy reflected in the bubbles that float upon the spring-tide of human life.' Not only did Hazlitt make great use of and have a great love of creating his own mix of words but he relished the words of others. In his essay 'On Reading Old Books'[9] he describes the formative influence of his earliest reading and how the first books which capture our imagination are 'links in the chain of our conscious being. They bind together the different scattered divisions of our personal identity. They are landmarks and guides in our journey through life. They are pegs and loops on which we can hang up, or from which we can take down, at pleasure, the wardrobe of a moral imagination, the relics of our best affections, the tokens and records of our happiest hours.' To open such an old book transported him back in time to how he felt when he first read it. Sometimes he found that all that was needed was the sight of the volume on the library shelf and 'twenty years are struck off the list, and I am a child again'. Sometimes the transportation is a complete one and he finds 'not only are the old ideas of the contents of the work brought back to my mind in all their vividness, but the old associations of the faces and persons of those I then knew, as they were in their life-time – the place where I sat to read the volume, the day when I got it, the feeling of the air, the fields, the sky – return, and all my early impressions with them'.

Chapter 14

A Compass of Soul

Many men set their minds only on trifles, and have not the compass of soul to take an interest in anything truly great and important beyond forms and minutiae.[1]

In his essay on 'The Difference between Writing and Speaking' Hazlitt invited us into the room of the solitary writer, and at the same time invited us into the inner recesses of his own mind. What are the truly great and important things which he asks us to look at with him? He calls them 'the sacred cause of truth' and wrote with an awareness that nature was his 'mistress truth his idol.' Nature as we have seen is more than the world of trees and mountains, but includes human nature. Here lie the great truths and here we see Hazlitt the philosopher, working in secret, concerned with general moral and spiritual issues. As Roy Park[2] has emphasised, Hazlitt sought to protect fundamental human values because he saw them as vital to civilised living.

A mind which is set on trifles and which cannot see beyond forms and minutiae is unable to detect these important truths. A mind which is focused on the trifle of human behaviour has no capacity to look beyond, has no compass to guide it to the inner world. It is preoccupied with patterns of action; it skims the surface and never pauses to search for what might be below its feet. Hazlitt believed that 'the whole of a man's thought and feeling cannot lie on the surface, made up for use' and the necessary words 'do not lie at the orifice of the mouth ready for delivery'. One must delve into the unconscious, into the dark recesses, into the inner regions of one's self.

The reflection which Hazlitt described cannot be simply labelled philosophical introspection in the ordinary sense of the term. It is not just the thoughts which are 'registered in the chambers of the brain' but also that which 'is wrapped in the folds of the heart'. A man needs to be honest about what he thinks and about what he experiences and feels. His emotional truth is as sacred as his rational and intellectual truth. Here again we see how the *Essay* found its way into his popular essays and how concrete, lived experience has become infused with a depth of thought. As we sit in Hazlitt's room we will hear him say that his written work is 'the thoughts of a metaphysician expressed by a painter'.

If we listen we will hear Hazlitt telling us about his method of reflection. It is not easy to describe because it is not a simple logical mind at work. Like Keats' nightingale who sings with 'full throated ease' it has a relaxed determination or, as Keats would describe in his letters, 'a diligent indolence'. Hazlitt tells us that he uses 'the levers of imagination and reflection'. Having allowed a truth to come within his hands, having received it with patience, we can see him shifting into another gear. He is plucking an argument by its roots and tearing out the very heart of his subject, great effort being employed to drag the ideas, and their words, from their lurking places. Here is Hazlitt digging with his pen, (like Heaney), strenuously unearthing the solid thought. If Hazlitt seems to have grown in size and if we find ourselves in awe of what is taking place, it is because there is indeed an awesome event in progress. Here we have 'mind' and 'heart' working together; we have conscious and unconscious living in partnership. The nature of this partnership as Hazlitt saw it is significant and it points to my assertion in chapter 1 that Hazlitt was a psychoanalytically-minded man, aware that much of life lies beyond our conscious control. Mutual respect must characterise the relationship between these two parts of the self. There is no master and slave. One is not 'above' the other and cannot claim pride of place. If condescension or inferiority is introduced an imbalance occurs. If the language of each is not listened to by the other, communication breaks down.

Another way of looking at this marriage of mind and heart, of conscious and unconscious, of imagination and reflection, is to explore the interplay between the conception of a piece of art and its subsequent creation. Charles Morgan identified the creative moment as the time of impregnation. This he distinguished from the making of the picture, the poem, the piece of music or the essay, which he calls 'the harvesting of the original truth'. This is how he described it:

> The authentic experience of the artist is not by him to be mistaken. It may be isolated and final, like the falling of seed from which a plant springs, or, like rain, be continually renewed upon him. In each case his joy of it, ordinarily called creative, is a receptive joy; there is a close analogy in the feminine act of love, which is at once fierce and peaceful, a fulfilment and an initiation. The making of the work of art – the harvesting of the original truth – is a less intense experience than the conceiving of it, for in the moments of conception, and perhaps at no other time, the artist fully apprehends his gods and sees with his own eyes their reality. The power to be impregnated, and not the writing of poems, the painting of pictures, or the composition of music, is the essence of art, the being an artist.[3]

The sum of impregnation and of harvesting is greater than their individual parts. Hazlitt's gusto celebrates the fermentation of this union. This whole he says 'must be a greater quantity, a mightier power'. Here we see the secret of Hazlitt's fierce independence of mind, the Hazlitt who has told us that he has brooded over his ideas until they became a type of substance in his brain. This is the freedom which is only possible when vanity has been put aside, when he does not court the favour of the audience.

Hazlitt is not just protecting certain values which he saw as necessary for civilised life. He is also protecting the freedom to have a life of the imagination, a life of the spirit. These are the gateways to the actual values. You cannot allow one to suppress the other. Freedom is not a matter of forms and minutiae, it is not a matter of laws. Man has the right to freedom of thought and freedom of expression. When all of these are threatened what else can be the retort but obstinacy, unbendingness and incorrigibility?

Each individual human life has within it the potential for greatness, its vast quantity of experience providing continual material for reflection. This greatness may not manifest itself in activity of which the world takes notice. To live a life where one can say 'I have never given the lie to my own soul' points to the nature of the greatness being addressed. Hazlitt takes us to the broad canvas of a human life in his essay 'On the Past and Future':

> Indeed it would be easy to show that it is the very extent of human life, the infinite number of things contained in it, its contradictory and fluctuating interests, the transition from one situation to another, the hours, months, years spent in one fond pursuit after another; that it is, in a word, the length of our common journey and the quantity of events crowded into it, that, baffling the grasp of our actual perception, make it slide from our memory, and dwindle into nothing in its own perspective. It is too mighty for us, and we say it is nothing! It is a speck in our fancy, and yet what canvas would be big enough to hold its striking groups, its endless subjects! It is light as vanity, and yet if all its weary moments, if all its head and heart aches were compressed into one, what fortitude would not be overwhelmed with the blow! What a huge heap, a 'huge, dumb heap,' of wishes, thoughts, feelings, anxious cares, soothing hopes, loves, joys, friendships, it is composed of! How many ideas and trains of sentiment, long and deep and intense, often pass through the mind in only one day's thinking or reading, for instance! How many such days are there in a year, how many years in a long life, still occupied with something interesting, still recalling some old impression, still recurring to some difficult question and making progress in it, every step accompanied with a sense of power, and every moment conscious of 'the high endeavour or the glad success'; for the mind seizes only on that which keeps it employed, and is wound up to a certain pitch of pleasurable excitement or lively solicitude, by the necessity of its own nature.[4]

This volume of experience is awaiting every thinking person. For some it will simply pass by, their thoughts and feelings meeting no mind to hold them. Others remember, recall, return to difficult questions and by doing so develop a sense of power. Hazlitt is again echoing Richard Dyer – 'My mind to me a kingdom is' – and he asserts the inherent goodness of thoughtfulness and a basic trust in the action of his mind in its work when he says that 'the mind seizes only on that which keeps it employed'. This good pursuit is also a pleasurable one and can reach 'a certain pitch of pleasurable excitement or lively solicitude, by the necessity of its own nature'.

In his book *William Hazlitt: Critic of Power*, John Kinnaird addressed problems inherent in approaching works of literature. In highlighting the inability and unwillingness to judge and to damn, he points to a preoccupation with the ideas that surround such phrases as 'interpret a writer', 'looking for structure and convention', 'placing something in a tradition', examining 'the autonomy of a work of art'. He believes that a fascination with words such as 'irony' and 'paradox' hold sway because of an unwillingness to put a person's character on the line.

Like Kinnaird, Hazlitt saw the creation of elaborate 'systems' of analysis as diversions where a preoccupation with minutiae and trifles and forms become a substitute for a compass of soul. A compass of soul leads us intuitively beyond forms, and if these faculties are to operate effectively in us there is a need to retain a certain childlike innocence, a natural trust that our inner nature will guide us to what we seek. We can turn again to Charles Morgan whose eloquence and accuracy on the operation of these qualities in the child and in the artist are hard to surpass.

> Have you ever watched a child, in the full activity of childhood, halt as though an invisible hand had touched his shoulder, and stare? I remember such occasions in my own childhood, and in my manhood also, when a thing seen, which a moment ago was one of many and of no particular significance, has become singular, has separated itself from the stream of consciousness, and has become not an object but a source. What is the child staring at? Not at the flower or the drop of water or the face. The thing seen, which ordinarily halts our observation, has become not a wall but a window. The opaque has become the serene; he is looking through it, through the disparate appearances of life, which we falsely call reality, towards the origin of that light by which all things are seen. What awes the child is not that he has arrived at an intellectual understanding of the order of things but that he has perceived that there is an order of things … An artist is a child who stares, not at the imprisoning walls of life, but outward through the window.[5]

The invisible hand that touches the shoulder is this compass of soul. It takes you beyond what is in front of your face. It is the seeing of a harmony among the various disparate objects in view. It is a transformation because it uses the new understanding with creative imagination. The harmony is not merely an additional object to be placed alongside the previous ones. It becomes a window not a wall. It thus transforms everything in its line of sight. But there is more. The mind which sees is itself transformed and has acquired the ability to stare. It is now characterised by serenity. A great work of art stimulates not just a feeling of beauty but it takes a person beyond, and through awakening the aesthetic passion, leads on to an appreciation of the essence of what is beautiful. It is not merely an agent of utility; it opens a window to the world of beauty.

While the artist needs to be a child and acquire or regain a sense of awe, he does not thereby establish sole and exclusive rights in this regard. To be a true artist he must have this capacity, but all human beings have the opportunity to see like a child sees. They have all been children. Too often, perhaps, they have been expected to outgrow this way of seeing, this way of being, as if maturity implies the subjugation of such qualities. Invisible hands, like Santa Claus don't exist anymore!

Throughout all of Hazlitt's writing we find this distinction being drawn between the person who is dominated by his head and the one who can trust his heart. One instance is when he compares the performances of two singers, Madame Pasta (Giuditta Pasta 1798–1865) and Mademoiselle Mars (Anne Francoise Boutet-Mouvel 1779–1847). Of the latter he wrote:

> When she speaks, she articulates with perfect clearness and propriety, but it is the facility of a singer executing a difficult passage. The case is that of habit, not of nature … Her acting is an inimitable study or consummate rehearsal of the part as preparatory performance: she hardly yet appears to have assumed the character … if Mademoiselle Mars has to smile, a slight and evanescent expression of pleasure passes across the surface of her face, twinkles in her eyelids, dimples her chin, compresses her lips, and plays on each feature.[6]

This he compares to Madame Pasta. She:

> gives herself entirely up to the impression of the part, loses her power over herself, is led away by her feelings either to an expression of stupor or of artless joy, borrows beauty from deformity, charms unconsciously, and is transformed into the very being she represents … when Madame Pasta smiles, a beam of joy seems to have struck upon her heart, and to irradiate her countenance. Her whole face is bathed and melted in expression … when she speaks it is in music.[7]

He is attributing to Madame Pasta a greater compass of soul. She can be like a child and trust her intuition to guide her. She has acquired a certain power of expression which occurs spontaneously, naturally. But if we remember Hazlitt's distinction between talent and genius it is not simply a matter of free expression, a triumph of the laissez-faire. Hazlitt's author in his room has truth as his idol. 'The personal is to him an impertinence: so he conceals himself and writes.' Mademoiselle Mars seems to be playing unduly to the audience, courting their favour. Who is she singing to? Perhaps the distinction between the good and the great in the performing arts, (aside from their inherent skill and artistic ability), is whether one sees beyond the audience. Is there a greater good to which the performance is bearing witness? Does the part and the playing of it say something universal and does the player, while mindful of the audience also play to that greater good? I sometimes wonder if the incidence of stage fright among the experienced and accomplished results from this loss of vision. The audience has become the god; the artist has lost track of the good; their compass of soul has lost its bearings.

One of Hazlitt's great attractions is his ability to move into different states of mind. I am not here referring to the variety of moods within which he found himself and from which he honestly wrote. Rather I point to the different classes of mind within which he could take up position. He could be the philosopher, the painter, the plain speaker. To be able to speak from these positions successfully requires an awareness of the boundaries of different orders of discourse. Hazlitt believed it was very important not to take things beyond the limits we are capable of, and if something is doubtful, why should it not be left so. He said that:

> It cannot be expected that abstract truths or profound observations should ever be placed in the same strong and dazzling points of view as natural objects and more matters of fact. It is enough if they receive a reflex and borrowed lustre, like that which cheers the first dawn of morning, where the effect of surprise and novelty gilds every object, and the joy of beholding another world gradually emerging out of the gloom of night, 'a new creation rescued from his reign,' fills the mind with a sober rapture.

That he could enjoy the contemplation of subtle ideas and at the same time poke fun at his temptation to bide his time within them and forget about the daily practicalities is shown by a story he told at the end of his lectures on philosophy:

> We feel that some apology is necessary for having thus plunged our readers all at once into the middle of metaphysics. If it should be asked what use such studies are of, we might answer with Hume, *perhaps of none, except that there are certain persons who find more entertainment in them than in any other.* An account of this matter, with which we were amused ourselves, and which may therefore amuse others, we met with some time ago in a metaphysical allegory, which begins in this manner: 'In the depth of a forest, in the kingdom of Indostan, lived a monkey, who, before his last step of transmigration, had occupied a human tenement. He had been a Bramin, skilful in theology, and in all abstruse

learning. He was wont to hold in admiration the ways of nature, and delighted to penetrate the mysteries in which she was enrobed; but in pursuing the footsteps of philosophy, he wandered too far from the abode of the social Virtues. In order to pursue his studies, he had retired to a cave on the banks of the Jumna. There he forgot society, and neglected ablution; and therefore his soul was degraded to a condition below humanity. So inveterate were the habits which he had contracted in his human state, that his spirit was still influenced by his passion for abstruse study. He sojourned in this wood from youth to age, regardless of everything, save cocoa-nuts and metaphysics.' For our own part, we should be content to pass our time much in the same manner as this learned savage, if we could only find a substitute for his cocoa-nuts! We do not, however, wish to recommend the same pursuit to others, nor to dissuade them from it. It has its pleasures and its pains – its successes and its disappointments, it is neither quite so sublime nor quite so uninteresting as it is sometimes represented. The worst is, that much thought on difficult subjects tends, after a certain time, to destroy the natural gaiety and dancing spirits; it deadens the elastic force of the mind, weighs upon the heart, and makes us insensible to the common enjoyments and pursuits of life.[8]

***

Luckily for us Hazlitt was unable to provide himself with a substitute for coconuts and through his pen applied his fine mind and allowed the compass of his soul to attend to great and important things to the benefit of all who have inherited his writings. To give an instance of how his mind worked, I will turn to his fourth lecture of the series on the dramatic literature of the Age of Elizabeth. While displaying the weightiness of his thoughts, it also illustrates the way his mind can turn from one aspect of the subject to another. Let us examine what he said in the first ten minutes of this lecture which occupies a little over three pages of text.

He examined the literary partnership of the Elizabethan playwrights Francis Beaumont (1584–1616) and John Fletcher (1579–1625). They were contemporaries of Shakespeare and over a ten year period between 1606 and 1616 they collaborated on many plays and poems. Fletcher may have collaborated with Shakespeare in the writing of *Henry VIII* and *The Two Noble Kinsmen*. Hazlitt describes Beaumont and Fletcher as lyrical poets of the highest order. He adds that in his opinion 'they are dramatic poets of the second class, in point of knowledge, variety, vivacity, and effect; there is hardly a passion, character, or situation, which they have not touched in their devious range, and whatever they touched they adorned with some new grace or striking feature ... in comic wit and spirit, they are scarcely surpassed by any writers of their age.'[9]

This is praise indeed and some critics might be happy to leave it at that. But the phrase 'their devious range' might have alerted us to the fact that he would have more to say. He marks out their serious poetry for more extensive comment. This he says stimulates more than it gratifies and leaves the mind in a certain sense exhausted and unsatisfied. 'Everything', he says, 'seems in a state of fermentation and effervescence, and not to have settled and found its centre in their minds.'

The word nature keeps cropping up and needs some elaboration if we are to grasp what Hazlitt is on about. When he is speaking about 'nature' here what he is pointing to is the necessity for symmetry of character. If an artist of whatever kind sets out to depict human nature, in some dramatic form, he must first of all understand that nature. He must be a keen and accurate observer. He needs to have an eye for how people are in themselves. Whatever faculties he uses to do this, whether they operate intuitively or scientifically, the aim is the same. If the artist's faculties are not operating well, if his capacities to see others as they are in themselves are limited or diminished or have never developed, the vacancy will be filled by imposition. This imposition is another way of talking about projection. Hazlitt draws the important distinction between a projective imposition that occurs within a process of sympathetic identification guided by a disinterestedness, and one which does not. Without disinterestedness, affectation and vanity fill the vacancy and the artist has become more pre-occupied with a display of self rather than using his ability to paint a picture of the other. When Hazlitt says of Beaumont and Fletcher that 'they do not wait nature's time, or work out her materials patiently and faithfully, but try to anticipate her, and so far defeat themselves,' he is highlighting both a lack of receptivity and a lack of knowledge. It has not settled and found its centre in their minds. Hazlitt's point is that if we try to control nature we not only end up failing but we deceive and diminish ourselves. If we go for display rather than substance, if we seek praise rather than the truth, everything we produce is short-lived and we are required to answer to the clamour for more excitement. One's taste has become corrupted and impaired. 'Their subject becomes their master', said Hazlitt.

To illustrate his points, Hazlitt describes Beaumont and Fletcher as pitching their characters in too high a key, and with all the prodigality of youth, with richness running riot, their beauty dissolves in its own sweetness. He gathers in his sense of their strengths and weaknesses with the following. 'Their productions shoot up in haste, but bear the marks of precocity and premature decay. Or they are two goodly trees, the stateliest of the forest, crowned with blossoms, and with the verdure springing at their feet; but they do not strike their roots far enough into the ground, and the fruit can hardly ripen for the flowers!'[10]

In their characterisations Hazlitt senses that something is out of place and the parts of the character do not hang together. Their proportions do not fit, their colours do not match. This is similar to the notion of 'keeping' in painting.

Instead of a character being allowed to grow, to build itself up, to evolve at a natural pace, there is a forced and artificial construction of a person.

Returning to his text we can see that Hazlitt is taking up the relevance of morality. Before we get to the end of the third page he will be talking about the splitting of the mind, and we might be forgiven the passing thought that Fairbairn had wandered across the page! 'The peccant humours of the body or the mind break out in different ways,' he will tell us. Our two writers, Beaumont and Fletcher, he says are not 'safe teachers of morality'. If this all seems like a change of direction, a wild swing of the compass, then we need to clarify something fundamental about Hazlitt's thought. What seems to be a small step will, on closer examination, prove to be a large bridge by which he joins up and makes solid links in his mind. The moral problem follows on from the faults which he has itemised. Because in their construction of characters they manufacture artificial 'people', they cannot be relied upon to explain comprehensively the nature of dealings between people or dealings within individuals. 'There is', says Hazlitt, 'a too frequent mixture of voluptuous softness or effeminacy of character with horror in the subjects, a conscious weakness (I can hardly think it wantonness) of moral constitution struggling with wilful and violent situations, like the tender wings of the moth, attracted to the flame that dazzles and consumes.' Hazlitt understands that many conflicts within the person are unconscious. The person or the 'character' is seldom sitting there weighing up the dilemma as on a scale. His life seesaws as he lives through his struggles, and emotionally he is pulled this way and that. This is Hazlitt as the depth psychologist who understands the complexity of the mind. The good artist successfully dramatises this complexity and this inner conflict, and he does not make it into his own play-thing. Beaumont and Fletcher make a play-thing of this issue. 'In the hey-day of their youthful ardour, and the intoxication of their animal spirits, they take a perverse delight in tearing up some rooted sentiment, to make a mawkish lamentation over it; and fondly and gratuitously cast the seeds of crimes into forbidden grounds, to see how they will shoot up and vegetate into luxuriance, to catch the eye of fancy.'[11] They make up people and play about with them but Hazlitt is saying that this is a serious business. Artistic licence is not a free-for-all. 'They seem to regard the decomposition of the common affections, and the dissolution of the strict bonds of society, as an agreeable study and a careless pastime.' These 'common affections' and the 'strict bonds of society' refer to what emotionally holds individuals and people together. They meddle in places which they ought to leave alone. Shakespeare by comparison 'never disturbs the grounds of moral principle; but leaves his characters, (after doing them heaped justice on all sides) to be judged of by our common sense and natural feeling'. The earlier exploration of criticism and judgement in chapters 10 and 11 are relevant here. Shakespeare does justice to his characters because he is true to how they are. The question of favouring one or another is irrelevant. Shakespeare had the ability to identify with such a range of humanity, that he could himself enter into the complexity of each character and then by describing people from the inside do them justice, be true to what they were and describe them accurately.

Shakespeare left space for our judgement. Beaumont and Fletcher do not create the conditions for such natural feeling to arise and so in place of judgement and good thinking the issues are 'set up to be debated by sophistical casuistry'.

When Hazlitt sums up what is taking place he says that 'the dramatic paradoxes of Beaumont and Fletcher are, to all appearances, tinctured with an infusion of personal vanity and laxity of principle'. But then before we quite know where we are he has opened up for us a new level of debate. Like the tour guide who suddenly ushers us into an unexpected room, Hazlitt has led us into another chamber of the mind. What he follows on with is 'I do not say that this was the character of the men; but it strikes me as the character *of their minds.* The two things are very distinct.' (my italics) What is he talking about?

To understand what he means we need to return to his forest metaphor: 'Their productions shoot up in haste, but bear the marks of precocity and premature decay. Or they are two goodly trees, the stateliest of the forest, crowned with blossoms, and with the verdure springing at their feet; but they do not strike their roots far enough into the ground and the fruit can hardly ripen for the flowers!' The productions lack a certain robustness, and are likely to crumble in our minds and hearts. Because they are not rooted in an understanding of the unconscious aspects of life, they have no firm roots to substantiate the complexity of the human mind. The evidence of growth is deceptive. In a natural state of affairs, blossoms give way to fruit. The fresh, beautiful blossom must die if the fruit is to grow and ripen. The artist playing to the gallery holds on to the blossom. He becomes addicted to making new blossom because he is addicted to applause.

Apart from the issues which I have been drawing out from this piece of text I also wish to illustrate that certain pieces which Hazlitt wrote do not lend themselves to speed reading. Sometimes we are jauntily carried along by his prose but at times, and with writing like this, we are required to move at a snail's pace if we are to follow the laser-like precision with which he can zoom in on an issue. Tom Paulin makes a similar point when he describes Hazlitt's essay 'On a Landscape of Nicholas Poussin' as having 'one of the finest opening paragraphs in the history of criticism, a paragraph so long and carefully moulded, so epic in its momentum, that it's like a concentrated essay in itself'. Paulin dedicates a lengthy chapter to unfolding effectively the successive layers on meaning in this single paragraph.[12]

***

When Coleridge wrote of Hazlitt's ability to send well-headed and well-feathered thoughts straight forward to the mark with a twang of the bow-string he also described him as *strange*. This strangeness has proved a stumbling block to many who were introduced to him in his lifetime or who have met him through his writing. To understand this strangeness we need to go beyond any particular aspect of his personality, his dislike of shaking hands, his melancholic moods, his inability or unwillingness to be the centre of conversation when others demanded it of him. William Bewick has described a scene when he and Hazlitt were fishing with Sheridan Knowles. Bewick observed how Hazlitt marvelled at the grace of Knowles' casting and then when Knowles later opened his basket to show the now lifeless fish Hazlitt recoiled 'as if he were looking into a cradle of dead babies.' I think some explanation for this strangeness is to be found in his essay 'On the Love of the Country' when Hazlitt wrote 'there is no object, however trifling or rude, that has not, in some mood or other, found the way to my heart; and I might say, in the words of the poet,

> 'To me the meanest flower that blows can give
> Thoughts that do often lie too deep for tears.' [13]

Hazlitt's compass of soul was attracted to all points on the circumference of human experience. The meanest flower touched him. That which repelled others found a way into his heart. That which is called great also touched him and found a way into his heart. The Unitarian College in Hackney, London which Hazlitt attended until its closure in 1796 was set up to provide an education for the sons of Unitarians. The universities were closed to Dissenters and those who did not profess the Anglican/State faith. Lack of funds led to the college's closure as did its failure to produce an adequate number of ministers of religion. The liberal education provided was held responsible by some for many of the young men losing their faith and the place was dubbed by Henry Crabb Robinson as 'the slaughterhouse of Christianity' and Hazlitt is reported by him to have left the place 'an avowed infidel'.

These labels can be misleading. While Hazlitt's faith in the god of his father did not endure, he never spoke disparagingly of his parents' beliefs and in developing the notion of disinterestedness, he was in part borrowing from the theology of his father who wrote of Jesus – 'never was there any other son of man so totally disinterested'. When we read the introduction to 'The Age of Elizabeth' we find him treating the Bible with the utmost respect. 'The translation of the Bible was the chief engine in the great work [of liberating men's minds]. It threw open, by a secret spring, the rich treasures of religion and morality … it revealed the visions of the prophets, and conveyed the lessons of inspired teachers (such they were thought) to the meanest of the people'. There was in Scripture he said 'an originality, a vastness of conception, a depth and tenderness of feeling, and a touching simplicity in the mode of narration, which he who does not feel must be made of no penetrable stuff. Here, true to form, Hazlitt is ferreting out the lazy commentator in matters religious. A wholesale disposal of that which contains truth, beauty and goodness within it is the action of a long narrowing of the mind. 'Sceptics and philosophical unbelievers appear to me to have just as little liberality or enlargement of view as the most bigoted fanatic.' Hazlitt once caused great offence to a group of unbelievers when he said that Jacob's dream was finer than anything in Shakespeare and that Hamlet bore no comparison to at least one character in the New Testament. The character in question was Jesus of Nazareth and far from engaging in Crabb Robinson's 'slaughter' Hazlitt put Jesus Christ forward as a unique individual emphasising his humanity. Hazlitt wrote:

> There is something in the character of Christ too (leaving religious faith quite out of the question) of more sweetness and majesty, and more likely to work a change in the mind of man, by the contemplation of its idea alone, than any to be found in history, whether actual or feigned. This character is that of a sublime humanity, such as was never seen on earth before nor since. This shone manifestly both in his words and actions ... He was the first true teacher of morality; for he alone conceived the idea of a pure humanity. He redeemed man from the worship of that idol, self, and instructed him by precept and example to love his neighbour as himself, to forgive our enemies, to do good to those that curse us and despitefully use us. He taught the love of good for the sake of good, without regard to personal or sinister views, and made the affections of the heart the sole seat of morality, instead of the pride of the understanding or the sternness of the will ... The gospel was first preached to the poor, for it consulted their wants and interests, not its own pride and arrogance. It first promulgated the equality of mankind in the community of duties and benefits. It denounced the iniquities of the chief priests and pharisees, and declared itself at variance with principalities and powers, for it sympathises not with the oppressor, but the oppressed. It first abolished slavery, for it did not consider the power of the will to inflict injury, as clothing it with a right to do so. Its law is in good, not power. It at the same time tended to wean the mind from the grossness of sense, and a particle of its divine flame was lent to brighten and purify the lamp of love![14]

Quoting the writer John Decker, who described Jesus as 'the first true gentleman that ever breathed', Hazlitt suggested that this gentleman should be of interest whether one was interested in theistic religion, natural religion, philosophy, humanity or true genius. He saw in Jesus disinterestedness writ large, someone who reached out to others in sympathetic identification. 'He redeemed man from the worship of that idol, self.' This concurs with Hazlitt's understanding of vanity and affectation and its central position in determining the quality of human life. 'Redemption' for Hazlitt was dependent upon a resolution of one's vanity and narcissism. Human redemption is the capacity to see beyond oneself, to escape from the idolatry of our own being. Those who, when they look around themselves, forever see a reflection of themselves are blind to what is behind them. Hazlitt is not shy to use such phrases as the spark of divinity in mankind because he is thus referring to a world larger than one's self. The peace that he saw embodied in Jesus was a peace and happiness which followed from the ability to think about other people. A loving act arises from an accurate perception of the needs of someone else and is not measured by whether in the performance of a good deed it makes one feel good.

Hazlitt saw the gospel as a message for the poor, attending to their needs, proclaiming the equality of all people. Human dignity and equality were good things in themselves. In essence his politics has a very Christian flavour as the gospel proclaimed the 'equality of mankind in the community of duties and benefits'. We have also seen how much of Hazlitt's political writings served to expose the pride and arrogance of political machines, the systemic corruption which served the vanity of the few.

Chapter 15

Remembrance of Things Present

The objects that we have known in better days are the main props that sustain the weight of our affections, and give us strength to await our future lot. The future is like a dead wall or a thick mist hiding all objects from our view; the past is alive and stirring with objects, bright or solemn, and of unfading interest. What is it in fact that we recur to oftenest? What subjects do we think or talk of? Not the ignorant future, but the well-stored past.[1]

It has been observed that in the latter years of his life Hazlitt's writings took on a distinctive sense of the finite nature of existence, that the pictures he painted with his words acquired an autumnal hue. His disappointments in politics and in life are pointed to, the defeat of Napoleon, the reinstating of absolute monarchy in Europe and of the Inquisition in Spain, the lack of parliamentary reform in England.

We can find evidence to support this point of view that his return to the past is simply a reaction to disappointments. In 1827 he wrote:

> For my part, I started in life with the French Revolution, and I have lived, alas! to see the end of it. But I did not foresee this result. My sun arose with the first dawn of liberty and I did not think how soon both must set. The new impulse to ardour given to men's minds imparted a congenial warmth and glow to mine; we were strong to run a race together, and I little dreamed that long before mine was set, the sun of liberty would turn to blood, or set once more in the night of despotism. Since then I confess, I have no longer felt myself young, for with that my hopes fell.
>
> I have since turned my thoughts to gathering up some of the fragments of my early recollections, and putting them into a form to which I might occasionally revert. The future was barred to my progress, and I turned for consolation and encouragement to the past. [2]

Whilst these words support the common view, in my opinion it is an incomplete reading of the situation. A glance at some essay titles will tell us that the transience of life had long impressed itself upon his mind and the theme of time and its passing is not a totally new one. We need to look beyond a simple ageing process and the simple passage of time if we are to comprehend what was on his mind. Behind his references to time there is often a reference to other things. The time which we measure by the planetary movements and which we transfer to our time-pieces is always on the move. It can become something we latch other things onto. We become preoccupied with time, the next hour, tomorrow, next week and year. We have to get on, we have things to do, places to visit. The measurement of time, which originates as a tool to help us order our lives, becomes our master.

In the essay 'On The Past and Future', Hazlitt points to the way time can become our master and we become slaves to its measurement:

> Sir Joshua Reynolds was never comfortable out of his painting-room, and died of chagrin and regret because he could not paint on to the last moment of his life. He used to say that he could go on retouching a picture for ever, as long as it stood on his easel; but as soon as it was once fairly out of the house, he never wished to see it again. An ingenious artist of our own time has been heard to declare, that if ever the Devil got him into his clutches, he would set him to copy his own pictures. Thus secure, self-complacent retrospect to what is done is nothing, while the anxious, uneasy looking forward to what is to come is everything.[3]

Here time has become a distraction and a diversion, and something more fundamental than the ticking of a clock needs attention. The rhythms keep running in the head, the body is so used to habitual movement and action that it has difficulty standing still. Rest that is one's due after a job well done is not forthcoming. But when Hazlitt refers to Sir Joshua Reynolds he is taking us beyond any kinetic over-stimulation. He is asking if a painter's work-space can become to its occupant a perpetual stage. The outer circumstances are poles apart and yet the same conditions prevail. What, we might ask, was the relationship Sir Joshua and his 'ingenious artist' had to their art? In the light of our exploration of the 'good enough' and 'the perfect' we might conjecture that Sir Joshua was not content with 'the good enough' and the ingenious artist had a very low opinion of his own work. He might also be so constantly driven to do new things that he is lost in the future. We can also wonder why, when an artist sells his work, does he so disown it, that he never wants to see it again? Is it because someone else now legally possesses it, and so the artist is left feeling as though a theft has taken place, as if virtue has gone out of him, and he is empty and bereft?

These numerous inquiries lead to one fundamental question. What judgement of value has the artist made of his work? Has he been his own good critic? When this has not taken place a vacuum is created. What can rush in to fill the void is often an issue of time. The problem is expressed in terms of time and frequently it is embodied in some anxiety about the future. From all I have already said it will be clear I am not here singling out one group called artists. The problem which the artist illustrates is ubiquitous. All human daily activity, big and small is subject to the same necessities. What judgement of value do we make of ourselves and our work?

We are now firmly in the realm of value. What is valuable in life? What retains its worth regardless of the passage of that humanly-invented entity called time? By what do we judge our own worth and the worth of what we do? In my reading of Hazlitt I think it is fundamental to come to grips with what time meant to him. To assist in this exploration I call upon my most prominent luminary, Shakespeare, and in particular his great speech on time as spoken by Ulysses in *Troilus and Cressida*. Hazlitt made many references to this passage and also quoted it in full twice (in *Characters in Shakespeare's Plays*[4] and in 'On Application to Study'[5]). He was (and I am) aware that it is long but, as he said, worth the quoting because it shows 'the thankless nature of popularity'. It has a still great 'depth of moral observation and richness of illustration', and although the 'throng of images [are] prodigious…and though they sometimes jostle against one another, they every where raise and carry on the feeling, which is metaphysically true and profound.'

> ULYSSES: Time hath, my Lord,
>   A wallet at his back, wherein he puts
>   Alms for oblivion, a great-sized monster
>   Of ingratitudes. Those scraps are good deeds past,
>   Which are devoured as fast as they are made,
>   Forgot as soon as done. Perseverance, dear my lord,
>   Keeps honour bright. To have done is to hang
>   Quite out of fashion, like a rusty mail
>   In monumental mockery. Take the instant way,
>   For honour travels in a strait so narrow,
>   Where one but goes abreast. Keep then the path,
>   For emulation hath a thousand sons
>   That one by one pursue: if you give way,
>   Or hedge aside from the direct forthright,
>   Like to an entered tide they all rush by
>   And leave you hindmost;
>   Or, like a gallant horse fall'n in first rank,
>   Lie there for pavement to the abject rear,
>   O'errun and trampled on. Then what they do in present,
>   Though less than yours in past, must o'ertop yours.
>   For time is like a fashionable host,
>   That slightly shakes his parting guest by th' hand
>   And, with arms outstretched as he would fly,
>   Grasps in the comer. Welcome ever smiles,
>   And Farewell goes out sighing. O let not virtue seek
>   Remuneration for the thing it was;

For beauty, wit,
High birth, vigour of bone, desert in service,
Love, friendship, charity, are subject all
To envious and calumniating time.
One touch of nature makes the whole world kin –
That all with one consent praise new-born gauds,
Though they are made and moulded of things past,
And give to dust that is a little gilt
More laud than gilt o'er-dusted.
The present eye praises the present object.
Then marvel not, thou great and complete man,
That all the Greeks begin to worship Ajax,
Since things in motion sooner catch the eye
Than what not stirs.

Act 3.3, 145–184

Here we have Shakespeare full of swift transitions and glancing lights. Certainly, the ideas and images jostle with each other and we run the risk of having our senses overloaded. We will hold on, if we hold to the question of value as it runs through the entire piece. When Hazlitt decided to give his series of lectures on Elizabethan drama in 1819, the sentiments in this passage acted as a guidance to him and he quoted from it in his introductory lecture. He believed the riches of the age had been lost. 'They went out one by one unnoticed, like evening lights; or were swallowed up in the headlong torrent of puritanic zeal which succeeded, and swept away everything in its unsparing course, throwing up the wrecks of taste and genius at random.'

Here is, perhaps, the place to deal with the issue of his preference for old or new works. But as we have seen (by his remarks on Beaumont and Fletcher) he did not like old works merely because they were old. He made a judgement of the value of a work. Hazlitt's attitude might be summed up by referring again to the comments he made about Joseph Fawcett. 'He did not care a jot whether something was old or new, in prose or in verse. What he wanted was something to make him think.' Hazlitt found much to make him think in the works of Marlowe, Heywood, Decker and others. Time had been cruel to these great people and he set about playing his part in redeeming their reputation, their knowledge and their wisdom. But what he was doing was part of a larger project, part of a greater view of things, part of articulating his ideas on time and value. Yet again, the notion of vanity and affectation infuse his thought on these subjects.

At the centre of Ulysses' piece we can see the fashionable host and he is as real today as he was two hundred and four hundred years ago in Hazlitt's and Shakespeare's day (and I dare say in the time of the original Ulysses). Yesterday's star, the departing guest, gets a limp handshake of farewell and the latest thing on the block is ushered in enthusiastically. Welcome ever smiles and farewell goes out sighing. This fashionable host is a monster of ingratitudes. He owes nothing to anyone who is not the latest fashion. In the action of turning to the latest excitement, yesterday's good is destroyed, devoured. Images of appalling destructiveness pile up one upon the other in this passage. The force of a tide relentlessly pushing into an estuary may strike fear in us if we have ever been caught in one, but the gallant horse who falls and is trampled on and used as pavement leaves no doubt about the degree of devastation involved.

Not only is the degree of destruction highlighted in the words spoken by Ulysses, but also the extent and the amount of it. Beauty, love, friendship, charity are among the good things destroyed. Calumniating and envious time are the agents of destruction. Not only is an act of obliteration in progress, but there is also the claim there never was any good there in the first place. It never existed!

In all of this the stakes are high. Great things are destroyed; the scene is one of a scorched earth and scorched flesh. Its horrific nature may tempt us to diminish our discussion by referring to time as some impersonal entity and our language and culture has a ready supply of aphorisms which are used to do just that: 'All things come to an end'. 'Time rolls on'.

The truth however is that it is human beings who do all these things. It is human beings who behave monstrously, who devour and trample and praise new-born gauds. Time can be a container into which we throw all the things we do not want to accept responsibility for, and if we do it often enough we soon believe it is the master and we are its slave.

But what awaits us if we don't do this, if we refuse to displace our responsibility and accept that the mastery lies in our own hands? In the autumn of 1819 Hazlitt returned from his months of reading in Winterslow. In preparation for his lectures he came back to London not just with a greater understand of the writers of the age but with a heightened sense of gratitude to those great figures. His task is not merely one of conveying information and knowledge. He had long felt a sense of gratitude to good books and now these Elizabethan writers of drama were added to his list. If we read Hazlitt carefully, when he talks of the past being alive and stirring with objects he calls it 'the well-stored past'. Do we have a well-stored past or do we behave like a fashionable host to ourselves? Do we pass over what we have done, throw our good deeds over our shoulder, forgot as soon as done? If we do not value what we have done, if we have not learned to be a good critic of ourselves and our worth, we do not build a well-stored past.

Hazlitt captures another significant moment in the human struggle to value what is good and to hold on to that value in his essay 'On Application to Study'.

There, having quoted this same passage from *Troilus and Cressida,* he says some people become afraid of their success and having produced good work they come to a halt. They are stuck in the middle of the road to fame and are 'startled at the shadow of their own reputation'. In providing an explanation for this he takes us back to a familiar human struggle, to live to oneself or to become captured by vanity and affectation. But here instead of these words he approached a language more familiar to the modern tongue, namely narcissism. 'Such delicate pretenders tremble on the brink of *ideal* perfection, like dew-drops on the edge of flowers; and are fascinated like so many Narcissuses, with the image of themselves, reflected from the public admiration.'[6]

When Hazlitt wrote about the past it is often with a painful awareness of how life is wasted if we do not have a well-stored reservoir within us. The riches he felt within himself and which he saw as available to others are described in 'A Farewell to Essay-Writing'. There he wrote:

> We walk through life, as through a narrow path with the curtain drawn around it; behind are ranged rich portraits, airy harps are strung – yet we will not stretch forth our hands and lift aside the veil, to catch glimpses of the one or sweep the chords of the other. As in a theatre, when the old-fashioned green curtain drew up, groups of figures, fantastic dresses, laughing faces, rich banquets, stately columns, gleaming vistas, appeared beyond, so we have only at any time to 'peep through the blanket of the past' to possess ourselves at once of all that has regaled our senses, that is stored up in our memory, that has struck our fancy, that has pierced our hearts: yet to all this we are indifferent, insensible, and seem intent only on the present vexation, the future disappointment.[7]

∗∗∗

In 1913 Freud spent part of August walking in the Dolomites. This experience prompted him to write a short essay called 'On Transience'. He was, along with other writers, invited by the Berlin Goethe Society to contribute a piece as an introduction to a commemorative volume called *Goethe's Country*. This short essay, only three pages in length, reveals Freud at his literary best. The text speaks for itself:

> Not long ago I went on a summer walk through a smiling countryside in the company of a taciturn friend and of a young but already famous poet. The poet admired the beauty of the scene around us but felt no joy in it. He was disturbed by the thought that all this beauty was fated of extinction, that it would vanish when winter came, like all human beauty and all the beauty and splendour that men have created or may create. All that he would otherwise have loved and admired seemed to him shorn of its worth by the transience which was its doom.

The proneness to decay of all that is beautiful and perfect can, as we know, give rise to two different impulses in the mind. The one leads to the aching despondency felt by the young poet, while the other leads to rebellion against the fact asserted. No! it is impossible that all this loveliness of Nature and Art, of the world of our sensations and of the world outside, will really fade away into nothing. It would be too senseless and too presumptuous to believe it. Somehow or other this loveliness must be able to persist and to escape all the powers of destruction.

But this demand for immortality is a product of our wishes too unmistakable to lay claim to reality: what is painful may none the less be true. I could not see my way to dispute the transience of all things, nor could I insist upon an exception in favour of what is beautiful and perfect. But I did dispute the pessimistic poet's view that the transience of what is beautiful involves any loss in its worth.

On the contrary, an increase! Transience value is a scarcity value in time. Limitation in the possibility of an enjoyment raises the value of the enjoyment. It was incomprehensible, I declared, that the thought of the transience of beauty should interfere with our joy in it. As regards the beauty of nature, each time it is destroyed by winter it comes again next year, so that in relation to the length of our lives it can in fact be regarded as eternal. The beauty of the human form and face vanish for ever in the course of our lives, but their evanescence only lends them a fresh charm. A flower that blossoms only for a single night does not seem to us on that account less lovely. Nor can I understand any better why the beauty and perfection of a work of art or of an intellectual achievement should lose its worth because of its temporal limitation. A time may indeed come when the pictures and statues which we admire to-day will crumble to dust, or a race of men may follow us who no longer understand the works of our poets and thinkers, or a geological epoch may even arrive when all animate life upon the earth ceases; but since the value of all this beauty and perfection is determined only by its significance for our own emotional lives, it has no need to survive us and is therefore independent of absolute duration...

My conversation with the poet took place in the summer before the war. A year later the war broke out and robbed the world of its beauties. It destroyed not only the beauty of the countrysides through which it passed and the works of art which it met with on its path but it also shattered our pride in the achievements of our civilisation, our admiration for many philosophers and artists and our hopes of a final triumph over the differences between nations and races. It tarnished the lofty impartiality of our science, it revealed our instincts in all their nakedness and let loose the evil spirits within us which we thought had been tamed forever by centuries of continuous education by the noblest minds. It made our country small again and made the rest of the world far remote, it robbed us of very much that we had loved, and showed us how ephemeral were many things that we had regarded as changeless.[8]

Freud's young walking companion illustrates the dilemma which Hazlitt is addressing. The future and some idealised version of it so preoccupies him that he was unable to enjoy the present.

Hazlitt opposed the belief that the more information you accumulate, the more knowledge and wisdom you acquire. Perhaps it is the case that as you travel along the line of information-gathering you run the risk of losing touch with where you started out from. You have forgotten the basic principles upon which your search was founded. Hazlitt despised those thinkers who behaved towards their readers like the juggler whose art is to mystify and deceive the onlooker. 'These intellectual Sysiphuses are', he says, 'always rolling the stone of knowledge up a hill, for the perverse pleasure of rolling it down again.'[9] Hazlitt stands out as a first-principles man. Despite his many diversions and digressions he remains within the gravitational field of his essentials, his timeless classics. 'Value dwells not in particular will, it holds its estimate and dignity.' He did not feel forced to be always producing something new. He could live by husbanding the interest in his true classics. The lesson here is to keep a living pride in what one has done well and not always be driven to do something new. True genius springs from inspiration and not ambition. Such an attitude allows a person to build up solid stores which remain timeless.

In reading Hazlitt you will find repeated references to time, and in this chapter I have sought to go beyond the commonly accepted interpretation of the word. In understanding the whole notion of time I have drawn considerably on Hazlitt's 'Age of Elizabeth'. This is not one of his books you are likely to find in the local library. I bought my copy from a bookstore in the Lower East Side of Manhattan. It was the 1845 edition published in New York by Wiley and Putnam, and it cost less than a week's supply of my daily newspaper. I was intrigued by the state of the book. It had not had an easy life – as if it had doubled as a resting place for coffee cups, one of them at least having spilt its contents and seeped through the final thirty pages, leaving them badly stained and in places difficult to read. No name had been written on the cover page, unusual for the second-hand Hazlitt books I have bought. Apart from the stains the text had a rather pale complexion as if the pages had seldom seen the light of day, as if the book might never have been actually read. I thought of Tom Paulin's experience, recounted in the opening pages of The Day Star of Liberty, how he found some of the pages Hazlitt's Life of Napoleon uncut. So had this book remained unread for a century and a half? I found the irony of that possibility rather amusing. Maybe those of us who have glimpsed the genius of this man and write about him are now attempting to do for him what he did for those forgotten writers.

Chapter 16

A Spirit for Our Age

He brought his subjects along with him; he drew his materials from himself. The only limits which circumscribed his variety were the stores of his own mind. His stock of ideas did not consist of a few meagre facts, meagrely stated, of half a dozen commonplaces tortured in a thousand different ways: but his mine of wealth was a profound understanding, inexhaustible as the human heart, and various as the sources of nature. He therefore enriched every subject to which he applied himself, and new subjects were only the occasions of calling forth fresh powers of mind which had not been before exerted. It would therefore be in vain to look for the proof of his powers in any one of his speeches or writings: they all contain some additional proof of power…I shall speak of the whole compass and circuit of his mind – not of that small part or section of him which I have been able to give: to do otherwise would be like the story of the man who put the brick in his pocket, thinking to show it as the model of a house. I have been able to manage pretty well with respect to all my other speakers, and curtailed them down without remorse. It was easy to reduce them within certain limits, to fix their spirit, and condense their variety; by having a certain quantity given, you might infer the rest; it was only the same thing over again. But who can bind Proteus, or confine the roving flight of genius? [1]

This is Hazlitt writing about Edmund Burke. As I reach this final chapter I shall allow the piece to speak for me as I try to gather in what I have wished to achieve in this book. I have not tried to lay brick upon brick of Hazlitt's life, nor methodically sum up the content of his thought. I have instead sought to call forth his spirit and display the compass of his heart and mind. From my first meeting with him, my first hearing him speak in *On Living to One's Self* I was struck by his generosity and I have not wavered in that opinion of him. Hazlitt takes you into his mind, his heart, his soul, his company. 'I laugh, I run, I leap, I sing for joy … I am like an infant on the edge of a precipice…as to my old opinions, I am heartily sick of them … Later impressions come and go, and serve to fill up the intervals; but these are my standing resources, my true classics. If I have had few real pleasures or advantages, my ideas, from their sinewy texture, have been to me in the nature of realities; and if I should not be able to add to the stock, I can live by husbanding the interest.'

In revealing himself he is also revealing us to ourselves. The expansive ease by which he carries us along and the fluency of his prose can leave us forgetting the amount of back-breaking digging which was required along the way. The French Impressionist painter Claude Monet, famous for the scenes of his own garden, did not inherit a garden ready to be painted. He bought some land. He cultivated it. He designed and planted it. His sweat and labour built it. He tended it with his own toil. Then he painted. Like Monet's water lilies painted at different times of day and in changing seasons, Hazlitt's essays take us through the shifting states of mind and the altering moods of mankind. He takes us through the pain and the hard work of life; he also shows us its delight and sparkle.

If you read Hazlitt and try to set him up as your guru or teacher, to decipher a system and apply it to your life, you will meet with disappointment. His *Liber Veritatis,* as an overarching definition of his life's writings, requires your company not as a spectator but as an active participant. As we have seen, he lectured and wrote as if he were a dinner guest. As we eat his partridge and drink his wine or partake of his strong black tea, we as good mannered guests must enter into the spirit of the conversation and speak our minds and hearts.

By now we will not be surprised that he can be a disquieting presence. As our frailties, our mistakes, those parts of ourselves which arrive in our peripheral vision and we would wish to go unseen, have an uncanny habit of attracting his gaze we can easily find ourselves shifting uneasily in his company. If we remind ourselves of the fabled Hazlitt spleen, we could be tempted to draw some comfort around ourselves and rest assured in our righteousness. But as we move to turn the next page of his essay, a hesitation must set in. There he is waiting for us. He won't go away. To move on we need, as he has already told us, courage.

If we read Hazlitt as he deals with hate, envy, cant, egotism, hypocrisy, pedantry and believe he is writing about someone else, then we have missed the whole point. He is writing for us and about us. He is writing for himself and about himself. To avert our gaze from the truth of who we are and who we have been is to deny our own nature. If we look away we join those who accused Hazlitt of being testy and peevish, of being 'at feud with the world'. Hazlitt was at feud with the world because he loved it. As Leigh Hunt wrote he was a 'splenetic but kindly philosopher'; he did not merely dissect human frailty but also exhibited it. In *Liber Amoris* he exposed himself to the world. As Hunt added, it was his sympathy and empathy with all aspects of the human condition which motivated him and 'his regard for human nature, and his power to love truth and loveliness in their humblest shapes, survived his subtlest detections of human pride and folly'.[2] Shakespeare's words spoken by Mariana in Act 5 of *Measure for Measure* are meant for Hazlitt and for us all:

> They say, best men are moulded out of faults;
> And, for the most, become much more the better
> For being a little bad.

Harold Bloom in his book *Shakespeare: The Invention of the Human* outlines his belief that Shakespeare did not merely dramatise and represent human character; he invented human identity in all its forms and shapes. He not only created characters for the stage, he created people for life, he defined us and invented us. 'His plays remain the outward limit of human achievement: aesthetically, cognitively, in certain ways morally, even spiritually.'³ Hazlitt expressed the opinion that, if we had to, we could get by in life without reading anything but Shakespeare, and Bloom places himself within Hazlitt's tradition of thought, along with Johnson, Bradley and Goddard. If we look back at Hazlitt's comments on Shakespeare's ability with words, we find a thesis similar to Bloom's:

> His language is hieroglyphical. It translates thoughts into visible images. It abounds in sudden transitions and elliptical expressions. This is the source of his mixed metaphors, which are only abbreviated forms of speech. These, however give no pain from long custom. They have, in fact, become idioms in the language. They are *the building and not the scaffolding to thought'*. (my italics)⁴

As the builder and not merely the provider of the scaffolding to thought, Hazlitt is asserting that Shakespeare was not just depicting what was already there. He was involved not just in a supporting role, he was constructing human thought.

In chapter 1 I asserted that Hazlitt was a psychoanalytically-minded man and throughout the book have attempted to provide my reasons for this point of view. I have pointed out how his understanding of the working of the human mind dovetails with a psychoanalytical model. But I also suggest that he had an intuitive awareness of what takes place in a psychoanalyst's consulting room. If the man in the street asked me to tell him what takes place in such a room I would now refer him to Hazlitt's essay 'On Genius and Common Sense' and, in particular, to the story about John Thelwall. Let us listen to Hazlitt's story of Thelwall's visit to Wales after his acquittal:

> One of the people who had rendered themselves obnoxious to Government and been included in a charge for high treason in the year 1794, had retired soon after into Wales to write an epic poem and enjoy the luxuries of a rural life. In his peregrinations through that beautiful scenery, he had arrived one fine morning at the inn at Llangollen, in the romantic valley of that name. He had ordered his breakfast, and was sitting at the window in all the dalliance of expectation when a face passed, of which he took no notice at the instant – but when his breakfast was brought in presently after, he found his appetite for it gone – the day had lost its freshness in his eye – he was uneasy and spiritless; and without any cause that he could discover, a total change had taken place in his feelings. While he was trying to account for this odd circumstance, the same face passed again – it was the face of Taylor the spy; and he was no longer at a loss to explain the difficulty.

He had before caught only a transient glimpse, a passing side-view of the face; but though this was not sufficient to awaken a distinct idea in his memory, his feelings, quicker and surer, had taken the alarm; a string had been touched that gave a jar to his whole frame, and would not let him rest, though he could not at all tell what was the matter with him. To the flitting, shadowy, half-distinguished profile that had glided by his window was linked unconsciously and mysteriously, but inseparably, the impression of the trains that had been laid for him by this person;– in this brief moment, in this dim, illegible short-hand of the mind he had just escaped the speeches of the Attorney and Solicitor-General over again; the gaunt figure of Mr. Pitt glared by him; the walls of a prison enclosed him; and he felt the hands of the executioner near him, without knowing it till the tremor and disorder of his nerves gave information to his reasoning faculties that all was not well within.[5]

I would say to my questioner this is the type of listening which takes place in a psychoanalyst's consulting room; this is the way the psychoanalyst listens to the patient; this is the type of listening to oneself which the whole experience of psychoanalysis aims to promote. What is called free association encourages this state of reverie. If my questioner wanted to hear more, I would say that in this instance Thelwall was lucky. He did not take long to explain his unease and presumably, the story does not cover this detail, in having regained his sense of well being got on with enjoying his well-earned breakfast. But I know of people who can spend a long time, in some cases a lifetime, lost in a state of never-ending anxiety. Their reasoning faculties are of little assistance to them in explaining their disquiet. All medical and prescriptive remedies have failed them. I suppose I might say they have never been able to identify the 'Taylor' in their life. If in their early years, in the time beyond which their conscious memory cannot enter, they suffered a calamity, had for instance been abused or neglected by a parent, then in a way they have been at the mercy of a 'Taylor'. The 'Taylor' they sense within themselves is the ghost of things which have happened to them. Their body, their 'nerves', I would say their unconscious will remember. They live carrying around within themselves a sense of imprisoned pain. In later life the tragedy can become enlarged. All intimate human contact will bring anxiety and they struggle to trust anyone. They can even become a 'Taylor' to themselves; they distrust their own good deeds; they are suspicious of their own creative endeavors and they suspect, interrogate and seek to imprison their own true self. Interestingly, Fairbairn's name for this part of the self which interrogates was 'the internal saboteur'.

'It asks a troublesome effort to insure the admiration of others: it is a still greater one to be satisfied with one's own thoughts.' In writing about Hazlitt I have been aware of the extensive scholarship of others who have written before me, much of which has enriched my appreciation and understanding. From the beginning, however, all my reading and study has primarily been driven by a desire to be satisfied with my own thoughts. Since he has knocked and gained entry to my mind I have indeed brooded over Hazlitt's ideas and undoubtedly they have become a kind of substance in my brain. But as I have indicated, the ideas and insights which he spoke about at my table were not always unknown and unfamiliar. When this has been the case, he has collected and embodied what I have already known, riveted old impressions more deeply and made what was plain still plainer, infused life and energy and quickened and invigorated the pulse of thought.

Numerous writers have drawn attention to Hazlitt's understanding of human psychology. What individuals mean when they use the term 'psychology' can vary enormously. I have argued that Hazlitt has a place within psychoanalytic psychology and I have shown how this has gone largely unrecognised and if recognised, unacknowledged. Hazlitt has a capacity to quicken and invigorate my notion of unconscious mental and emotional life. I have, in my exposition on Ronald Fairbairn and in my own attempts to think of what took place in Hazlitt's mind in *Liber Amoris*, sought to explain that psychoanalysis as I think of it goes beyond what has in the past been termed the 'psycho-neurosis'. The so-called 'worried well' make up a small part of its clientele. As psychoanalysis has developed and matured during the century of its existence under the genius of people like Ronald Fairbairn, Melanie Klein, Donald Winnicott, Wilfred Bion and many others, the boundaries of its constituency have been enlarged. The splitting of the mind, the disintegration of human mental faculties, the loss of all sense of a coherent self have moved within the circumference of its concerns. Freud himself could see the direction which needed to be taken and in his final, unfinished paper (written in the year of his death, 1939, and published in 1940, called 'The Splitting of the Ego in the process of Defence') he called for a re-think. But, as I have pointed out above in his letter to Arthur Schnitzler, he knew that the creative and imaginative writers had explored this ground before him. 'You know through intuition – really from a delicate self-observation – everything that I have discovered in other people by laborious work.' What do we think Hazlitt knew when he wrote the following in 1820?

> Decker has given an admirable description of a mad-house in one of his plays. But it might be perhaps objected, that it was only a literal account taken from Bedlam at that time: and it might be answered, that the old poets took the same methods of describing the passions and fancies of men whom they met at large, which forms the point of communion between us; for the title of the old play, 'A mad world, my masters,' is hardly yet obsolete; and we are pretty much the same Bedlam still, perhaps better managed, like the real one, and with more care and humanity shown to the patients! [6]

Hazlitt knew about the madness of the world and not just the madness of those in Bedlam but also of those at large. This takes me back to his feud with the world. He understood that you cannot lock away your 'passions and fancies', you cannot deny or disavow any part of your inner experience of yourself. If you do you create an inner bedlam, your own personal madhouse within the secret recesses of your mind. He feuded because he knew the damage caused by such arrangements, how the full powers of the mind and heart are imprisoned, how that independence of mind so valuable and necessary for creative engagement with the world shrinks into a pitiable replica of what it ought to be. These are the processes to be hated and towards which the full venom of his spleen was directed and at which his pen slashed and struck. He saw the same sinister powers at work in many guises and he knew of the alliances people made with them. I have given many instances already from his work. Here is one more. As always his understanding has been arrived at not only through his observations of others, but also in his reflecting upon the workings of his own mind:

> A self-tormentor is never satisfied come what will. He always apprehends the worst, and is indefatigable in conjuring up the apparition of danger. He is uneasy at his own good fortune, as it takes from him his favourite topic of repining and complaint. Let him succeed to his heart's content at all that is reasonable or important, yet if there is any one thing (and that he is sure to find out) in which he does not get on, this embitters all the rest. I know an instance. Perhaps it is myself.[7]

When Scott Fitzgerald wrote an account of his mental breakdown and it was published as 'The Crack-Up' in 1939, he identified two types of stress, or more particularly two different places from which stress comes and overpowers the individual. The 'big sudden blows' come from outside, a misfortune or series of misfortunes which leave you stunned and traumatised. These are things which are easy to remember. They are dramatic; they can be spoken about to friends; they are the ones you 'blame things on'. The other sort of blow he says 'comes from within' and it is the type that that 'you don't feel until it's too late to do anything about it, until you realise with finality that in some regard you will never be as good a man again.' This sort of breakage 'happens almost without your knowing it but is realised suddenly indeed'.[8]

Hazlitt was very aware of the blows that come from outside and he attacked injustice and inequality with the deftness of a philosopher and the pugilistic determination of a bare-knuckled fighter. But, like Fitzgerald, he knew about another type of stress, another front where the battles are just as severe and the war is a lifelong necessity. This war takes place in the world inside, and it too has its kings and despots, its belief in Divine Right, is peopled by spies and characterised by tyranny, inequality, injustice, cruelty and hatred.

Hazlitt understood that the key to gaining access to this world was courage, the courage to dare to know oneself and the inner workings of one's mind and heart. Without this courage and this knowledge one can never acquire control of one's life. One has to listen to what one is experiencing. In Thelwall's case 'his feelings, quicker and surer had taken the alarm'. It is through an awareness of one's feelings that the 'dim, illegible shorthand of the mind' can be translated into knowledge. Montaigne was aware of the same necessity. 'The world always looks outward, I turn my gaze inward; there I fix it and there I keep it busy. Everyone looks before him; I look within. I have no business but with myself, I unceasingly consider, examine and analyze myself.'⁹ Fairbairn worked as a psychoanalyst with his 'actress' to help her to find the courage to be real, to understand the forces which had shaped her life and to acquire a sense of agency. Truth and falsity are the axis upon which everything turns. Can she see in herself her tendency to be the actress and how this leads to her absence from real relationships and to her inability to be creatively engaged with the world? Truth and falsity confront Troilus as he watched his lover Cressida becoming intimate with Diomedes. Troilus does not want to believe his eyes and ears. He contemplates a lie and looks to Ulysses, half hoping that he will lie to him. Ulysses refuses to juggle with reality.

> ULYSSES: I cannot conjure, Trojan.
> TROILUS: She was not, sure.
> ULYSSES: Most sure she was.
> TROILUS: Why, my negation hath no taste of madness.
> ULYSSES: Nor mine, my lord: Cressida was here but now.
> Act 5.2, 124–126

His struggle to believe is so powerful that the onlooker Thersites wonders if Troilus will 'swagger himself out of his own eyes'.

Ella Sharpe's school-girl similarly has a choice. Does she juggle with the truth of her experience and try to conjure up a different reality and then attempt to make herself and others believe it? Does she lie about her sexual knowledge and accept she not only has to face her actual parents but she is also presented with the choice of whether she has installed within her own mind a repressive authority?

The 'actress' saw glimpses of her inner state, her inner war and conflict and her dream conjures up the interplay between all the warring parties. Troilus speaks of 'a madness of discourse' within himself and he also tells us 'within my soul there doth conduce a fight of this strange nature'. Scott Fitzgerald could detect the operations of his mind; it happens *almost* without you knowing it.

Hazlitt understood these human dilemmas. 'Most men's minds are to me like musical instruments out of tune. Touch a particular key, and it jars and makes harsh discord with your own.' He also understood what can happen next, what can take place once we have become aware of what is going on. The act of telling yourself a lie has two parts. One part we could say relates to content and the other to process. In other words you tell yourself she is worthless, and that you never loved her anyway, that it is all your husband's fault, that your boyfriend corrupted you. That is the content of the lie. What I call the process part is that you also draw a veil over what you have done to your mind. The implications here are enormous. Hazlitt could not accept the truth that Sarah Walker did not love him. The lie he was telling himself had a huge emotional cost. He has already spelt out that cost to us:

> A raging fire is in my heart, that never quits me. The steam-boat (which I foolishly ventured on board) seems like a prison-house, a sort of spectre-ship, moving on through an infernal lake, without wind or tide, by some necromatic power – the splashing of the waves, the noise of the engine gives me no rest, night and day – no tree, no natural object varies the scene – but the abyss is before me, and all my peace lies weltering in it! I feel the eternity of punishment in this life; for I see no end of my woes ... I am tossed about (backwards and forwards) by my passion, so as to become ridiculous. I can now understand how it is that mad people never remain in the same place – they are moving on forever, *from themselves.* [10]

The dilemma is as old as Socrates: know thyself. In the passage above from 'On the Past and Future' Hazlitt has described the awful waste involved when this state of mind dominates. The soundness of the judgement, the serenity and buoyancy of feeling, a softness and elasticity are destroyed and the flower of love, hope and joy are all lost. As I read the passage again I realise how easily all these descriptions of freedom and growth could be submerged in the storm of violence and evil which Hazlitt conjures up. The serpent coils around the heart to gnaw and stifle it. But Hazlitt is, indeed, demonstrating that the good is lost sight of within the sandstorm of evil. He speaks of what he knows and he speaks with all his customary passion and gusto. He is also capturing the helpless state within which a person can get caught and shows how neither will nor reason are of much help.

Hazlitt did not stop here. He had more to say which was of greater importance. Before we investigate what journey Hazlitt might take us on from here, if we look around we will soon see that this is a very crowded junction. People have been arriving here for generations and have never moved on. They have been so incensed, so outraged, so scandalised, so horrified by what he has said and the way he has said it that they throw up their hands in horror at the avowed infidel. Hazlitt the damner! And yet there are those who listened to the same words and welcomed them. There was Keats who called him the only good damner and spoke of Hazlitt almost as if he awaited his criticism with a relish. Then there was Sheridan Knowles:

> He had an endearing tenderness of heart towards those whom he loved … There was ore in him, and rich, but his maturer friends were blind to it. I saw it. He was a man to whom I would have submitted my life.[11]

We might say it was understandable to be put off by Hazlitt. He could sound like a preacher standing above his congregation and showing them the evil of their ways. Those offended and hurt turn away and decide not to go beyond this junction. However, Hazlitt is so often reflecting on his own infirmities that it is hard to sustain the argument that he is placing himself in a pulpit. We have to ask if others place him there in order to knock him down! What seems central here is the distinction between two types of guilt. Guilt often gets a bad press, as if everything which goes under its name is harmful. In chapter 10 I have drawn attention to the muddle which commonly exists around jealousy and envy and made a distinction which draws a line between them and sees them as separate and distinct entities. Guilt can also be subdivided. Guilt can be the emotional state which informs me of the consequence of my actions. Through it I am made aware that I have harmed or hurt another. This type of guilt, while it does not feel pleasant, is, however, useful; in fact it is necessary because without it I would not have any feedback on the consequence of my actions. Without it being in others, they would have no feedback on the effects of their actions on me and social life would be intolerable. The Freudian term super-ego has entered into common parlance and mostly attracts a bad press in the sense that it is seen as a bad thing. I am arguing for the need to have a good super-ego. It is the essence of our conscience. This healthy guilt is more properly called a sense of responsibility.

The other type of guilt is felt to be a persecution and is called 'persecutory guilt'. I distinguish it from 'healthy guilt'. Healthy guilt allows thought and reflection; persecutory guilt does not. Fear and terror have taken the place of reflection and the threat of thinking is so great that the person's only response is flight, a flight to destroy awareness. This occurs in essentially two directions: an attack upon the messenger who has brought the news of the guilt or an attack upon one's own mind. Do not think! When this happens we have what Fairbairn aptly described when he wrote of how one part of the self takes up an uncompromisingly hostile attitude towards another part.

Time to go back to John Kinnaird and his concern that the word 'criticism' is ceasing to mean judgement, and how the fashion is for the critic to 'interpret', to look for 'structure' and 'conventions' in a work, to tease out 'irony' and 'paradox'. Hazlitt, he writes, 'reminds us that criticism, no matter how systematic its methods of analysis may become, can never escape the risk of a personal judgement of another's mind in its personality. Ignore or deride him how we will, our memory of Hazlitt will always be there reminding us that literature and criticism, whatever else they may be, end in the act of reading, in a dialogue that ensues; and he reminds us that these selves have brought themselves to write and read in order to know and judge, not "art" or "reality" or "the modern self" but themselves.' [12]

Are we in a position to take up John Kinnaird's questions and ask, 'Why has some artificial self been constructed and then set up as the object of criticism?' Why has the intellectual framework, within which human experience can be reflected upon, been mistaken for that experience itself? Why the unwillingness and inability to damn? Why destroy the measuring scales which we use to estimate a writer's character? I suspect it has much to do with guilt and confusion between persecutory guilt and healthy guilt. As these two entities collide and become muddled, an evaluation of a person's character becomes very difficult. There is reluctance to inflict such pain on another and also to expose oneself to a retaliation in kind.

Hazlitt knew the difference between the two types of guilt and I believe that is one of the faculties which made him such a powerful critic. I am not saying he did not feel a sense of persecutory guilt, but he could move from it and work through it. Sometimes we see this 'working through' taking place before our eyes as we read Hazlitt. There on the page he exposes himself. Full of indignation and hate and hurt he throws himself about like a child or a rebellious adolescent. Are we any different? Have we in our adult years left all semblance of childhood behind? Can a sudden sting from an unexpected quarter not raise our hackles and make our body ready for the strike? Or is all our emotion so mature, so ordered, so sanitised that it is only in others we notice such eruptions?

If you have followed thus far you have already left many behind at the junction. Those who insist on the primacy of their rational mind, who never weep and proclaim their self confidence to be everlasting, remain and converse with others of like mind. They are unlikely to recognize the sites on show because most of the objects which Hazlitt would point to are within themselves. Hazlitt will take us to the borders of our mind, to the outer regions of ourselves. Like Charles Morgan he offers a window through which a new order can be perceived. He is there in the moments of waking, speaking to us through a dream world and we will find he is a fellow traveler during all the moments and states of mind in between. It is tempting to turn to the text to take refuge in irony to perform emotional somersaults with paradoxical paradoxes. We can get so lost between 'the reader', 'the writer' and 'the text' that at best a mist has formed on our minds and at worst we are talking about nothing. The choice is between reality and filmy abstraction. I think one of the reasons why Hazlitt had such high regard for Shakespeare was because he himself felt explained by

Shakespeare, felt known by him. Shakespeare, in his presentation of character allowed for collision and contrast, for every variety of light and shade, for a continual composition and decomposition of its elements. No human plight or dilemma is beyond knowing and understanding. In the passage from 'On the Past and Future' and in many others of a similar kind where he described the human tragedy of being ensnared in something, I hear a man who is distressed. Sometimes I see him crying, sometimes he tells us he is crying. Maybe it seems unmanly to pause and look at his distress. Do we join those who read *Liber Amoris* and had no time to hear that his pain was so great that he thought of ending his life? Do we treat his depressive withdrawal of Christmas 1807 as a joke? Hazlitt had no interest in persecuting people for their faults and wrong doings. He was distressed by the terrible waste which takes place when the mind and heart move in ever-decreasing circles. This is what many could not see. Hope, love and joy, a softness and elasticity of mind; serenity and buoyancy of feeling; the capacities to make good judgement; these are all precious possessions. If we lose them we are bereft. This is why Hazlitt loved great works of art, be they great paintings, great writings or the greatest art work of all, nature. To look abroad into universality and be able to share its beauty and truth was how he found rest. He knew that when anyone, himself included, lost sight of these precious things, they were in a prison house, on a sort of spectre-ship without wind or tide, like Coleridge's ancient mariner.

When the spotlight of examination is turned on Hazlitt and his limitations as a critic, as will be the case in modern times with its love of systems, we need to listen to what type of critic he saw himself as. In the final part of his introduction to 'The Age of Elizabeth' he describes his views of creativity among the English: not good at painting or writing music but with a strength for poetry and philosophy. 'We have had strong heads and sound hearts among us' he wrote and the following description is an accurate summary of his method of criticism:

> We are slow to think, and therefore impressions do not work upon us till they act in masses. We are not forward to express our feelings, and therefore they do not come from us till they force their way in the most impetuous eloquence … We pay too little attention to form and method, leave our works in an unfinished state, but still the materials we work in are solid and of nature's mint; we do not deal in counterfeits. We both under and over-do, but we keep an eye to the prominent features, the main chance. We are more for weight than show; care only about what interests ourselves, instead of trying to impose upon others by plausible appearances, and are obstinate and intractable in not conforming to common rules, by which many arrive at their ends with half the real waste of thought and trouble. We neglect all but the principal object, gather our force to make a great blow, bring it down, and relapse into sluggishness and indifference

again … we may be accused of grossness, but not of flimsiness; of extravagance, but not of affectation; of want of art and refinement, but not of a want of truth and nature … Our understanding (such as it is and must remain, to be good for anything) is not a thoroughfare for common places, smooth as the palm of one's hand, but full of knotty points and jutting excrescences, rough, uneven, overgrown with brambles; and I like this aspect of the mind (as someone said of the country), where nature keeps a good deal of the soil in her own hands.[13]

Although he had a keen eye for what is good and beautiful, the actual perfection of man and the seeking of an ideal life is not on his agenda. Life is 'indeed a strange gift, and its privileges most mysterious'. Crabbe Robinson believed that Leigh Hunt 'caught the sunny side of everything' and would find fault in Hazlitt for being otherwise. The mingled yarn of life, the good and bad, gave it its zest. A theory which aims to eliminate this mixture, which tries to smooth out all the contradictions, which is uncomfortable with soil on its hands has no attraction for him. 'There must be,' he wrote, 'a spice of mischief and wilfulness thrown in the cup of our existence to give it its sharp taste and sparkling colour.'[14] Despite the mischief of life despite his own limitations and the abuse which was hurled his way, Hazlitt did not become embittered. The triumph of life in the face of adversity was not to seek revenge. I think Shakespeare's wisdom on this point had been internalized by Hazlitt so the world had no hold on him. During the sixth lecture on the drama of 'The Age of Elizabeth' Hazlitt digressed from his discussion of the poets to explain to his listeners his method of criticism:

If I did not write these Lectures to please myself, I am at least sure I should please nobody else. In fact, I conceive that what I have undertaken to do in this and former cases, is merely to read over a set of authors with the audience, as I would do with a friend, to point out a favourite passage, to explain an objection; or if a remark or a theory occurs, to state it in illustration of the subject, but neither to tire him nor puzzle myself with pedantic rules and pragmatical formulas of criticism that can do no good to anybody. I do not come to the task with a pair of compasses or a ruler in my pocket, to see whether a poem is round or square, or to measure its mechanical dimensions, like a metre and alnager of poetry: it is not in my bond to look after exciseable articles or contraband wares, or to exact severe penalties and forfeitures for trifling oversights…I do not think that is the way to learn the gentle craft of poesy, or to teach it to others: – to imbibe or to communicate its spirit; which, if it does not disentangle itself and soar above the obscure and trivial researches of antiquarianism, is no longer itself, a phoenix gazed at by all. At least, so it appeared to me; it is for others to judge whether I was right or wrong. In a word, I have endeavoured to feel what was good, and to give a reason for the faith that was in me, when necessary, and when in my power. This is what I have done, and what I must continue to do.[15]

Hazlitt made good judgements because he was not judgmental. He brought subjects alive and treated them with passion and gusto to make them present to us. There is always an invitation to take part and the force of his expression does not intend to subjugate us but to call forth an equally robust response. Sometimes the wear and tear on our mind as we sit in his company may feel excessive and we are tempted to offer some second-hand opinion. Are we prepared to search, not just like an anatomist but like a lover? Are we prepared to pass through a cool dissection of form and allow our eyes to sparkle and to soften and allow our enjoyment of beauty to be brightened by our acquaintance with its sources within us? Hazlitt could live very much alone because he did not feel alone. To him the dead could be more alive than the living. Listen to him talk of the company he kept in Winterslow when he was working on his 'The Age of Elizabeth' lectures:

> Here with a few old authors, I can manage to get through the summer or the winter months, without ever knowing what it is to feel ennui. They sit with me at breakfast; they walk out with me before dinner … I can take mine ease at mine inn, beside the blazing hearth, and shake hands with Signor Orlando Friscobaldo, as the oldest acquaintance I have. Ben Jonson, learned Chapman, Master Webster, and Master Heywood, are there; and seated around, discourse the silent hours away. Shakespeare is there himself…Spenser is hardly returned from a ramble through the woods, or is concealed behind a group of nymphs, fawns, and satyrs. Milton is on the table, as on an altar, never taken up or laid down without reverence. Lyly's Endymion sleeps with the Moon that shines on at the window; and a breath of wind stirring at a distance seems a sigh from the tree under which he grew old. Faustus disputes in one corner of the room with fiendish faces, and reasons of divine astrology. Bellafront soothes Matheo, Vittoria triumphs over her judges, and old Chapman repeats one of the hymns of Homer, in his own fine translation.[16]

The writer who had reached into the innermost recesses of his own soul, in his art was reaching out to all who can be touched. The magic of great literature is that it makes time stand still.

***

In 1802, when he was 24, Hazlitt met the painter James Northcote. Born in the same year as Grace Loftus (1746), Northcote was 56 at that time. They developed a particular sort of relationship which lasted all their lives, Northcote outliving Hazlitt by one year. Hazlitt loved to visit the old painter's studio; to sit among the paintings; to observe work in progress; to smell the paints and after he had relinquished his own brush take a vicarious satisfaction in the creation of art but above all to have the best of good talk. 'I have lived on his conversation with undiminished relish ever since I can remember, – and when I leave it, I come out into the street with feelings lighter and more ethereal than I have at any other time.'[17] Besides the company of many friends and acquaintances who used to drop in for a chat, to view their work in progress or to collect a work completed, Hazlitt was also treated to the older man's recollections of those from an earlier generation: Edmund Burke, Oliver Goldsmith, Joshua Reynolds and Samuel Johnson, whom Hazlitt had never met.

Later Hazlitt would make notes of their talk and one of his final works was a book entitled *Conversations of James Northcote* published in 1830. In the introduction to this volume Hazlitt tells us what was so important to him about these visits:

> The person, whose doors I enter with most pleasure, and quit with most regret, never did me the smallest favour. I once did him an uncalled-for service, and we nearly quarreled about it. If I were in the utmost distress, I should just as soon think of asking his assistance, as of stopping a person on the highway. Practical benevolence is not his forte. He leaves the profession of that to others. His habits, his theory are against it as idle and vulgar. His hand is closed, but what of that? His eye is ever open, and reflects the universe: his silver accents, beautiful, venerable as his silver hairs, but not scanted, flow as a river. I never ate or drank in his house; nor do I know or care how the flies or spiders fare in it, or whether a mouse can get a living. But I know that I can get there what I can get nowhere else – a welcome, as if one was expected to drop in just at that moment, a total absence of all respect of persons and of airs of self-consequence, endless topics of discourse, refined thoughts, made more striking by ease and simplicity of manner – the husk, the shell of humanity is left at the door, and the spirit, mellowed by time, resides within! All you have to do is sit and listen; and it is like hearing one of Titian's faces speak. To think of worldly matters is a profanation, like that of the money-changers in the Temple; or it is to regard the bread and wine of the Sacrament with carnal eyes. We enter the enchanter's cell, and converse with the divine presence.[18]

The piece speaks for itself but I should say that it also tells us something about Hazlitt's tetchiness. Would he have written it in the same manner if he had known that his old friend had provided for him in his will, leaving him an amount of £100?

***

I conclude in the hope that this piece of writing may enable you to place yourself in the man's company, that it will serve as an introduction to your own reading of the works of William Hazlitt. I have thought of it as an introduction to a complicated and intriguing person and one of the most independent spirits and creative minds of the Romantic period. What of all the statements made of him, that he was fitful, sullen, fiery etc.? It would seem to me he was all of these things. I also believe that he was the object of enormous envy from many of his contemporaries, particularly those who could swagger themselves out of their own eyes. The difference between him and many of those who damned him was that he knew his own character and did not try to hide these things about himself. 'I have, then, given proofs of some talent, and of more honesty: if there is haste or want of method, there is no common-place, nor a line that licks the dust; and if I do not appear to more advantage, I at least appear such as I am.' He revealed himself on every page. His essay titles have spoken for themselves: 'On the Love of Life', 'On Personal Character', 'On the Fear of Death', 'On the Pleasure of Hating', 'On Cant and Hypocrisy', 'On Envy'. He saw it as his duty to evaluate a man's work, being as honest with others as he was with himself. Any and every work of art was a commentary on life. Shoddiness in art or in criticism led to the same in life. Those who took it upon themselves to be such creators or commentators bore the highest responsibilities. Artists of any kind were not exempt from a social and political responsibility. My abiding sense of him is of a man who in the small matters of his daily life and in the big issues of his lifetime sought to know himself. Once, in exasperation, Leigh Hunt presented him with a paper listing all his faults. Hazlitt read it through slowly and exclaimed, 'By God, sir, there's a good deal of truth in it'. He expected a lot of himself and a lot from others and from his friends. He expected his friends to live to themselves, to be true to themselves and some of his sharpest criticisms were reserved for those who had reneged on their own truth and their own principles. 'We are something in ourselves,' he wrote, 'nothing when we try to ape others.'. Hunt also said of Hazlitt that he did 'justice to that real and interior spirit of things, which modifies and enlivens the mystery of existence'.[19] It will be obvious to all that I share the sentiments of Charles Lamb who, when his friend was being attacked from all sides and without ignoring Hazlitt's shortcomings came out fighting and declaring, 'I should belie my own conscience if I said less than that I think W. H. to be in his natural and healthy state one of the wisest and finest spirits breathing. So far from being ashamed of that intimacy which was betwixt us, it is my boast that I was able for so many years to have preserved it entire, and I think I shall go to my grave without finding, or expecting to find, such another companion.'[20] My abiding sense is of a man aware of a rich and complex inner life; a man capable of love and hate; a man who was both very fragile and extraordinarily robust; a human being with an irrepressible masculinity together with an unmanly, feminine gentleness of mind; a strident adult taking on the world around him; an infant on the edge of a precipice in desperate need of love and support. The task which I have set myself in this book is to share my sense of William Hazlitt, as I believe in our life and times we are in need of his spirit as it remains a spirit for our age.

Notes

Chapter 1

1 *My First Acquaintance with Poets* 1823: *Complete Works of William Hazlitt*, ed. P. P. Howe, 21 vols. (London: J.M. Dent and Sons 1928–1932). vol.17, p. 106.
2 *Characters of Shakespeare's Plays* 1817; [Howe 4.70–1]
3 *On Living to One's-Self* 1821; [Howe 8.90]
4 Quoted in Jones (1991), p. 247
5 *The Fight* 1836; [Howe 17.72]
6 Heaney (1998), p. 3
7 Keats (1960), p. 117–8
8 *Kinnard* (1978), pp. 367–8
9 Macdonald Maclean (1948)
10 Johnson (1907), p. v–xi
11 Quoted in Howe (1922), p. 205
12 Ibid., p. 262
13 Letter of 28/4/1817. Leigh Browne–Lockyer Collection at Keats House Hampstead
14 *On Depth and Superficiality* 1826; [Howe 12.347]
15 Grayling (2000), p. 92
16 *The Shyness of Scholars* 1836; [Howe 17.261]
17 Macdonald Maclean (1943)
18 *Lectures on English Philosophy* 1928; [Howe 2.124].
19 *On The Causes of Popular Opinion* 1828; [Howe 17.313]
20 *Characters of Shakespeare's Plays* 1817; [Howe 4.226]
21 *On Shakespeare and Milton* 1818; [Howe 5.47]
22 Howe (1922), p. 220
23 *A View of the English Stage* 1818; [Howe 5. 175]
24 *On the Pleasure of Painting* 1820; [Howe 8.14]
25 Martin (1920) *International Journal of Psycho-Analysis* 1:414–9
26 Quoted in Howe (1922), pp. 265–6
27 *Political Essays* 1819; [Howe 7.7–9]
28 *On the Conversation of Authors* 1820; [Howe 12.41–2]
29 Howe (1922), p. 386
30 Macdonald Maclean (1949), pp. xi–xii

Chapter 2

1 *A Project for a New Theory of Civil and Criminal Legislation* 1836; [Howe 19.302]
2 Trevelyan (1928), p. 71
3 Ibid., p. 157 footnote
4 Ibid., p. 27
5 *A letter to the Right Honourable William Pitt*, p. 38 quoted in Baker (1962), p. 23
6 Trevelyan (1928), p. 158
7 *Emancipation of the Jews* 1831; [Howe 19.321]
8 *A Project for a New Theory of Civil and Criminal Legislation* 1836; [Howe 19.312]

Chapter 3

1 Macdonald Maclean (1943), pp. 9–43 passim
2 Hazlitt, Margaret. (1967), p. 50
3 Ireland (1889), p. xiii

4   Hazlitt Margaret (1967), p. 30
5   Ibid., pp. 104–5
6   Ibid., p. 106
7   *On the Conduct of Life* 1836; [Howe 17.93]
8   Sikes (1978), p. 60 Letter of October 6, 1793
9   Hazlitt, Margaret (1967), p. 109
10   *On the Fear of Death* 1822; [Howe 8.326]
11   Hazlitt, Margaret (1967), p. 50
12   Paulin (1998), p. 14
13   Hazlitt, Margaret (1967), p. 82
14   Grayling (2000), p. 260
15   *On The Knowledge of Character* 1822; [Howe 8.311–2]
16   *On the Conduct of Life* 1836; [Howe 17.88]
17   Birrell (1902), p. 5
18   Hazlitt, Margaret (1967), p. 51
19   Ibid.
20   Park (1971), p. 66
21   Freud (1917a)
22   Bowlby (1944)
23   Bowlby (1951)
24   Bowlby (1969)
25   Bowlby (1973)
26   Bowlby (1980)
27   Parkes (1972)
28   *The Tatler* Tuesday June 6, 1710, Issue 181
29   *Lectures on the English Comic Writers* 1819; [Howe 6.98]
30   Steele (1923), pp. 50–1

Chapter 4

1   *Mind and Motive* 1815; [Howe 20.44]
2   Freud (1925)
3   Martin (1920), p. 418
4   Ibid., p. 419
5   Ireland (1889), p. xxxi
6   *On Depth and Superficiality* 1826; [Howe 12.354]
7   Freud (1920)
8   Quoted in Freud (1900), p. 103
9   Quoted in Freud (1920), p. 265
10   *Lectures on the English Comic Writers* 1819; [Howe 6.92]
11   Freud (1900), p. xxii
12   *On Dreams* 1823; [Howe 12.22–3]
13   Mordell (1919), p. 22
14   Ibid., pp. 22–3
15   Ibid., p. x
16   Jones, E. (1957), p. 474

Chapter 5

1   *On Cant and Hypocrisy* 1828; [Howe 17.346]
2   Fairbairn (1952)
3   *Essay on the Principles of Human Action* 1805; [Howe 1.1–91]
4   Schneider (1933), p. 39

5   *Mind and Motive* 1815; [Howe 20.44]
6   [Howe 1. 1
7   Ibid., p. 1.2
8   Ibid., p. 1.18
9   Ibid., p. 1.18
10 Fairbairn (1952), pp. 13–4
11 Fairbairn (1952), p. 95
12 Ibid., p. 96
13 *On Depth and Superficiality* 1826; [Howe 12.353]
14 Ibid., p. 348
15 [Howe 9.121;9.130]

Chapter 6

1   *Liber Amoris: Or, The New Pygmalion* 1823; [Howe 9. 99]
2   Ibid., p. 9.100
3   Ibid., p. 9.101
4   Ibid., p. 101–2
5   Ibid., p. 102–3
6   Ibid., p. 103
7   Ibid., p. 105
8   Ibid., p. 106
9   Ibid., p. 109
10 Ibid., p. 118
11 Ibid., p. 120
12 Ibid., *p.* 120–1
13 Ibid., p. 122
14 Ibid., p. 123–4
15 Ibid., p. 125–6
16 Ibid., p. 128–9
17 Ibid., p. 130
18 Ibid., p. 130–1
19 Ibid., p. 145–6
20 Ibid., p. 149–50
21 Ibid., p. 153
22 Ibid., p. 162
23 Quoted in Ireland (1889), p. xxxv–vi
24 Anon *Literary Register* May 17 1823
25 Anon *John Bull* June 15 1823
26 Anon *The Times* May 30 1823
27 *Noble Temple Bar* March 1881
28 Quoted in Neve (1985), p. 227–8
29 Ibid., p. 185
30 Ibid., p. 229
31 Anon *Athenaeum* July 15 1893
32 Ibid.
33 Howe, P. P. *Forthnightly Review* February 1916 *Hazlitt and Liber Amoris*
34 Priestley (1960), p. 9
35 Baker (1963)
36 Morgan (1960), p. 159
37 Ibid., p. 160
38 Ibid., p. 167
39 Ibid., p. 171

40   Ibid., p. 172
41   Connolly (1954), p. 59
42   Ibid., p. 63
43   Lahey (1980), p. 1
44   Ibid., p. 15
45   Ibid., p. 17
46   Ibid., p. 22
47   *Kinnard* (1978), pp. 367–8
48   Neve (1985), p. vii
49   Lahey (1980), p. 15

Chapter 7

1   **Quoted in Ireland (1889), p.** xxxvii
2   Stendhal *De L'Amour* Penguin 1975, p. 45
3   Ibid., p. 57
4   Ibid., p. 61
5   Ibid., p. 62
6   Ibid., p. 75
7   Ibid., p. 73
8   Ibid., p. 49
9   Ibid., p. 59
10   Ibid., p. 64 footnote
11   Ibid., *p. 60*
12   *Characters from Shakespeare's Plays* 1818; [Howe 4.225]
13   Cohen (1958), p. 190
14   Quoted in Ireland (1889), p. xxxvi
15   Macdonald Maclean (1943), pp. 246–253
16   Grayling (2000), p. 119
17   [Howe 9. 122]
18   Ibid., p. 123
19   Ireland (1889) xxxvii
20   [Howe 9. 162]
21   Haverty (2000)
22   O'Neill-Dean (2002)
23   [Howe 9. 133–4]
24   [Howe 9. 134]
25   Grayling (2000), p. 344
26   Wardle (1971), p. 267
27   Grayling (2000), p. 260
28   *On the Knowledge of Character* 1822; [Howe 8.305]
29   Ibid., pp. 310–11
30   *Whether Genius is Conscious of its Powers?* 1823; [Howe 12.123]
31   Keynes (1930)
32   Jones (1990)
33   *On the Knowledge of Character* 1822; [Howe 8.310–11]

Chapter 8

1   *Essay on the Principles of Human Action* 1805; [Howe 1. 75]
2   [Howe 1. 3]
3   Albrecht (1965), p. 23
4   [Howe 1., pp. 1–2]

5   Ibid., p. 1
6   Ibid., p. 12
7   Ibid., pp. 41–2
8   Ibid., p. 18
9   Ibid., p. 69
10   Ibid., p. 56
11   *On Genius and Common Sense* 1821; [Howe 8.47]
12   *Characters of Shakespeare's Plays* 1817; [Howe 4.226]
13   *On Shakespeare and Milton* 1817; [Howe 5.47]
14   *Character in Shakespeare's Plays* 1817; [Howe 4.183–4]
15   Quoted in Stanley Jones (1991), p. 247
16   Letter to William Gifford 1819; [Howe 9.13–59]
17   Macdonald Maclean (1943), p. 401
18   *The English Novelists* 1819; [Howe 6.109]
19   Ibid.; [Howe 20.46]
20   *On Reason and Imagination* 1826; [Howe 12.47]
21   *On Reason and Imagination* 1826; [Howe 12.54–5]

Chapter 9

1   *On Depth and Superficiality* 1826; [Howe 12.352]
2   *On Living to One's-Self* 1821; [Howe 8.90–1]
3   *On Criticism* 1822; [Howe 8.224–5]
4   *Characteristics* 1823; [Howe 9.224]
5   *On the Living Poets* 1818; [Howe 5.163]
6   *On Living to One's-Self* 1821; [Howe 8.92–3]
7   *Age of Elizabeth* 1819; [Howe 6.176–77]
8   *On the Knowledge of Character* 1821; [Howe 8.316]
9   Symington (1993)
10   *On the Pleasure of Painting* 1820; [Howe 8.6–7]
11   Bacon (1952), p. 27
12   *The Spirit of Philosophy* 1836; [Howe 20.375]
13   Cohen (1958), p. 190

Chapter 10

1   *The Spirit of Philosophy* 1836; [Howe 20.371]
2   *On Genius and Common Sense* 1821; [Howe 8.31–2]
3   *On Criticism* 1821; [Howe 8.214]
4   *Advice to a Patriot* 1806; [Howe 1., p. 112 footnote]
5   Grosse (1894), p. xxiv
6   *Sketches of the Principle Picture galleries of England* 1822; [Howe 10.65]
7   *On Gusto* 1816; [Howe 4.77]
8   *On Genius and Common Sense* 1821; [Howe 8.31]
9   *Character of Mr. Burke* 1807; [Howe 7.304]
10   Ibid., p. 305
11   Ibid., pp. 303–4
12   *On Genius and Common Sense* 1821; [Howe 8.47]
13   *A Farewell to Essay Writing* 1828; [Howe 17.317]

Chapter 11

1   Sharpe (1950)

2   Whelan (2000)
3   Sharpe (1950), p. 5
4   *On the Knowledge of Character* 1822; [Howe 8.316]
5   *A farewell to Essay Writing* 1828; [Howe 17.319]
6   *A View of the English Stage* 1818; [Howe 5.175]
7   *On The Causes of Popular Opinion* 1828; [Howe 17.313]
8   Jackson Bate (1964), p. 62
9   Keats (1960) Letter 32, p. 71, 21December 1817.
10   *The Spirit of Philosophy* 1836; [Howe 20.371]
11   Bacon (1952), p. 16
12   Park (1971), p. 34
13   *The Spirit of Philosophy* 1836; [Howe 20.371]

Chapter 12

1   *On the Aristocracy of Letters* 1822;[Howe 8.28]
2   *On the Conduct of Life* 1836; [Howe 17. 86–100]
3   Baker (1962)
4   *Guardian Weekly* Jan 24–30, 2002, p. 14
5   *The Spirit of Philosophy* 1836; [Howe 20.370]
6   Priestley (1960), p. 22
7   Howe (1922), p. 10
8   *Knowledge of the World* 1827; [Howe 17. 299]
9   *On Party Spirit* 1830; [Howe 20.322]
10   *A Reply to Malthus's Essay on Population* 1807; [Howe 1.177–364]
11   *Advice to a Patriot* 1806; [Howe 1.97–8]
12   *Life of Napoleon* 1828–30; [Howe 13.133footnote]
13   Hunt (1928), p. 344
14   *Life of Napoleon* 1828–30; [Howe 13.ix]
15   Ibid.
16   Ibid.; [Howe 13.x]
17   *Liber Amoris* 1823; [Howe 9. 145]

Chapter 13

1   *On the conversation of authors* 1820; [Howe 12.40]
2   Paulin (1998)
3   *Notes of a Journey through France and Italy* 1825; [Howe 10.186]
4   *On the Conversation of Authors* 1820; [Howe 12.41–2]
5   Keats (1960) Letter 44, p. 93 February 3, 1818
6   *My First Acquaintance with Poets* 1823; [Howe 17. 114]
7   *On the Pleasure of Painting* 1820; [Howe 8.14]
8   *My First Acquaintance with Poets* 1823; [Howe 17. 114]
9   *The Difference between Writing and Speaking* 1825; [Howe 12.278–9]
10   *On Reading Old Books* 1821; [Howe 12.220–9]

Chapter 14

1   *On Great and Little Things* 1822; [Howe 8.234]
2   Park (1971)
3   Morgan *Portrait in a Mirror* quoted in Groddeck (1951) *The World of Man*, p. 32
4   *On The Past and Future* 1821; [Howe 8.28]
5   Morgan (1960) *The Word 'Serenity'*, p. 50

6   *Madame Pasta and Mademoiselle Mars* 1825; [Howe 12.325]
7   Ibid., pp. 325–6
8   *Mind and Motive* 1815; [Howe 20.51]
9   *The Age of Elizabeth* 1819; [Howe 6. 183–184]
10   Ibid., p. 249
11   Ibid., p. 250
12   Paulin (1998) Chapter 9, pp. 205 –228
13   *On The Love of the Country* 1814; [Howe 4.20]
14   *The Age of Elizabeth* 1819; [Howe 6.183–4]

Chapter 15

1   *On The Past and Future* 1821; [Howe 8.25]
2   *On The Feeling of Immortality in Youth* 1827; [Howe 17.196–7]
3   *On The Past and Future* 1821; [Howe 8.30]
4   *Characters in Shakespeare's Plays* 1817; [Howe 4.223]
5   *On Application to Study* 1823; [Howe 12.63–4]
6   *On Application to Study* 1823; [Howe 12.63]
7   *A Farewell to Essay Writing* 1828; [Howe 17. 314–5]
8   Freud (1917b) S.E. 14:305–7
9   *On Dreams* 1823; [Howe 12.18]

Chapter 16

1   *Character of Mr. Burke* 1807; [Howe 7.301]
2   Quoted in Park (1971), p. 59
3   Bloom (1999)
4   *Lectures on the English Poets* 1818; [Howe 5.55]
5   *On Genius and Common Sense* 1821; [Howe 8.34]
6   *The Age of Elizabeth* 1819; [Howe 6.191]
7   *On Personal Character* 1821; [Howe 12.238]
8   Hamilton (1999), p. 73
9   Cohen (1958), p. 219
10   [Howe 9.121; 9.130]
11   [Howe (1922), p. 56]
12   *Kinnard* (1978), pp. 367–8
13   *The Age of Elizabeth* 1819; [Howe 6.191–2]
14   *On Depth and Superficiality* 1826; [Howe 12.349]
15   *The Age of Elizabeth* 1819; [Howe 6.363–4]
16   Ibid., [Howe 6.247]
17   *On the Conversation of Authors* 1820; [Howe 12. 40]
18   *On The Spirit of Obligations* 1824; [Howe 12.85–6]
19   Quoted in Park (1971), p. 31
20   Quoted in Howe (1922), p. 329

Bibliography

Notes on reference system

The standard reference for all of Hazlitt's writings is the *Complete Works of William Hazlitt*, ed. P.P. Howe, 21 vols. (London: J.M. Dent and Sons 1928–1932). Much of what we now read within the 21 volumes of the *Complete Works of William Hazlitt* was originally published as articles in newspapers or periodicals or was delivered as lectures before publication in book form. As a listener you would have heard his words or as a reader read him in your daily newspaper. Many books about Hazlitt have a reference system using Howe's *Complete Works*, where citation is to a volume and page number. Because this work is not readily available to the public I will provide two sets of references.

I will cite the particular work by name and give the date in which it was first published. For example *My First Acquaintance with Poets* 1823.

I will then cite the reference from the *Complete Works of William Hazlitt* by P.P. Howe. This will appear thus [Howe 17.106]. This refers to vol. 17. page 106. Thus individual books or collections of Hazlitt's essays which are more readily accessible to the general public can be followed up. A specific essay may be found in numerous publications. *My First Acquaintance with Poets* can now be found in more than a dozen books and collections of essays. Additionally a lecture which was then published as part of a book can later appear as a free-standing essay. *On Poetry in General* was the opening lecture in the series *Lectures on the English Poets* delivered by Hazlitt in 1818. It became the first chapter of the book by the same name and it can also be found as a free-standing essay in various collections of essays. To add to the complicated picture, the Everyman Library published editions of Hazlitt's works which combine two originally separate books. For example *Lectures on the English Poets* and *The Spirit of the Age* were printed in a single volume in 1910.

Abbreviations

Essay	=	*An Essay on the Principles of Human Action*
Howe	=	Howe, P.P., (1928–32), *Complete Works of William Hazlitt*, 21 vols., J.M. Dent and Sons
Int. J. PsychoAnal	=	*The International Journal of Psychoanalysis.*
Liber Amoris	=	*Liber Amoris: or, The New Pygmalion*
Life of Napoleon	=	*The Life of Napoleon Buonaparte*
S.E.	=	*The Standard Edition of the Complete Psychological Works of Sigmund Freud*, 24 vols., James Strachey (ed.) Hogarth, 1953–73
The Age of Elizabeth	=	*Lectures on the Dramatic Literature of the Age of Elizabeth*

Albrecht, W.P. **(1965)** *Hazlitt and the Creative Imagination.* Lawrence: University of Kansas Press.

Bacon, Francis. (1952) *The Advancement Of Learning.* William Benton.

Baker, Herschel. (1962) *William Hazlitt.* Harvard University Press.

Bate, Walter Jackson. (1964) *Keats.* Prentice Hall.

Birrell, Augustine. (1902) *William Hazlitt.* Macmillan.

Bloom, Harold. (Ed.) (1986) *William Hazlitt.* Chelsea House.

— (1994) *The Western Canon.* Harcourt Brace.

— (1999) *Shakespeare: The Invention of the Human.* Fourth Estate.

Bowlby, John. (1944) Forty-four Juvenile Thieves', *Int.J.Psycho-Anal.* 25: 19–52,107–27.

— (1951) *Maternal Care and Mental Health.* Geneva: WHO.

— (1969) *Attachment.* Hogarth.

— (1973) *Separation, Anxiety and Anger.* Hogarth.

— (1980) *Loss, Sadness and Depression.* Hogarth.

Brett, R.L. (1977) *William Hazlitt.* Longman.

Bromwich, David. (1983) *Hazlitt: The Mind of a Critic.* Oxford University Press.

Byatt, A.S., (1989) *Unruly Times: Wordsworth and Coleridge in their Times.* Hogarth.

Cohen, J.M. (Ed.) (1958) *Montaigne Essays.* Penguin.

Connolly, Cyril. (1954) *Hazlitt's 'Liber Amoris'* London Magazine. November.

Fairbairn, R. (1952) *Psychoanalytic Studies of the Personality.* Routledge.

Freud, S. (1917a) *Mourning and Melancholia* in *The Standard Edition of the Complete Psychological Works of Sigmund Freud,* 24 vols. James Strachey (Ed.) Hogarth, 1953–73, vol. 14:237–258.

— (1917b) *On Transience* S.E. vol.14: 303–307.

— (1900) *The Interpretation of Dreams* S.E. vol. 4:xxxii.

— (1920) *A Note on the prehistory of the technique of Analysis.* S.E. vol.18: 263–5.

— (1925) *An Autobiographical Study.* S.E. vol. 20:3–74.

— (1940) *The Splitting of the Ego in the Process of Defence.* S.E.

Grayling, A.C. (2000) *The Quarrel of the Age: The Life and Times of William Hazlitt.* Weidenfeld & Nicolson.

Groddeck, Georg. (1951) *The World of Man.* Vision Press.

Groose, Edmund. (Ed.) (1894) *Conversations of Northcote.* Richard Bentley and Son.

Hamilton, Ian. (1999) *The Crack-Up* by Scott Fitzgerald. The Penguin book of Twentieth Century Essays.

Haverty, Anne. (2000) *The Far Side of a Kiss.* Chatto & Windus.

Hazlitt, Margaret, *Journal,* Ernest J. Moyne (Ed.) (1967). University of Kansas Press.

Hazlitt, William. (1845) *Lectures on the Dramatic Literature of the Age of Elizabeth.* Wiley and Putnam.

Hazlitt William and Sarah (Stoddart), (1959) *The Journals of Sarah and William Hazlitt,* W.H.J. Bonner (Ed.). Buffalo University Press.

Hazlitt, Willaim Carew. (1897) *Four Generations of a Literary Family.* George Redway.

— (1911) *The Hazlitt's: An Account of their Origins and Descent.* Ballantyne, Hanson and Co.

Heaney, Seamus. (1998) *Opened Ground, Poems 1966–1996.* Faber and Faber.

Holmes, R. (1989) *Coleridge: Early Visions.* Hodder and Stoughton.

Houck, J.A. (1977) *William Hazlitt: A Reference Guide.* G.K. Hall and Co.

Howe, P.P. (1922) *The Life of William Hazlitt.* London. Hamish Hamilton.

— (1928–32) *Complete Works of William Hazlitt* 21 vols. J.M. Dent and Sons.

Hunt, Leigh. (1928) *Autobiography of Leigh Hunt.* Oxford University Press.

Ireland, Alexander. (1889) *William Hazlitt: Essayist and Critic.* Fred.erick Warne and Co.

Jeffares, Norman A. (1961) *A Review of English Literature.* Longmans.

Johnson, Brimley. (1907) Lectures on the English Comic Writers by William Hazlitt. Oxford University Press.

Jones, Ernest. (1957) *Sigmund Freud: Life and Work.* vol.3. Hogarth

Jones, Stanley. (1991) *Hazlitt: A Life.* Oxford University Press.

Keats, John, (1960) *Letters of John Keats*, Maurice Buxton Forman (Ed.). Oxford University Press.

Keynes, Geoffrey. (Ed.) (1930) *Selected Essays of William Hazlitt.* The Nonesuch Press.

Kinnard, John. (1978) *William Hazlitt: Critic of Power.* Columbia University Press.

Lahey, Gerald. (Ed.) (1980) *Liber Amoris: or, The New Pygmalion by William Hazlitt.* New York University Press.

MacDonald Maclean, Catherine. (1943) *Born Under Saturn: A Biography of William Hazlitt.* Collins. London.

— (1948) *William Painted by Himself.* C & J Temple.

— (1949) *The Essays of William Hazlitt.* Macdonald and Co. (Publishers) Ltd.

Mahony, John. (1981) *The Logic of Passion: The Literary Criticism of William Hazlitt.* Fordham University Press. New York.

Martin, L.C. (1920) 'A Note on Hazlitt', *Int. J. Psycho-Anal.* 1: pp. 414–19.

Mordell, Albert. (1919) *The Erotic Motive in Literature.* Boni & Liveright.

Morgan, Charles. (1960) *The Writer and his World.* Macmillan.

Motion, Andrew. (1997) Keats. Faber and Faber.

Murry, Middleton John. (1925) *Keats and Shakespeare.* Oxford University Press.

Natarajan, Uttara. (1998) *Hazlitt and the Reach of Sense.* Clarendon.

Neve, Michael. (1985) (Ed.) *Liber Amoris: The Book of Love.*

O'Neill-Dean, Richard. (2002) 'The Sussicranistic: a new diagnostic category?' In *Forum, The Journal of New Zealand Association of Psychotherapists.* Vol.8. August 2002.

Park, Roy. (1971) *Hazlitt and the Spirit of the Age.* Clarendon.

Parkes, Colin Murray. (1972) *Bereavement. Studies of Grief in Adult Life.* Tavistock.

Paulin, Tom. (1997) *Juices of the mind.* TLS Number 4932. pp 15–17. Oct. 10.

— (1998) *The Day-Star of Liberty.* Faber/Penguin.

Pearson, Hesketh. (1934) *The Fool of Love.* Harper and Brothers.

Priestley, J.B. (1960) *William Hazlitt.* Longman, Green and Co.

Ready, Robert. (1981) *Hazlitt at Table* Rutherford: Fairleigh Dickenson University Press.

Schneider, Elisabeth. (1933) *The Aesthetics of William Hazlitt.* University of Pennsylvania Press.

Shakespeare, William. *Works.*

Sharpe, E.F. (1927) Contribution to symposium on child analysis. *Int. J. Psycho-Anal.* 8:380–384.

Sharpe, E.F. (1950) *Collected Papers on Psychoanalysis.* Hogarth.

Sikes, H.M. Bonner, W.H. Lahey, G. (Eds.) (1978) *The Letters of William Hazlitt.* New York University Press.

Steele, L.E. (Ed.) (1923) *Essays of Richard Steele.* Macmillan.

Stendhal (1975) *De L'Amour.* Penguin.

Symington, Neville. (1993) *Narcissism: A New Theory.* Karnac.

Trevelyan, George Macaulay. (1928) *British History in the Nineteenth Century (1782–1901).* Longmans, Green and Co. Ltd.

Wardle, Ralph M. (1971) *Hazlitt.* University of Nebraska Press.

Whelan, Maurice. (Ed.) (2000) *Mistress of her own Thoughts: Ella Freeman Sharpe and the Practice of Psychoanalysis.* Rebus Press.

Whibley, Charles.(Ed.) (1906) *Essays by William Hazlitt.* Blackie and Son.

White, R.S. (Ed.) (1996) *Hazlitt's Criticism of Shakespeare.* Edwin Mellen Press

— (1987) *Keats as a Reader of Shakespeare.* The Athlone Press.

Wu, Duncan, (1998) *The Selected Writings of William Hazlitt* 9 vols. Pickering and Chatto.

— (2000) Hazlitt's Sexual Harassment' *Essays in Criticism* vol. 50 no.3.

Zeitlin, Jacob. (1913) *Hazlitt on English Literature.* Oxford University Press

Publications by William Hazlitt

1805	*An Essay on the Principles of Human Action*
1806	*Free Thoughts on Public Affairs: or, Advice to a Patriot*
1807	*Preface to an Abridgement of Abraham Tucker's Light of Nature Pursued*
	Advertisement and Biographical and Critical Notes from *The Eloquence of the British Senate*
1809	*A Reply to Malthus's Essay on Population*
1810	*Lectures on English Philosophy* (delivered 1812–13, and published in *Literary Remains* 1836)
1816	*Memoirs of Thomas Holcroft*
1817	*The Round Table*
	Characters of Shakespeare's Plays
1818	*Lectures on the English Poets*
	A View of the English Stage, A Series of Dramatic Criticisms
	A Reply to 'Z'
1818–25	Prefatory Remarks to Oxberry's *New English Drama*
1819	*Lectures on the English Comic Writers*
	Political Essays
	A Letter to William Gifford, Esq.
1820	*Lectures on the Dramatic Literature of the Age of Elizabeth*
1821–2	*Table Talk*
1823	*Liber Amoris; or, The New Pygmalion*
	Characteristics: in the Manner of Rochefoucauld's Maxims
1824	Preface and Critical List of Authors from *Select British Poets*
	Sketches of the Principal Picture Galleries in England
1825	*The Spirit of the Age*
1826	*The Plain Speaker*
	Notes of a Journey through France and Italy
1828-30	*The Life of Napoleon Buonaparte* (4 vols)
1830	*Conversations of James Northcote*

Volumes 16–20 of Howe's *Complete Works of William Hazlitt* contain various miscellaneous writings as follows:

Vol. 16	*Contributions to the Edinburgh Review*
Vol. 17	*Uncollected Essays*
Vol. 18	*Art Criticism & Dramatic Criticism*
Vol. 19	*Literary Criticism & Political Criticism*
Vol. 20	*Miscellaneous Writings*

Index